THE CHANGS NEXT DOOR TO THE DÍAZES

The Changs Next Door to the Díazes

. . . .

Remapping Race in
Suburban California

Wendy Cheng

University of Minnesota Press
Minneapolis • London

Portions of this book have been published previously in Wendy Cheng, "The Changs Next Door to the Díazes: Suburban Racial Formation in Los Angeles' San Gabriel Valley," *Journal of Urban History* 39, no. 1 (2013): 15–35 (Sage Publications Ltd.); and in Wendy Cheng, "'Diversity' on Main Street? Branding Race and Place in the New 'Majority-Minority' Suburbs," *Identities: Global Studies in Power and Culture* 17, no. 5 (2010): 458–96; reprinted by permission of the publisher (Taylor & Francis Ltd., http://www.tandf.co.uk/journals).

Published by the University of Minnesota Press
111 Third Avenue South, Suite 290
Minneapolis, MN 55401–2520
http://www.upress.umn.edu

Library of Congress Cataloging-in-Publication Data
Cheng, Wendy, 1977–
The Changs Next Door to the Díazes : Remapping Race in Suburban California / Wendy Cheng.
        Includes bibliographical references and index.
        ISBN 978-0-8166-7981-2 (hc)
        ISBN 978-0-8166-7982-9 (pb)
        1. Los Angeles Suburban Area (Calif.)—Race relations. 2. Asian Americans—California—Los Angeles Suburban Area. 3. Hispanic Americans—California—Los Angeles Suburban Area. I. Title.
        F869.L89A25174 2013
        305.8009794'94—dc23   2013028358

Printed in the United States of America on acid-free paper

The University of Minnesota is an equal-opportunity educator and employer.

20 19 18 17 16 15 14   10 9 8 7 6 5 4 3 2

Contents

Preface and Acknowledgments

WHEN I WAS A CHILD growing up in North County San Diego, about once every couple of months my parents would pack up an empty ice chest, along with me, my grandparents, and my brother, and we would drive the hundred miles to Monterey Park, in Los Angeles's San Gabriel Valley, to stock up on ingredients to make the food that made my parents remember their native Taiwan: twenty-pound sacks of rice, glossy plastic bags full of dried shitake mushrooms and tiny dried shrimp, densely leaved heads of napa cabbage, pork spare ribs expertly hacked into one-inch pieces, boxes of brown Asian pears cradled in padded netting, and for us kids, Japanese chocolate-covered Pocky sticks and the green and pink packs of Botan rice candy sold at the register. Besides going to the market, we would meet my uncle and his family for a meal at one of the Hong Kong banquet-style restaurants, where efficient servers would deliver a seemingly endless series of courses—platters of sliced barbecued pork, chewy strands of jellyfish, and chicken cooked in white wine; freshly sautéed baby pea sprouts; and steaming chunks of crab or lobster in ginger and scallion sauce. Afterward, the adults would sit contentedly, eating orange slices and cleaning their teeth, one hand cupped discreetly over the other wielding the toothpick.

For me as a child, then, the San Gabriel Valley represented things that were both strange and deeply familiar. Compared to the predominantly white suburb in which we lived, places like these in which everyone I saw seemed to be Taiwanese, or some kind of Chinese, were in some sense unfathomable. Yet it was where my uncle and his family lived, as well as many of my parents' Taiwanese friends, and many of the children with whom my brother and I grew up. So even as we made our daily lives a hundred miles away, our family was oriented toward the San Gabriel Valley—and for many years, until the Nationalist government lifted martial law in 1987, it was the closest we could get to Taiwan.

I didn't discuss these excursions with my friends, most of whom were white. Perhaps I understood at some level these trips were part of a circuit to which my friends had neither access nor understanding, which over-lapped but did not intersect at all with North County's predominantly white, suburban beach culture. Driving between San Diego and Mon-terey Park, stopping sometimes in Irvine, Rowland Heights, or Hacienda Heights, was how my parents traced what it meant to be Taiwanese in Southern California. For my brother and me, it instilled a sense of what it meant to be a young "Asian" in America—or at least Southern Califor-nia's version of it. This included lowered Honda Civics with dark-tinted windows and exaggeratedly high spoilers, speaking English with an accent though one had been born and raised in the United States, and neighbor-hood after neighborhood of faux-Mediterranean tract homes full of other Asian families. Though of course these were vast oversimplifications, it was already apparent to me that Taiwanese and other Asian groups in the San Gabriel Valley were making worlds of their own, in Southern Califor-nian suburbs, strip malls, and car culture.

It did not become clear to me until more than fifteen years later, when I had moved to the area myself, that there were many other people living alongside and within what I had conceived of as exclusively "Asian" worlds who were not Asian. In fact, in many of the San Gabriel Valley communi-ties that are popularly conceived as "Asian," Latinas/os make up between a third to one-half of the population. I observed the old Asian American ladies and men with their portable radios who started each day at Almansor Park in Alhambra with a little tai chi and disco amid what seemed to be a nearly 100 percent Asian American and Latina/o world. I watched as Asian American and Latina/o skater kids plodded along to school, virtu-ally indistinguishable from one another in their black skinny jeans, black T-shirts, and strategically disheveled hair. I sat among Asian immigrant and Mexican American families eating late at night at Noodle World or in the Taiwanese cafeteria-style restaurants. What stood out was not an unusual level of interethnic or interracial interaction—most often Lati-nas/os and Asian Americans appeared to move in separate though tightly overlapping orbits—but the everyday banality of it all, the sense of ease with which people moved through this majority-nonwhite, predominant-ly middle-income and suburban, world. What did this sense of ease—even complacency—mean in a nation that has historically excluded nonwhites from access to such spaces and confined them, literally and figuratively, to poor central city areas in which they are pitted against one another for scarce resources and represented as deadly enemies? The streets, shops, schools, and restaurants of the San Gabriel Valley did not seem inclined toward conflict or coalition—the other pole to which the representational pendulum swings—but rather more modulated and nuanced daily codes of coexistence. I began to wonder, how did this particular, majority–Asian American and Latina/o racial configuration come to be? What did place have to do with it? What multiethnic and multiracial histories and present realities have been obscured by the area's contemporary designation as a "suburban Chinatown"—and what possible futures?

As these questions coalesced into my dissertation research, I was fortunate to have the support and mentorship of a remarkable community in the Department of American Studies and Ethnicity at the University of Southern California. For my place there, and for so much else, I thank my mentor and dissertation chair, Ruth Wilson Gilmore, whose formidable intellect, ready laughter, and unwavering commitment to the people in her life no less than her political convictions have deeply informed my thinking and aspirations. Laura Pulido provided generous and challenging mentorship, from supporting me in exploring concepts important to her work in my own terms, to giving me the opportunity to collaborate with her and Laura Barraclough on *A People's Guide to Los Angeles*—a dream project. During the home stretch of writing this manuscript, she even shared precious office space in Los Angeles with me. Viet Thanh Nguyen pushed me to approach Asian American studies with an independent mind and offered an inspiring example of how critical and creative work can be complementary to one another. David Lloyd was supportive from early on, and Fred Moten urged me to think seriously about the virtue and meaning of people simply coexisting and "leaving each other alone." Leland Saito offered insight and support for my research from its beginning stages, and Karen Tongson was an energizing interlocutor in shaking up conventional thinking (including my own) on the suburbs. Lanita Jacobs, Dorinne Kondo, Josh Kun, Jane Iwamura, and David Román taught me skills and inspired me with their research and knowledge. Kitty Lai, Sandra Hopwood, Jujuana Preston, and Sonia Rodriguez made the department run for students and faculty alike. Jujuana in particular continued to provide much-appreciated assistance long after I graduated. My coconspirators and dear friends during graduate school and beyond, especially Michelle Commander, Laura Fugikawa, Emily Hobson, Viet Le, Jesús Hernández,

Jason Goldman, Nisha Kunte, Araceli Esparza, Imani Kai Johnson, Cam Vu, Sionne Neely, Micaela Smith, Perla Guerrero, Isabela Seong-Leong Quintana, Jian Chen, Michelle Dizon, Andrew Burridge, Jenna Loyd, Shiloh Krupar, Jennifer Casolo, and Trevor Paglen, made it better. Jake Peters was supportive and unfailingly kind. Daniel Martinez HoSang and Laura Barraclough consistently helped me see the way ahead.

At numerous conferences and presentations as well as informal communications over the years, I benefited enormously from conversations with and feedback from Lan Duong, Karen Tongson, Cindy I-Fen Cheng, Glen Mimura, Christine Bacareza Balance, Laura Liu, Clement Lai, Craig Gilmore, Alexandro Gradilla, Jerry González, Hillary Jenks, Michan Connor, Andrew Wiese, Charlotte Brooks, Genevieve Carpio, Catherine Michna, Yen-fen Tseng, Naiteh Wu, Mau-kuei Chang, Jonathan Ying, Isabela Seong-Leong Quintana, Rudy Guevarra Jr., Nikhil Singh, Crystal Parikh, Neil Brenner, Nhi Lieu, Sarah Wald, Thomas Chen, and Frank Cha. Arlene Dávila, Johana Londoño, Christopher Niedt, and Matthew Lassiter offered critical guidance on two journal articles based on materials included in this manuscript. Michael Omi and two anonymous readers provided invaluable feedback on the manuscript. Laura Barraclough and Daniel Martinez HoSang read and commented on the manuscript in its entirety, and I am grateful for their insightful suggestions. At University of Southern California, an Urban and Global Fellowship, Haynes Dissertation Fellowship, and Oakley Fellowship helped me complete the research and writing for the dissertation; a semester of course releases from Arizona State University provided crucial time to finish the book.

I owe the most to the sixty-eight people who generously gave their time to share with me their life experiences and thoughts regarding growing up in the West San Gabriel Valley, many of them deeply personal. During the course of my interviews, I was frequently inspired, moved, humbled, and awed. Translating experiences and perspectives from their lives into a book has been a daunting and, in many ways, impossible task, but I hope those who may eventually read it will find at least part of their lives accurately reflected within it. I especially thank Laura Aguilar, Karen Toguchi, Bill Gin, Deshawn Holmes, Helena McCrimmon, Russell Lee-Sung, Albert Huang, Stephen Sham, Eloy Zarate, Mike Murashige, Anita Marie Martinez, Milo Alvarez, and Paul Chan for their trust and generosity. The Alhambra Latino Association permitted me to attend several of their meetings and events, and I thank Dora Padilla in particular for her encouragement and interest in my research. I am grateful to Susie Ling for her historical knowledge about the area and Sharon Gibbs's assistance at the Alhambra Chamber of Commerce. Karen Yonemoto helped me make important connections early on. Former *Los Angeles Times* reporter Jia-Rui Chong first brought to my attention the excellent article she had written on the controversy over Robin Zhou's column at Alhambra High. Her article served as a starting point for my own research, and she assisted me in making several key contacts. I thank Jennifer Tran, Julienne Gard, and John Emerson for their cartography skills and patience in converting my mental images into readable maps. At the University of Minnesota Press, Pieter Martin has been an exemplary editor whose steadfast support for this book is much appreciated. Kristian Tvedten, Rachel Moeller, Brittney Estes, and Kyriaki Tsaganis also provided important assistance, while David Martinez completed the index.

Within the School of Social Transformation at Arizona State University, in particular my home units of Asian Pacific American studies and Justice and Social Inquiry, I am thankful to Mary Margaret Fonow, Kathy Nakagawa, and Mary Romero for their mentorship and support. My days in the office would be much worse without the help, patience, and kindness of staff members Maureen Roen and Johnny Roldán-Chacón, and Roisan Rubio always comes through to save the day. My friends and colleagues Karen Leong, Myla Vicenti Carpio, H. L. T. Quan, Crystal Griffith, Rudy Guevarra Jr., Wei Li, Brandon Yoo, Karen Kuo, Michelle Téllez, Elizabeth Sumida Huaman, Alan Gómez, Merlyna Lim, Joanne Rondilla, Beth Blue Swadener, Lee Bebout, Sujey Vega, and Patrick Grzanka—among others—are amazing human beings who can make a desert bloom. The ASU Ethnic Studies Working Group, including stellar graduate students Meghan McDowell and Grace Gámez, and Arizona Ethnic Studies Network have also been important and generative sources of sustenance.

My family is always in my heart. While completing this book, I found myself living in my own Asian American and Latina/o SGV household: I am grateful to Juan De Lara for his love and constant intellectual provocation and to Ixchel and Emiliano for sharing their unique worlds with me. My brother Eric has always been one of my greatest supporters, and I am consistently heartened by my sister-in-law Pam's cheerful company. My parents, Edward Teh-Chang Cheng and Shu-Ching Cheng, are the original intellectuals in my life, and I will never stop learning from them.

Theorizing Regional Racial Formation

*Places are fragmentary and inward-turning histories, pasts that others
are not allowed to read, accumulated times that can be unfolded
but like stories held in reserve, remaining in an enigmatic state,
symbolizations encysted in the pain or pleasure of the body. "I feel good
here": the well-being under-expressed in the language it appears in like
a fleeting glimmer is a spatial practice.*

—Michel de Certeau, *The Practice of Everyday Life*

*The SGV is a region of America where a lot of Chinese and Mexicans
have learned to live together, most of the time in harmony.*

—SGV brand "Chimexica Flag T-shirt" description

L AURA AGUILAR, A forty-seven-year-old[1] Chicana artist living in Los
Angeles's West San Gabriel Valley (SGV), can trace her family back
five generations in the area, since before the U.S. conquest of Alta California. In 2007, when I interviewed her for the research that would eventually
become this book, she recounted family stories of bandit-hidden treasure, recalled memories of her grandfather working as a caretaker for
Texaco among oil wells in the hills, and described patches of land along
the Rio Hondo that used to be all strawberry fields. She fondly recalled
picnicking with her mother and siblings at the San Gabriel Mission as a
child and described the cemetery there as "comforting," since her great-
grandmother and great-great-grandmother were buried there and it
reminded her of her family's long history in the area.[2] Attending junior
high in the early 1970s, Aguilar met and befriended Lisa Beppu, a third-
generation Japanese American whose family had taken advantage of the
lack of racial restrictions in unincorporated South San Gabriel to buy a
house there in the 1960s. As adults, both women lived not far from where
they had grown up and maintained a close friendship.

In nearby Monterey Park in the 1970s, young Japanese Americans Karen and Ed Toguchi were persuaded by a Japanese American realtor to purchase a home, following in the footsteps of earlier Japanese Americans, Chinese Americans, and Mexican Americans who had heard that Monterey Park—unlike the vast majority of suburbs during that time—was open to nonwhite homebuyers. In the same neighborhood, multiple generations of Bill Gin's Chinese American family purchased homes within a mile of one another, as longtime white residents moved out in droves around them. A stone's throw away in South San Gabriel, in the late 1980s, teenager Anita Martinez, a fourth-generation Mexican American whose parents had been activists in the Chicano movement, was best friends with Tina, whose Vietnamese parents had fled Vietnam after the fall of Saigon. The two girls were so close they shared clothes, fought over a boy, and even occasionally experimented with passing as each other's ethnic backgrounds—Anita as Vietnamese and her friend Tina as Mexican. Around the same time, a young, Monterey Park-raised, Chinese Mexican American man named Russell Lee-Sung started a teaching career that would eventually lead him to become principal of nearby Alhambra High School, which by 2000 would be made up of over 90 percent Asian and Latina/o students.

By the mid-2000s, the particular ethnic and racial mix of the West SGV had given rise to polyglot cultural representations such as the "SGV" street wear brand, the brainchild of West SGV locals Paul Chan, the son of well-heeled professionals originally from Hong Kong, and Eladio Wu, a self-described "Asian *paisa*" (a Spanish term referring to a fellow countryman), whose ethnically Chinese family hailed from Costa Rica and Mexico. The SGV brand featured slogans such as "SGV; not just an area east of Los Angeles, but a state of mind" and designs featured a mix of Chicano and Asian immigrant references.[3] In mid-2012, the SGV brand released a "Chimexica Flag" T-shirt design, featuring an altered American flag with the Mexican flag's eagle and People's Republic of China's arc of four stars in place of the usual rectangle of stars representing the fifty states.[4] Paul Chan, who designed the shirts and managed the website, thought the SGV area had finally come into its own. Living there "used to be something to be ashamed of," he said, but now he and the rest of the SGV "crew" were proud to claim it.[5] The SGVers' public claim to a prevalent Latina/o and Asian world, whether or not it was widely shared, was certainly of a specific historical moment in which at least one full generation had come of age in a racial mix that, in this area, was over 90 percent Latina/o and Asian.[6]

How do we understand the cumulative experiences of these diverse, present-day residents of the West SGV and how their experiences and perspectives might constitute a place-specific state of mind? Or, to put it another way, how do people's daily paths, and whom they encounter on them—shaped by family histories, regional and global economies, and localized knowledge—inform their racial and even political consciousness? How do people experience these shifting formations daily, especially in an area in which the local hierarchy does not match up easily to national racial ideologies? Based on the experiences and perspectives of residents of this pocket of Los Angeles County, this book posits everyday landscapes as crucial terrains through which racial hierarchies are learned, instantiated, and transformed. Combining a cross section of people's everyday experiences with a critical focus on landscape, it develops a theory of racial formation that looks at the West SGV through sharply focused lenses of race and place.

First, however, we need some background on the place in question. Los Angeles County's SGV as a whole is vast, encompassing forty-five municipalities and unincorporated communities stretching from just east of the city of Los Angeles to the western edge of the Inland Empire.[7] For the purposes of this book, what I refer to as the *West* SGV is the portion closest to central Los Angeles—a densely populated suburban region just minutes by car east of downtown, with a landscape characterized by sprawling strip malls, clusters of industry, and housing ranging from nondescript apartment complexes to faux-Mediterranean town homes to stately mansions (see Figure 1). Although geographically this western part of the valley arguably includes whiter, wealthier communities to the north (e.g., South Pasadena and San Marino), more heavily Latina/o areas to the south (e.g., Montebello), and poorer areas to the southeast (e.g., South El Monte, El Monte), the smaller area I focus on can be considered its core: the four adjacent municipalities of Alhambra, Monterey Park, Rosemead, and San Gabriel, and—at times—the small unincorporated area of South San Gabriel.[8] In the contemporary period, this subregion's distinct features have been shaped by processes including differentially racialized suburbanization and global economic restructuring—forces that have restructured the landscape and created

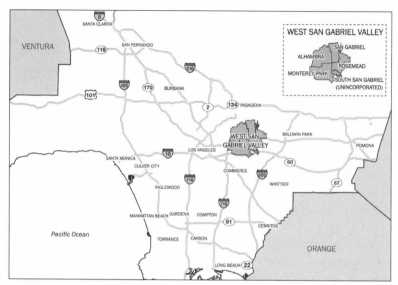

Figure 1. *Map of the West SGV in the context of the metropolitan Los Angeles region. Map by Jennifer Tran and John Emerson.*

a unique Asian American and Latina/o majority characterized by shared residential spaces and relative class parity.

This area gained fame in the 1990s as what has been described as a suburban, "spectacular eight-mile-long linear Chinatown."[9] Indeed, Asians and Asian Americans make up three-fifths of the population here. Chinese and Taiwanese make up about two-thirds of this group, and three in four are foreign born.[10] Despite such overwhelming emphases on the immigrant "Chinese" character of the region, however, as the histories and experiences of the previously mentioned residents show, these West SGV communities are actually highly diverse in terms of race, ethnicity, national origins, and immigrant-generational status. Most strikingly, Latinas/os make up nearly a third of the populations of these municipalities,[11] whose total population numbered nearly a quarter-million residents in 2010 (see Figure 2).[12] Indeed, the relative balance between Asian American and Latina/o populations in this area was an important factor in a successful 1991 redistricting campaign, involving a coalition of Asian American and Latina/o political organizations, to unite these four cities into one electoral district (state assembly district 49).[13]

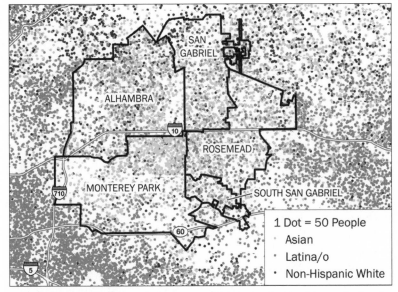

Figure 2. *Map of West SGV cities showing racial/ethnic distribution of Asians, Latinas/ os, and non-Hispanic whites. Data from 2010 U.S. Census: Summary File 1, 100 percent Census Tract Level Data. Map by Jennifer Tran and John Emerson.*

Mexican Americans constitute over four-fifths of the Latina/o popula-tion of 73,136 in the area and have a long history in the SGV, dating from before the U.S. conquest of Alta California and continuing through the formation of citrus labor communities in the East SGV from the early to mid-twentieth century.[14] Since the 1950s, a significant population of middle-income Mexican Americans has moved east from East Los Angeles into the West SGV, and cities such as Montebello and Monterey Park were referred to (albeit sometimes with tongue in cheek) as the "Mexican Beverly Hills."[15] Asian Americans also have a longer history in the area—a fact that is often obscured by the contemporary "suburban Chinatown" narrative. In the early twentieth century, Japanese Americans and Filipinos labored in the citrus groves alongside Mexican Americans, and Japanese Americans farmed fruits and vegetables. A small, early Chinese American population sold produce off trucks or worked as ranch hands or domestic labor.[16] Suburban-izing later-generation Japanese Americans and Chinese Americans began to arrive with their Mexican American counterparts beginning in the 1950s as well, unwittingly laying the groundwork for the massive ethnic Chinese immigration that would begin after the 1965 Immigration Act. In the 1970s and 1980s, new Asian immigrants—Vietnamese and other Southeast Asian political refugees, many of them ethnic Chinese, and immigrants from Taiwan and Hong Kong seeking to escape political uncertainty—flowed into the area, as well as eastern SGV cities like Rowland Heights and Hacienda Heights. Latina/o immigrants moved into cities slightly further east such as El Monte and La Puente. The 1980s saw an increase in Asian American as well as Latina/o political power on the area, with the election of several Latina/o and Asian American politicians.[17]

The contemporary racial and economic development of the SGV has very much been part of metropolitan and global economic restructuring, especially processes of deindustrialization and reindustrialization since the 1970s. Beginning in the 1960s, in response to successful labor organization and a decline in the rise of profit rates, firms in the United States began to look elsewhere for cheap labor as well as develop new production platforms in the global south and east, leading to the loss of manufacturing jobs and economic polarization in the United States and the depression of wages on a global scale.[18] Deindustrialization left warehouse and manufacturing spaces empty and available in the SGV, which also had well-developed infrastructure in large part due to the construction of freeways in the 1950s and 1960s. Changes in immigration laws in 1965 opened the door to an influx of Asian immigrants both at the top (e.g., professionals) and at the bottom (e.g., low-wage labor) of the economic spectrum. The West SGV, especially Monterey Park, with its proximity to Chinatown, relatively cheap land, and growing ethnic Chinese business networks (e.g., banks and real estate agents), became a top point of entry for ethnic Chinese.[19] In particular, the growth of Chinese American banking institutions, concurrent with global economic cycles and political and economic factors that prompted the migration of an ethnic Chinese "bourgeoisie" from Taiwan and Hong Kong, played an important role in facilitating ethnic Chinese business growth and home ownership.[20]

Asian and Latina/o immigrants are directly implicated in this latest round of global capitalist restructuring, which seeks a "two-prong" solution via technological innovation and cheap labor: Asian immigrants participate in both parts of the solution, furnishing highly educated professionals in technical fields as well as joining their Latina/o immigrant counterparts in low-wage jobs.[21] This is true in the SGV, in which Latina/o immigrants work alongside Chinese and other Asian immigrants in the

Figure 3. *A typical Mediterranean-style, single-family tract home sits at the end of a cul-de-sac in San Gabriel, with the San Gabriel Mountains in the background. Photograph by the author, 2007.*

kitchens of ethnic-Chinese-owned restaurants, garment factories, and manufacturing firms. However, recent Latina/o immigrants are less likely to live in the West SGV than recent Asian immigrants, favoring instead communities with larger immigrant Latina/o populations and lower rents further to the east such as El Monte and La Puente. As of 2010, only a third of Latinas/os living in the Monterey Park, Alhambra, San Gabriel, and Rosemead were foreign born (compared to two-thirds of the Asian population), and just one in eight had immigrated since 2000 (compared to about one in four Asians).[22]

Most of the West SGV's Latina/o population, then, are later-generation Mexican Americans with lower-middle-class to middle-class incomes. Importantly, in comparison to its surrounding areas, Asian Americans and Latinas/os living in this core region have relative parity in terms of socioeconomic status, both earning median household incomes slightly below the countywide median income.[23] Both earn significantly less than area whites, who in 2010 earned double the income of Latinas/os and nearly double the income of Asians.[24] Compared to their countywide counterparts, Latinas/os in this area are relatively wealthier, and Asians are significantly poorer (see Figures 4 and 5).[25] In Alhambra and Monterey Park, Latinas/os earn higher median household incomes than Asians, perhaps due to a higher proportion of workers employed in government jobs.[26] Compared to Latinas/os, Asians have somewhat better rates of homeownership and are also slightly better represented in management and professional occupations, although the same percentage of both groups hold service jobs.[27] Asians, however, own a much larger proportion of businesses than Latinas/os: as of 2007, approximately three in five businesses in Alhambra and San Gabriel were owned by Asians, while only one in seven in Alhambra and one in eight in Monterey Park were owned by Latinas/os—a clear indication of the degree to which (mostly) ethnic Chinese have been able to transform the landscape of the West SGV.[28] As a result, large numbers of Asian-owned businesses, many of which serve a predominantly Asian

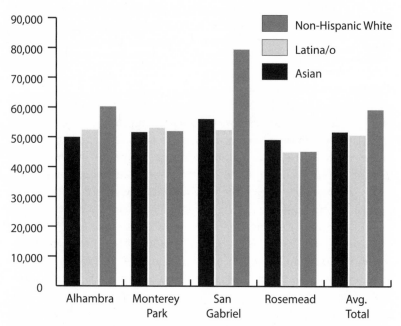

Figure 4. *West SGV median household income by race/ethnicity, 2010. Calculated from American Community Survey data, 2006–10.*

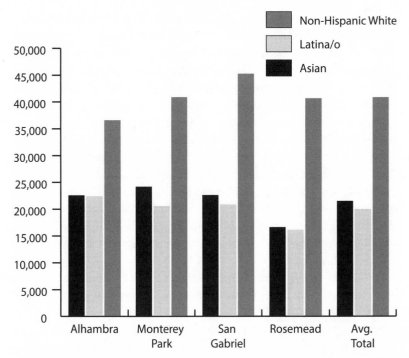

Figure 5. *West SGV per capita income by race/ethnicity, 2010. Calculated from American Community Survey data, 2006–10.*

clientele, characterize significant swaths of the West SGV's commercial landscape, compared to a relatively small number of Latina/o-owned or Latina/o-serving businesses.

The SGV thus constitutes not only an important site of Asian American and Latina/o suburbanization in the contemporary period but also a place rich in multiracial political, economic, and social history.

Of the four core West SGV cities, Monterey Park, adjacent to East Los Angeles, is probably the most well known. In 1990, it became the first majority Asian American city in the continental United States. Journalists promptly dubbed it "the first suburban Chinatown," and a cluster of scholars researched social, political, and economic changes and conflicts there between newly arrived Asian immigrants and established Asian Americans, Latinas/os, and whites.[29] In particular, Leland Saito detailed how these groups negotiated racial discourses to make political alliances and how race played prominently into struggles over public space. In doing so, Saito pointed to an important gap in the discourse on so-called suburban Chinatowns—that in most cases they were not *mono-* but *multiethnic* places, not "ethnic enclaves" in the traditional sense but dynamic sites of coexistence and contestation. Subsequently, geographer Wei Li developed the concept of "ethnoburb" to describe the area, denoting a transitional multiethnic space characterized by class diversity and both formal and informal ethnic business networks.[30] Most recently, Min Zhou, Xiaojian Zhao, and others have further elaborated on the local and transnational dynamics of these West SGV cities, as well as the class and intraethnic heterogeneity among ethnic Chinese immigrants in the area, many of whom hail from Taiwan, Hong Kong, and Southeast Asia. Tritia Toyota has described how such complex dynamics have informed the development of political activism among ethnic Chinese immigrants and naturalized citizens in this area.[31]

While *The Changs Next Door to the Díazes* is certainly indebted to these earlier studies, it also departs from them in several important ways. Instead of focusing primarily on political struggles or single ethnic community-based cultural and economic processes, this book also shines a light on people who will likely never attend a city council meeting, run for office, or make pan-Pacific business deals—people who are beneath the public radar, so to speak—and how they make sense of race and place in their everyday lives. I call this process *regional racial formation*. Building on Michael Omi and Howard Winant's influential definition of racial formation as "the sociohistorical process by which racial categories are created, inhibited, transformed, and destroyed," I define regional racial formation broadly as place-specific processes of racial formation, in which locally accepted racial orders and hierarchies complicate and sometimes challenge hegemonic ideologies and facile notions of race.[32] While Omi and Winant considered racial formation in terms of large-scale, national social processes and movements, regional racial formation is concerned instead with the ways in which these are situated in smaller-scale contexts (neighborhoods, localities, regions), important to the production of these scales themselves and intertwined with complex geographies of race.[33] How and where do racial projects and moments of racial formation *take place*, and what do these have to do with regionally specific identities?[34]

Focusing on the regional scale, I am less interested in using the lenses of specific political or historical events than the "sedimentation" of generations of social relations in the landscape.[35] While scholarship in this vein has been concerned primarily with the entrenchment and compounding of social inequalities in and through space, we might also utilize the metaphor to consider how sedimentation refers to the coexistence of complex and multiple histories and identities in a given moment—the "accumulated history of a place"[36]—and how these congeal into particular ways of making sense of the world. The geologic metaphor is also useful if one considers that in any landscape only the uppermost layer may be visible, but nonetheless the cumulative processes that formed all the layers below still shape the uppermost layer and may cause shifts and ruptures at any time. Seen as a sociospatial dialectic, then, regions or localities are "not simply spatial areas you can easily draw a line around," but "defined in terms of the sets of social relations or processes in question."[37] With regard to racial formation in particular, looking at the regional scale allows a "fine-grained analysis" of the everyday processes that shape racial hierarchies.[38]

A focus on regional racial formation therefore allows for (1) a level of analysis that focuses on everyday actions and movements, which are formed temporarily and shift more quickly and subtly than those formed at a larger scale, and (2) an analysis of the *dynamic* and *dialectic* between larger-scale ideologies and the micropolitics of local, everyday life. We might understand the latter as Gramscian common sense in formation, in dialogue with yet also apart from the state's and civil society's ascribed ideologies. Attention to processes at the regional scale allows a close analysis of the formation of "regional common sense" as provisional, daily, and constantly shifting, even as certain givens and structural (ideological) formations or limitations remain constant. Through the regional, we can articulate a set of practices intertwined with the production of local, daily knowledge that exceeds what national frameworks and top-down ideologies can dictate. Centering regional racial formation reveals an openness of meanings and outcomes rooted in place-based, everyday knowledge and interactions, which create the possibility of unexpected social and political consequences of proximity.

A growing body of scholarship and activism, as well as long-standing traditions of radical thought, has located the formation of racial hierarchies and the development of oppositional identities and world views as integrally tied to places, localities, and regions.[39] A handful of scholars working at the intersections of geography and ethnic studies have explicitly sought to create what Ruth Wilson Gilmore has described as "the political geography of race" or "a research agenda that centers on race as a condition of existence and as a category of analysis" and is grounded in the knowledge that "the territoriality of power is a key to understanding racism."[40] To take an important example, in Clyde Woods's study of political-economic development in the Lower Mississippi Delta region of the South, the vital connections between race and region emerge as what Woods calls a "blues epistemology"—an African American world view that grew out of the Delta in opposition to the dominant plantation regime and subsequently spread around the world.[41] This "ethno-racial epistemology" informs a "black geography," or dialectic of knowledge and spatial production in which "black histories, bodies, and experiences disrupt and underwrite human geographies."[42] Black geographies teach us that the situated knowledge of subordinated communities and their contributions to real and imagined human geographies, although often hidden, are significant political acts and expressions. These have the potential to disrupt dominant modes of geographic thought rooted in normative claims to place and allow us to consider alternate ways of imagining the world.

In a similar vein, Laura Pulido discusses "regional racial hierarchies," arguing that while we must always be cognizant of national racial narratives, it is "primarily at the regional or local scale that more nuanced discussions of the relationship between race and class emerge." Focusing on a local or regional scale enables analysis of how racial hierarchies "are shaped by local demographics, regional economies, local history," as well as larger-scale racial ideologies.[43] In ethnic studies, a number of important studies of differential racialization—or how distinct sets of racial meanings are attached to different groups with profound legal, social, and economic consequences—have been grounded in discussions of regional racial hierarchies, even if they are not explicitly theorized as such.[44] These include studies of how Chinese immigrants in Mississippi initially confounded but ultimately fit into the South's Black–white binary[45]; the differential racialization of Native Americans, Mexicans, African Americans, and Chinese and Japanese in California's early days of statehood; how Mexicans, African Americans, and poor whites negotiated the borderlands of central Texas; and regional hierarchies shaped in relation to citizenship status and labor between Black and white people in the South, Mexicans and Anglos in the Southwest, and Japanese and Haoles (whites) in Hawaii.[46] Other works focus on Southern California and especially Los Angeles, showing the immense fruitfulness of the region for scholars interested in the social, political, and cultural possibilities of regional processes of racial formation. For instance, Natalia Molina traces the development of a "regional racial lexicon" in public health discourse in Los Angeles in the late nineteenth and early twentieth century, based on interdependent meanings between white, Chinese, Japanese, and Mexican, and anthropologist Karen Leonard explores the early twentieth-century world of Punjabi men working in agriculture in the Imperial Valley who married Mexican women and made "biethnic" families and communities.[47]

The regionally specific histories of these shared multiethnic spaces are important not only because they challenge liberal democratic narratives of ever-increasing integration (into a normatively white polity) but also because of the radical possibilities often embedded within the residents' daily paths. As Scott Kurashige points out, "[T]he rapid and dramatic transformation of the United States from a majority-white society toward one in which people of color are in the majority must be taken as a challenge to do more than simply add new story lines to a preexisting narrative." Thus the mid- to late twentieth-century paradigm of racial progress, in which racial integration was conceived of as incorporation into a white majority, must be "revitalize[d]" as "a movement to construct a new polyethnic majority," in which integration depends less on the "spatial distribution of whites and blacks" and more on the relationships among multiple ethnic and racial communities.[48] In keeping with this goal, in recent years scholars have sought to unearth "the neglected history of multiracial coalitions and solidarities."[49] These emphasize coalition building in labor and political activism and the day-to-day formation of interracial friendships and alliances, which have previously been ignored or overlooked by urban historians as well as ethnic-studies scholars more concerned with single-group histories.[50] An important facet of this work is its positing of majority nonwhite spaces as "worlds of their own," in which white people are peripheral to the main act: people remaking their everyday lives and places within particular constraints but also emphatically on their own terms.[51]

With regard to the specific racial, ethnic, class, and historical contexts of the West SGV, three important themes emerge: the development of an emergent "nonwhite" identity rooted in middle-class and suburban contexts; the intertwined relationship of race, property, homeownership, and privilege; and the essential role of institutions of civil society in reconciling regional epistemes and practices with national ideologies.

The development of a distinct nonwhite identity in the West SGV grounded in lower-middle to middle-class, suburban neighborhood spaces stands in contrast to "people of color" identifications traditionally rooted in working-class affiliations and central urban areas. In Mary Pardo's book *Mexican American Women Activists*, Pardo refers to "the disordering of meanings and ethnic and racial categories" in the wake of rapid demographic change in Monterey Park from majority white to majority Asian and Latina/o—evidenced, for example, in the fact that as early as 1987, an Alhambra School District survey categorized whites as "other" and "minorities."[52] Indeed, in the course of my interviews, many people referred to whites as "minorities" or "token whites," sometimes matter-of-factly and sometimes in a pleased tone, connoting a subversive delight that supposedly normative categories had been inverted. When describing the West SGV, both Asian Americans and Latinas/os evoked peaceful Asian and Latina/o settings, which they felt might be "ruined" by white people (as twenty-one-year-old Vietnamese American Nancy Do put it).[53] Others expressed a sense of comfort tied to growing up as part of a nonwhite, Asian and Latina/o majority, which would influence their decisions as adults regarding where to live or in which schools to enroll their children.

While people-of-color identities have been mobilized for the most part on the left and in pursuit of specific political aims, an emergent nonwhite identity in the West SGV is instead characterized by frequently shifting alliances, with uncertain political outcomes depending on the individuals involved and the situation.[54] It is nonetheless significant to name, however, since most studies of racial minorities in suburban or middle-income settings to date assume a trajectory toward assimilation to white American norms (albeit with varying degrees of "success" or "failure") or are at least premised on the aspiration to such.[55] Asian Americans and Latinas/os are particularly believed to be desirous and capable of assimilating into whiteness, although most scholars still characterize them as "the racial middle," or—as I believe to be more accurate—perpetually triangulated vis-à-vis Black and white *and* present at all levels of a complex triracial racial order.[56]

A shared nonwhite identity does not, however, preclude the continued production of privilege and inequality. For one, a generalized "nonwhite" category can easily reify whiteness and white dominance by stabilizing whiteness as a category in itself. As Natalia Molina has pointed out, in

California's multiracial history, the development of a "nonwhite" category in the early decades of the twentieth century helped to stabilize a new
racial order, with "whites" at the top and "nonwhiteness" dictating degrees
of access to privilege and fluidly changing its composition "in response
to both national factors (e.g., labor needs, immigration laws, and economic cycles) and more regional pressures (e.g., the presence or absence
of other marginalized populations)."[57] Certainly, in the West SGV, posi-
tionality within a generalized nonwhite identity varies by race, ethnicity,
immigrant-generational status, and class. With regard to Asian Americans
and Latinas/os, one must also pay attention to differential racialization
vis-à-vis Asian American model minority discourse and the ambiguously
white status of Mexican Americans (referring to both day-to-day experiences of "passing" and historical and legal factors). These differentiated
statuses of relative valorization coexist with a "forever foreign" racialization
of Asian Americans—stemming from a long history of exclusion from citizenship, civic participation, and even the nation itself—and a combined
"foreign" and devalorized class stigma for Mexican Americans, whose
position in the racial hierarchy shifted over the course of the last century to reflect many Mexican immigrants' niche in the American economy
as cheap labor.[58] All these discourses paper over the tremendous ethnic,
class, political, generational, and racial (in the case of Latinas/os) heterogeneity of U.S. Asians and Latinas/os—yet all "Asians" and "Latinas/os"
must contend with the effects of the most salient racialized meanings.[59]

California—and especially Southern California—is particularly
important in the study of the differential racialization of Asian Americans
and Latinas/os for at least two reasons. First, it was here that whiteness
was solidified by both literal and figurative Asian exclusion and troubled
by the "doubly colonized" and ambiguous racial status of Mexican Americans.[60] Racialized labor competition in California served as the impetus
for the Chinese Exclusion Act of 1882, as well as the exclusion of Asians as
"persons ineligible for citizenship" from property ownership. The "ideological baggage"[61] that developed hand in hand with such laws prevented
Asians from full participation in civil society and enabled and perpetuated
their containment in segregated spaces. The ambiguous racial and social
status of Mexican Americans was also formed to a great degree in California, where, after the vast majority of what is now the American Southwest
was ceded by Mexico to the United States in 1848, Mexicans wishing to
remain in the United States were granted access to naturalized, American

citizenship and therefore legal whiteness. Anglo whites married wealthy Californios (Spanish-speaking, often landholding elites) and a "Spanish fantasy past" was valorized in the landscape.[62] At the same time, however, Mexican Americans were regularly denied the full social and material benefits of whiteness, and the constant presence of a large Mexican immigrant and Mexican American working class, in tandem with shifting immigration policies, led, during the second half of the twentieth century, to the racialization of Mexicans as the archetypal "illegal alien."[63] Second, as the two largest nonwhite groups in Southern California, Asian Americans and Mexican Americans have often shared space and similar (or at least adjacent) positions in racialized labor hierarchies. This has yielded relationality, various degrees of familiarity, and sometimes intimacy.[64] Thus, as Natalia Molina has argued, in Los Angeles, "Mexican" was "a category constructed from what it was not: not white, not Chinese, not Japanese . . . what it meant to be 'Mexican' . . . was determined in part by what it meant to be 'Japanese.'"[65]

In the case of the contemporary West SGV, the residues and continuing effects of such dynamics lead to regionally grounded expressions of racial formation, such as what I call *racialized privilege* and *strategic uses of whiteness*. Racialized privilege refers to a highly context-dependent enjoyment of greater expectations and opportunities among one nonwhite group relative to others. It is distinct from white privilege, though, because it depends on rather than negates racial otherness. For example, in the West SGV, a form of racialized privilege among Asian Americans manifested particularly in the schools and in comparison to Latina/o students, although predicated on racial otherness as well as attributes that applied unevenly to a heterogeneous "Asian" population, the relatively privileged status of Asians. As a result, Latina/o students tended to be devalorized in schools. In other contexts, however, such as in neighborhoods and civic issues, Latinas/os were able to claim a "mainstream" status as legitimate Americans that functioned implicitly as whiteness. Since this was an identity constructed in large part in opposition to "Asianness," it was one from which "Asians" were decisively excluded. At the same time, Asian Americans and Latinas/os often enacted a strategic use of whiteness (whether "honorary" or "ambiguous") that did not lose sight of legacies of historical and structural racism and often coexisted with a strong nonwhite identity.[66] Therefore although both Asian Americans and Latinas/os strongly expressed a multiracial nonwhite identity, I use the term *nonwhite* with caution, to indicate the ways in which an emergent nonwhite identity in the West SGV brushes histories and narratives of suburban and middle-class racial formation against the grain yet must still contend with the pervasiveness of whiteness and structures of white domination implicit at a basic level in the very construction and maintenance of racial categories.[67]

A second and related current throughout the book is the intertwined relationship of race and property, particularly as expressed through homeownership, conceptions of privilege, and notions of proper uses of space. Family histories in the West SGV are deeply informed by racialized relationships and differential access to property. While this is arguably true everywhere in the United States, and perhaps especially in urban areas, this has played out in the West SGV as well as the region as a whole in ways that have particular historical and theoretical significance. The significance of suburban, middle-income, majority people-of-color neighborhoods cannot be separated from the historical intertwinement of race, property, and citizenship in the United States—in particular, the centrality of linked notions of whiteness and property to the production and perpetuation of material racial inequality from the inception of the United States.[68] Homeownership is a central element of the perpetuation of racial inequality vis-à-vis literal property. For much of the twentieth century, housing discrimination was written into law, and indelible links between housing discrimination, inheritance, and life chances continue into the present.[69]

More specifically, I consider how particular components of Asian and Latina/o racialization in the United States and their differential relationships to whiteness and property have been mutually constitutive—in particular, the "honorary white" status of Asian Americans as model minorities and the ambiguously white status of Mexican Americans.[70] Asian Americans' and Latinas'/os' movements into the West SGV have been shaped by and are subsequently productive of differentially racialized relationships to property, which are expressed in and through distinct social relations, uses of space, and symbolic notions of homeownership. I also consider how ideological linkages between race and property—broadened into questions of access and ownership of public space—are formative of civic landscapes. Actions and attitudes in this realm are frequently shaped by long-standing historical geographies of race and expressed through racialized categories and tropes. In the West SGV, recurring motifs that buttress and reproduce white domination through the containment or erasure of specific racial groups in space or time include tropes of Chinatown and a "Spanish fantasy past" and flexibly exclusive notions of Americanness.[71]

The third theme concerns the essential role of institutions of civil society in reconciling regional epistemes and practices with national ideologies. Many a theorist of modernity has argued that institutions of civil society (e.g., schools, churches, community organizations) are key to the inculcation and production of hegemonic ideologies.[72] Institutions of civil society, especially school but also civic organizations such as the Boy Scouts of America, serve to inculcate a sense of a national culture and ideologies that mold their participants (compulsorily, in the case of school) to enter the working world as productive and loyal citizens. To use an expression from Marx, these institutions render people "free" to bring their hides to the market for tanning: to be exploited for their labor and participate in reproducing capitalist relations of production. In their capacities as everyday "racialized landscapes," institutions of civil society are essential to normalizing particular social, racial, economic, and political orders into "common sense."[73] Under the cover of ideological neutrality and egalitarianism, civic institutions normalize stratification and inequality. Because of this uniquely powerful function, they are also what Louis Althusser characterizes as both the "stake" and "site" of ideological struggle—so at moments of crisis, outcomes are not fixed, and reconfigurations of power can occur.[74]

Paying attention to the dynamics of social relations within institutions of civil society is particularly important in suburban, middle-class settings, which specialize in the ideological valorization of home, family, school, and nation. The West SGV, as a majority–Asian American and Latina/o lower-middle-income to middle-income, semisuburban space, is distinct from mainstream conceptions of nonwhite spaces (as poor, central urban ghettoes, barrios, or enclaves) as well as mainstream conceptions of suburbs (as normatively white and economically homogeneous). As such, institutions of civil society constitute key sites in which the West SGV's particular "disordering of meanings and ethnic racial categories" is taking place and where disjunctures between dominant and emergent alternative ideologies can be most readily observed.[75]

Based on the theoretical underpinnings I have just outlined, my methods and analysis proceed from two main assumptions. First, I consider that sites of everyday life—homes, neighborhoods, schools, civic organizations, and civic landscapes—are crucial terrains through which racial orders are produced, contested, and reproduced. Bearing in mind the concept of regions as sets of constantly shifting social relations and processes, I engage an episodic approach, focusing on pivotal episodes occurring in and through these sites as "articulated moments in networks of social relations and understandings."[76] At these moments of (regional) racial formation, an emergent structure of feeling or "meanings and values as they are actually lived and felt," which are as yet ideologically unthinkable but perched "at the very edge of semantic availability,"[77] collides with dominant institutional practices and discourses. In such moments, which arise from a disruption or challenge to an existing order, outcomes are not fixed and prevailing patterns of social relations, usually taken for granted, are illuminated by their disruption. In ensuing struggles to "make sense" of existing social relations as well as the challenges to them, each has the potential to transform the other.

Second, I believe that people's accounts of their daily lives—the decisions they make, the people they regularly interact with, and even their seemingly mundane interactions—cumulatively add up to a not necessarily fully articulated, yet definitely formed, regional racial consciousness. This can be conceived of as the *gestalt*—the "feeling" people have living in a particular area that feeds into their general satisfaction and long-term investment in the area despite existing tensions or conflicts. It is a sense of self and place that is rooted in the past but not fixed. As Stuart Hall puts it, while "the past continues to speak to us" with "real, material, and symbolic effects," identities are never fixed but are rather "the names we give to the different ways we are positioned by, and position ourselves within, the narratives of the past." They are "not an essence but a positioning." Thus it is quite important to pay attention to "the points of identification . . . or suture, which are made, within the discourse of history and culture."[78]

In the West SGV, I translate this into a concern with how people *position* themselves vis-à-vis their individual and family histories in the area. With this in mind, I chose as primary methods in-depth interviews and cognitive mapping. The interviews, which took place primarily over a period of two years (from fall 2006 through fall 2008, with a handful of additional and follow-up interviews in 2011 and 2012), included sixty-eight

Asian American and Latina/o residents of Monterey Park, Alhambra, San Gabriel, Rosemead, and South San Gabriel, across a range of ages, income levels, and ethnic backgrounds. Interviews typically lasted between forty-five minutes and two hours. I located interviewees through snowball sampling: first through my immediate circle of acquaintances and eventually through people I had already interviewed. In a semistructured fashion (with a list of questions I wanted to be certain to cover but allowing conversations to develop organically), I inquired about people's family histories in the West SGV area, everyday social worlds and geographies, and conceptions of race, ethnicity, and place. For chapters 2 and 3, discussing incidents at a local high school and in a Boy Scout troop, I interviewed students, teachers, and parents, as well as troop affiliates and regional Boy Scouts of America officials, respectively. For chapter 4, discussing civic landscapes, I conducted interviews with local officials and examined relevant public documents and newspaper articles.

At the conclusion of about two-thirds of the interviews, I also asked people to draw personal cognitive maps of their regular pathways in the region, in order to understand the variety of spatial experiences among residents of the same area and the coherence of the West SGV as a region in everyday experiences (see appendix). In Dolores Hayden's discussion of cognitive mapping, Hayden describes how urban planner Kevin Lynch studied mental images of the city "by asking people to draw maps or give directions."[79] Lynch's first study of this kind showed—perhaps unsurprisingly—that not everyone saw the city in the same way. In subsequent studies, Lynch and others explored the roles of class, gender, age, and ethnicity in shaping people's "mental maps." Hayden reproduces several maps from a 1971 study of Los Angeles residents that "showed graphically the differences between the residents of an affluent white suburb, an inner-city African American neighborhood, and a mixed neighborhood close to downtown that had long been home to new immigrants working in downtown factories and using a few downtown bus lines." As "the space of the city, as understood by these different groups, varied greatly in size as well as in its memorable features," Hayden concluded that "the maps are striking images of inequality of access to the city."[80]

While this is certainly true, in my approach, I focused more explicitly on the relationship of such maps to ideas about race, place, and region,

and what Hayden, citing Fredric Jameson, describes as the potential of
such exercises (constituting, in Jameson's words, "an aesthetic of cognitive
mapping") to engender "a heightened sense of place" and even raise political consciousness.[81] In asking people to draw maps of the places they went
to regularly in their daily/weekly paths, I was able to see both commonalities and variety among sociospatial experiences of people of different
races and ethnicities living in the same areas. Sometimes, people also used
the map exercise as a way to elaborate on themes we had already talked
about during the course of the interview. Cognitive maps are therefore
an expedient way to learn about individuals' often sophisticated understandings of relationships between race and place, built up over lifetimes
of daily observations and experiences. Cognitive maps are also shaped by
everyday experiences and dialectically with racial ideologies, constituting
racial geographies.[82]

As delineated in this book, a theory of regional racial formation con-
tributes to an emerging dialogue on the social and political possibilities
of multiracial, majority nonwhite spaces by conceptualizing the roles of
place and place making within processes of racial formation. By focusing on "the multiplicity of histories that is the spatial" as a key aspect
of racial formation,[83] we can better understand how place-specific
knowledge may illuminate histories and ways of thinking that offer
alternative world views to prevailing hegemonic ideologies. These
highly regional world views then have the possibility to "jump scale,"
become materialized in everyday landscapes, or disrupt a given context in another location.[84] Understanding processes of racial formation
within a small region such as the SGV in the contemporary moment is
also important not only in itself but also in the context of significant spatial and demographic shifts at the national level. As the population of the
United States as a whole rapidly follows California's lead in tilting toward
a nonwhite majority,[85] the SGV stands as a site where a multiracial,
majority-nonwhite population has already established itself over multiple
generations. Thinking critically about the spatialized racial history of the
area and how it has become the place it is today through a regional racial
formation framework will be instructive in analyzing other places that are
going through, or will soon go through, similar shifts. Further, the stories
and life histories of SGV residents in the contemporary moment challenge the old trinity of whiteness, suburban, and American—both what

we may think each of these terms means as well as their easy conflation with one another. Culturally, ideologically, and politically, the voices in this book unsettle the United States' long-held image of itself as a white suburban nation, with significant implications for the presumed conditions and terms through which people form class, racial, and national identities.

CHAPTER 1

Not "For Caucasians Only"

Race, Property, and Homeownership

O NE SUMMER AFTERNOON not long ago, Milo Alvarez, a thirty-seven-year-old, fourth-generation Mexican American who grew up in Alhambra, went for a drive in the Monterey Park hills with a friend, also Mexican American. His friend, who was not familiar with the area, wanted to look at a house that was for sale. As Milo tells it, when they arrived at the house,

there were these Japanese guys over there. I knew they were Japanese 'cause most of the old guys of that generation, they dress a certain way. . . . And [one of them] grabs a flyer and tells my friend, oh you're thinking about moving here. [My friend's] like, yeah. He goes, "That's cool." He goes, "I'm tired of all these damn chinos moving in, and just knocking down these nice houses and building their damn Hong Kong mansions. They think they're in fucking Hong Kong" . . . he says it like that. And then he tells him, "My mom owned this house"—it wasn't the house for sale, it was the house next to it—"she's been here for years," since like the forties or the thirties, I don't know how long it was he said . . . "but now you have all these damn chinos moving in." And he's a Japanese dude, right? . . . I'm used to it because I knew folks like that [growing up] . . . [but] my friend was just shocked and stunned, and he almost wanted to laugh . . . in the sense that, if he's talking about these "damn chinos," but in the eyes of somebody from outside . . . all Asian folk are chinos, right? So he just kind of blew him away. . . . We got back in the car and [my friend's] like . . . "I'm stunned. What is his perception of identity? Who does *he* think he is?"[1]

Milo, on the other hand, while amused by his friend's reaction, was unimpressed. Having grown up in the area, he was accustomed to its particular racial and cultural alignments. While he acknowledged that it might "sound kind of strange . . . it's very common if you grew up here."

Several facets of this story are significant. Its setting in the West San Gabriel Valley (SGV), adjacent to Los Angeles's Eastside, and the basic outlines of the interaction—an older Japanese American man expressing cultural familiarity (using the Spanish term *chino*, meaning "Chinese," but often used to refer to all Asians, regardless of ethnicity) as well as attempting to bond with two Mexican Americans—point to common group histories in the region. These began in the late nineteenth and early twentieth centuries with shared labor niches in the citrus groves and ranches of the SGV and extended through patterns of residential discrimination that formed multiracial neighborhoods such as Boyle Heights in the 1940s and 1950s.[2] However, post–World War II processes of suburbanization, urban renewal, and resegregation have left few remnants of the older history, which is hardly known outside of individual and family histories and certain neighborhoods like Boyle Heights, Crenshaw, and parts of the West SGV such as Monterey Park—as evinced by the dumbfounded reaction of Milo's friend. Further, the multiple ways in which the Japanese American man sought to make common cause—through disparaging more recent ethnic Chinese immigrants via their architectural choices, letting Milo's friend know that he would welcome him as a neighbor, and affirming his own family's long status as homeowners in the neighborhood—are both highly specific to the contemporary history of the West SGV and speak more broadly to the ways in which relationships to property, and especially homeownership, are central to regional processes of racial formation and productive of particular social relations.

What were the historical patterns and processes that informed Asian American and Latina/o residents' movement into, and subsequent lives in, these suburban spaces? How were these movements shaped by, and subsequently productive of, differentially racialized relationships to property? What kind of "worlds of their own" have present-day residents of the West SGV made collectively, in what have become largely nonwhite, suburban, middle-income neighborhoods, and what do these worlds mean to them? Finally, what possibilities do such spaces allow (or foreclose) that are distinct from those articulated in majority-white settings? In this chapter, I explore these questions through an analysis of differential racialization vis-à-vis property. Differentially racialized access to property is a key aspect of regional racial formation in the West SGV as a formative condition and also produces particular social relations. For many West SGV residents, what is produced is a form of what George Lipsitz has called a "moral geography of differentiated space," or an ethos that departs from the exclusionary mandates of normatively white suburban space in American history.[3] Lipsitz makes a distinction between a "moral geography of differentiated space," developed by "aggrieved communities of color," and a "moral geography of pure space," originating from American frontier ideologies. A moral geography of pure space is the basis of a "white spatial imaginary," which privileges the generation of exchange value via property over all else, while a moral geography of differentiated space, the basis of a "black spatial imaginary," promotes use value and the communal social good. In this formulation, *Black* and *white* refer not literally to Black and white people but are signifiers of ideological stances with deep historical and material implications. Blackness

Figure 6. A modest, single-family home coexists with multifamily housing and a larger, more recently built single-family home on a single block in Monterey Park. Photograph by the author, 2012.

denotes an ethos that subverts and eludes structures of domination in which capitalism and racialism are intertwined.[4] Whiteness, in contrast, refers to advantages accrued from structural discrimination, both historically and in the present.[5]

Even while their initial movements were to a large degree shaped by differential racialization in the housing market, Asian and Latina/o residents who came to the West SGV beginning in the 1950s and 1960s participated in producing a moral geography of differentiated suburban space. In doing so, they developed a particular sense of nonwhite identity, in which their motivations and long-term actions differed significantly from those of white residents, who fled en masse and virtually ceased moving to the area between 1960 and 1990.[6] This "moral geography" is both continuous with earlier histories of multiracial communities in the greater Los Angeles region and distinctively new in that it has been transformed by transnational ethnic Chinese settlement and economic globalization. I focus first on West SGV family histories that began between the 1950s and 1970s, a formative period that laid the groundwork for the "spectacular suburban Chinatown"[7] that would later take root. This earlier period was shaped not only by distinctive post–World War II patterns of residential development but by longer histories of shared multiracial residential spaces in the Los Angeles region, as well. I then consider how second-generation experiences growing up in the West SGV from the 1970s to the 1990s, as well as experiences of new arrivals during that time period, further trouble commonly accepted notions of race, homeownership, and property. Three key themes emerge: (1) the implications of differentially racialized relationships to homeownership via the distinct racial positions of Asian Americans and Mexican Americans; (2) the development of a moral geography of differentiated space through actions and neighborhood social relations; and (3) reconfigurations of relationships between race and property (encompassing differentiated material opportunities as well as expectations, understood or expressed through racialized categories and tropes and racialized uses of space). Throughout, I trace articulations of a distinctive majoritarian, nonwhite identity among Asian Americans and Latinas/os, which while selectively complicit with dominant racial hierarchies, is nonetheless deeply informed by antiracist principles.

Not "For Caucasians Only": Residential
Development in the West SGV since 1950

Although a few developers made forays into the West SGV in the 1920s—particularly in Monterey Park—it was really after World War II, in the 1950s and 1960s, that the West SGV began its rapid transformation from a semirural farming region into a suburb of Los Angeles.[8] Newly built freeways offered proximity and easy access to downtown as well as East Los Angeles, Chinatown, and Little Tokyo. Advertisements in the 1950s boasted that new developments in Monterey Park were a mere seven-minute drive from downtown.[9] Proliferating subdivisions attracted World War II veterans looking to buy homes (facilitated by the GI Bill's home loan guaranty program) and drew Mexican Americans from East Los Angeles, Japanese Americans from the West Side and East Side, and Chinese Americans from Chinatown.[10] Federal programs and policies in the postwar decades made homeownership available to Americans on a mass level unprecedented in history and in a way that would be lucrative for generations. However, nonwhites were largely and often explicitly excluded from such opportunities, in effect enacting a mass transfer of white people and resources out of central cities and hugely subsidizing the wealth of newly suburban whites and their descendants.[11] In a time of charged political struggle around race and housing rights in California and the nation as a whole, nonwhite homebuyers, especially Japanese Americans recently released from World War II internment camps, approached home buying cautiously, gathering information from intraethnic networks and gauging the attitudes of real-estate agents. Although racially restrictive covenants had been rendered legally unenforceable in *Shelley v. Kraemer* (1948), the Fair Housing Act, which explicitly prohibited racial discrimination in the sale of a house or in more institutionalized forms such as redlining and racial steering, was not instituted into law until 1968. In California, state laws passed in the late 1950s as well as the Rumford Fair Housing Act (1963) outlawed racial discrimination in segments of the housing market but was effectively disabled a year later by the real estate industry–led voters' initiative Proposition 14.[12]

Thus Asian Americans and Mexican Americans attempting to buy homes in the West SGV in the 1950s and 1960s approached the task with a full awareness of the realities of structural racial discrimination and the concomitant limitations it imposed on where they could and could not live. As largely well-waged, working-class, and middle-income home-buyers, however, they did have a much greater degree of choice than their poorer nonwhite counterparts and, compared to African Americans of all incomes, a larger ambit within which to exercise that degree of choice. This pattern was consistent with regional and national racial trends during the 1950s and 1960s, in which both Asian Americans and Mexican Americans gained acceptability in formerly all-white suburbs, even as African Americans continued to face virulent and often violent resistance.[13] In fact, in California, by the early 1960s, some Mexican Americans felt that issues of housing discrimination no longer applied to them.[14] In Los Angeles, the racially differentiated suburban housing market post–World War II particularly separated Asian American and African American populations who had formerly occupied many of the same neighborhoods.[15] However, there is evidence that at least in a few incidents occurring in Monterey Park (discussed in more detail later on), Mexican Americans and Asian Americans were reluctant to cooperate with Black exclusion, indicating early on the presence (however subtle) of a racial consciousness distinct from other suburban areas.

The generation that can now be considered "old-timers" in the West SGV, for the most part, moved to the area between the 1950s and the 1970s. While some families had already lived in the region for some time, most Mexican Americans who moved into the West SGV during the postwar decades were second-generation immigrants from East Los Angeles, looking to buy their first homes. Four-year-old Alice Ballesteros moved to Monterey Park with her family in 1952. As an adult, Ballesteros recalled that it was definitely seen as a "sign of upward mobility"; indeed, Monterey Park was known to many in East Los Angeles as the "Mexican Beverly Hills."[16] Throughout the Japanese American community, word circulated that Monterey Park was a white and Japanese American "bed-room community."[17] These various reputations evidenced the strong desire among different racial/ethnic groups for a suburban space to call their own. By 1970, Japanese Americans and Mexican Americans, as well as Chinese Americans, were well established in Monterey Park. In only two decades, the city had gone from almost exclusively white to "major-ity minority" (36 percent Latino, 10 percent Japanese American, and 5 percent Chinese American).[18]

In the 1970s, Karen and Ed Toguchi, Japanese Americans from Hawaii, were a young married couple living in an apartment in Los Angeles. Karen, now sixty-three, describes how they found their first house in Monterey Park during that time:

> We lived in an apartment in an alley in what's called K-Town now. And then, one day . . . we decided on getting a place of our own— and we really didn't think that would happen. But we contacted some gentleman . . . and I believe he was from a place called Kashu Realty, down here in Monterey Park. And of course, we had no clue what Monterey Park was . . . It's a Japanese name, but we don't know who owned it. . . . I don't know how we got in touch with this gentleman or how he got in touch with us. And he came over [to our] little apartment in K-Town and he says, "you guys would like to find a little place? I'll help you. . . . I know a place called Mon- terey Park." And I says, "Oh, I don't think I want to live there . . . it's a bedroom community, white and Japanese Americans, I don't think I want to live in a place like that." I want to live in a place that's mixed. And he says, "Well, just come on down and take a look." And so we went down and took a look. And we found a house there.[19]

Even though the Toguchis, according to Karen, did not initially want to live in a "white and Japanese American bedroom community," ethnic net- works, in a way they could barely recall, nonetheless led them to purchase a home in Monterey Park, where they had lived for the past thirty-plus years, with no intention of leaving. (As Karen put it, "We're gonna die here.") The Toguchis' home purchase through Kashu Realty was also significant: Unbeknownst to them, this was a branch office of Japanese American real- tor Kazuo Inouye's agency in Los Angeles's Crenshaw neighborhood. In the 1950s and 1960s, Inouye had been credited with single-handedly opening up large portions of Crenshaw to nonwhite homeowners.[20]

The successful entrée of Japanese Americans also attracted second- and later-generation Chinese Americans who, despite their distinct histories and cultures, as fellow "Orientals" occupied the same racial niche in the housing market. Seventy-eight-year-old Winston Gin, who moved to Monterey Park in 1958, heard that "it was one of the few areas where it was said that uh, Orientals might be welcome. . . . The fact that there were . . .

some Japanese families here already, we thought that we would belong."[21] Chinese American Howard Jong, who, like Gin, worked as an aeronautics engineer, purchased a home and moved to Monterey Park in 1964. Although he had heard that Monterey Park was "for Caucasians only," "Bill and Ernie"—two Chinese American friends—"had already purchased homes here at the time. I followed them."[22]

Others, following in the footsteps of earlier generations of racial minorities as well as working-class whites, bought land or homes in unincorporated areas outside the purview of municipal regulations.[23] Lisa Beppu's Japanese American family in 1961 and Anita Martinez's Mexican American parents, moving from Boyle Heights in the 1970s, took advantage of the relative lack of racial restrictions to buy homes in unincorporated portions of Los Angeles County in South San Gabriel and what is now Rosemead.[24] Mike Murashige, whose Japanese American family has been in San Gabriel for three generations, dating back at least to the 1920s, recalled a "weird pocket of Japanese Americans" in unincorporated land in South San Gabriel, who bought houses in new developments built in the 1960s and became the center of a vibrant Japanese American community in the West SGV.[25]

However, even though prospective Asian American and Latina/o homeowners like the Gins, Toguchis, and Martinezes had in some ways unprecedented opportunities to settle in the West SGV during this time, nearly all of them had experienced instances of discrimination in their lives that pointed to the ways in which racially differentiated access to space— public and private—delimited the boundaries of their social worlds. For instance, eighty-one-year-old David Tong, a third-generation Chinese American who has resided in Alhambra since 1973, recalled growing up the son of a grocer in Watts, "way on the southwest side" of Los Angeles, in the 1930s and 1940s, which was then a predominantly white area. Although he maintained that "we didn't feel any prejudice after they . . . got to know us," as a high school student during World War II, he also recalled passing through "the neighborhood" on his way home from school and being mistaken for Japanese by strangers, who "would holler out, 'You Jap. . . . Why don't you go back to where you're from?'"[26] He recalled another incident as a teenager, in which he—the only nonwhite in his group of friends—was refused admission to a public swimming pool on a club excursion to the San Fernando Valley. After the war—in which he served in the army in Saipan—Tong studied engineering in college and eventually embarked on a stable career as a civil engineer but was always aware not only of the "glass ceiling" but of racial boundaries inscribed in the landscape as well. He recalled that it was generally known that in certain areas, nonwhite professionals could work but not live: "It used to be a joke. Glendale [a suburban Los Angeles County municipality about 10 miles northwest of Alhambra] invites you if you're an Asian businessman and all that—you can open your business here in Glendale, but please leave at night, go back to where you're from." While Tong and his friends could laugh about it, in actuality nobody was kidding: he recounted the "shocked" reaction of a Chinese American engineer who moved from the Bay Area to work in Glendale when he could not find an apartment, "although there were plenty of them." The man ended up staying in a Glendale YMCA. Indeed, in 1949, Glendale realtors openly advertised their city as "a '100 percent Caucasian Race Community,'" and the city remained close to 100 percent white into the 1970s.[27] Thus, even for middle-income, professional people of color, public and private space were clogged with racial boundaries. Racial restrictions on where professionals like Tong could live often constituted a lingering reminder of their subordinated status in society, even as they found stable employment and made progress at work.

The ability of large numbers of Asian Americans and Latinas/os to buy homes in the West SGV beginning in the 1950s and its reputation as a place where Chinese Americans like Winston Gin "thought we could belong," was both significant and unusual. However, the West SGV suburbs' relative openness was not uniform across racial minority groups. Indeed, the increasing ability of Asian Americans and Latinas/os to buy houses was characterized by grudging acceptance posed in contradistinction to and often facilitated by racism against African Americans. For instance, when Kazuo Inouye, founder of Kashu Realty (the same company that would later lead the Toguchis to purchase a house in Monterey Park), opened a branch office in Monterey Park, he recalled that the local real estate board "wouldn't let us in because they were afraid that we were going to sell to blacks. So they said we had to wait two years. Nobody had to wait two years. They're always begging for members. Way in the back page, it says you had to wait two years. So we waited two years." When the two years was up, Inouye and his partner met with the board:

So they had a meeting with about eight or nine guys. They're all kind of looking at you with their arms folded and kind of glaring at you. They say, "Mr. Inouye, what type of people are you going to sell homes to here in Monterey Park?" I thought about it, and I said, "I would only sell to people who would be an asset to the city of Monterey Park." I didn't say I'm not going to sell to blacks or purples or whatever it is. I just told them [chuckles] that. They couldn't answer.

My partner was Chinese, and he went in there. He was taking a Berlitz course on memory. There were these eight or nine guys, and when he [my partner] left, he got up and called them by their first and last name. It shook each and every one up [chuckles]. So we kind of shook them up a little over there.[28]

Inouye and his partner's knowing evasion of the board members' questions and delight in "shaking them up" show how while they were willing to take advantage of opportunities afforded by their privileged racial status relative to Black people, this did not indicate a uniform willingness to comply with the existing racist hierarchy.[29]

A reluctance to conform to exclusionary scripts even while deriving relative benefits from racist practices—especially opportunities for homeownership—was also evident in many residents of the West SGV, as the experience of Bob and Helen Liley in Monterey Park in the early 1960s illustrates. Although significant numbers of Japanese Americans had already purchased homes in new tract developments in the area by that time, no "outright racial confrontation" occurred until February 1962, when the Congress of Racial Equality (CORE) charged that developer Montgomery Fisher refused to sell a house to Bob and Helen Liley, a Black physicist and his wife. Although the Monterey Highlands Homeowners Association (at that time still largely white) refused to get involved, stating that such matters were a matter of "individual conscience," the Monterey Park City Council took a more active stance to support the Lileys: Al Song, a Korean American who had recently been elected to the council, and Howard Fry, a white man who had previously lived on a South Dakota Indian reservation, issued a joint resolution endorsing state laws that prohibited discrimination and segregation. Unlike in other cases of housing activism, in which the primary antagonists were would-be Black residents' own neighbors (almost invariably whites), the Lileys also had the support of their neighbors in Monterey Park. When they were finally able to purchase the house, Bob Liley said, "We're happier over the response of the community than anything else." According to Eli Isenberg, the Jewish American editor of the *Monterey Park Progress*, "No city in the Southland, no large group of people have dealt with a problem as potentially explosive as the Liley case as well as Monterey Park has."[30]

The differentiated racial hierarchy that allowed Asian Americans and Mexican Americans, but few African Americans, to purchase homes in the West SGV marks the area as undeniably shaped by anti-Black racism, which hardened spatially in Los Angeles County during the same time period through the concentration and hypersegregation of Black Angelenos in South Central Los Angeles.[31] However, during the Liley incident, Monterey Park residents' refusal to uphold the suburban color line, which many of them had so recently crossed, indicates that some of them had distinct notions about race, homeownership, and property that departed from the usual narratives of movement into the suburbs as an inevitably whitening, assimilationist practice.

Property and Differential Racialization

The significance of suburban, middle-income, majority people-of-color neighborhoods is intimately tied to the imbrication of race, property, and homeownership in the United States. Legal scholar Cheryl Harris has discussed the centrality of interlinked notions of whiteness and property to the production and perpetuation of material racial inequality in the United States.[32] Thomas Shapiro, in *The Hidden Cost of Being African American*, highlights the links between housing discrimination, inheritance, and life chances. According to Shapiro, "inheritance is more important in determining life chances than college degrees, number of children in the family, marital status, full time employment, or household composition." Currently, almost all inherited wealth in the United States is rooted in white property ownership via gains from overtly discriminatory housing markets prior to 1968.[33] Discrimination was not an unfortunate incidental aspect of federal policies beginning in the 1930s but rather was written into the laws themselves.[34] David Freund argues that post–World War II patterns of suburban residential development, to which federal policies and practices were central, also marked a shift in white racial attitudes about race and property.[35] White homeowners, veiling the continuance of racist practices with professions of color-blind self-interest,[36] grew to embrace a "market imperative" explanation and justification for racial segregation

in which race and economics were conflated—an explanation that, ironi-
cally, was only possible due to the overtly discriminatory housing and loan
policies that had segregated their neighborhoods in the first place. Within
this logic, white homeowners were not personally racist; they were simply "concerned citizens" defending their right to property and following
the dictates of the market in upholding the neighborhood color line. The
terms *white*, *homeowner*, and *citizen* became increasingly conflated.

It follows, then, that the specific components of Asian and Latina/o
racialization in the United States and their differential relationships
to whiteness, homeownership, and property have been mutually
constitutive—in particular, the "honorary white" status of Asian Americans as model minorities and the ambiguously white status of Mexican
Americans.[37] However, while the linkages between property and the
continuance of white privilege have been relatively well documented,
aside from many excellent studies of the historical, structural, and ideological underpinnings of ghettoization, scholars have paid less attention
to theorizing differentially racialized relationships of nonwhite groups to
property and privilege, especially with regard to nonwhite homeowners.[38]
A growing body of work that seeks to recover the history of majority nonwhite spaces both within and on the fringes of metropolitan centers has
begun to correct this lacuna. Here are a few examples: Scott Kurashige
evokes a history of shared spaces among African Americans and Japanese
Americans in Los Angeles and illuminates access to homeownership as a
site of active struggle among both groups; Andrew Wiese catalogs a long
history of Black residential settlement and property ownership on the
fringes of U.S. cities; and Matt Garcia describes how Mexican American
citrus laborers made "worlds of their own" outside of the purview of white
employers in the early twentieth-century colonias of the eastern SGV.[39]
Recent scholarship on "suburban Chinatowns" has been somewhat disconnected from these histories, focusing more prominently on intraethnic
dynamics, economic flows, and transnational connections.[40] However, no
discussion of race and residential settlement can be complete without a
sustained consideration of how in the United States private property, symbolized by the "properly-ordered and prosperous domestic dwelling," has
come to serve as the "the nation's key symbol of freedom, harmony, and
virtue . . . the privileged moral geography of American society."[41] Just as
notions of whiteness and property have been bound to one another since
the founding of the United States, racialized minority groups' relationship

to, or terms of exclusion from, whiteness has been defined by differential access to property—and, more recently, to homeownership. Put another way, if conceptions of whiteness and property have been inextricably linked, so too have varying constructions of *non*whiteness and denial of rights to property. Therefore discourses concerning race and property are also significant in that they delineate "good" and "bad" citizens.[42]

Mexican Americans' ambiguous racial status dates from the United States' forcible acquisition of Mexican land in the 1848 Treaty of Guadalupe Hidalgo, in which all former citizens of Mexico in those territories were given U.S. citizenship, rendering them effectively white by law.[43] While most scholarship emphasizes systemic disenfranchisement and discrimination against Mexican Americans in housing, references to at least two midcentury cases in the Los Angeles area point to instances in which ambiguous racial status under the law allowed Mexican Americans access to homeownership in ways that were denied at the time to other racial groups. In the first case, as recounted by Kazuo Inouye, a "Mrs. Lopez" recounted to the realtor how, after she had bought her house previous to World War II, "the neighbors all took her to court saying that she wasn't white." Ultimately, the courts ruled in Mrs. Lopez's favor ("that the Mexicans were white"), and Mrs. Lopez kept the house and stayed but "it cost her a lot of money."[44] In another case around the same time, *A. T. Collison and R. L. Wood v. Nellie García et al.* (1945), the Los Angeles Superior Court dismissed a suit brought by property owners in El Monte to prevent Nellie García, a Mexican American woman, from occupying a property covered by a covenant that barred those of the "African," "Asian," and "Mexican" races. García's attorney, David Marcus, successfully requested dismissal on the grounds that "there was no Mexican race."[45]

With regard to homeownership, then, although there is plenty of evidence of pervasive discrimination against Mexican Americans, their ability to be considered white by law nonetheless stands in contrast with laws that explicitly forbade Asian Americans to own land or become citizens in the early twentieth century, effectively blocking fundamental entry points to the privileges of whiteness. Because of this ambiguous racial status under the law, Mexican Americans tended not to join other groups in battling whites-only restrictive housing covenants.[46] However, although some Mexican Americans certainly benefited materially from their ambiguous whiteness, relative to other racial groups, it is clear that legal status as white often did not translate into acceptance by white neighbors as such. The battles Mexican American homeowners in predominantly white neighborhoods fought on the ground, where there were no judges or lawyers to adjudicate that "there was no Mexican race," were also significant to the formation of racial and political identities. For instance, when Mrs. Lopez, the Mexican American woman homeowner whose neighbors had contested her whiteness in court, later decided to sell her house, she approached Inouye, a Japanese American, and insisted that he sell her house to a person of color: "Mrs. Lopez . . . called up one day, she says . . . 'I want to sell my house, but I do not want to sell to the whites.' I said, 'That's all right with me. I got all kinds of customers that are not white.'"[47] When Inouye asked why, Mrs. Lopez cited her white neighbors' efforts to prove that she was not eligible to live in her own house. Although the legal battle had been costly, Mrs. Lopez had persevered. In the process, her house became not just a commodity to be sold to the highest bidder but a symbol of a moral imperative: to pass on her right of homeownership, gained via access to whiteness, to a person of color. Inouye obliged and sold the house to a Japanese American family, standing up to white intimidation and threats of violence in the process.[48]

The actions of Mrs. Lopez and Inouye reiterate that, as mentioned earlier, Asian American and Latina's/os' relatively better access to homeownership than African Americans did not necessarily translate into complicity with a "white spatial imaginary" of exclusion, suggesting that theirs was often a strategic use of whiteness (whether "honorary" or "ambiguous") that did not lose sight of legacies of historical and structural racism. In what follows, we will see how Asian Americans and Mexican Americans in the West SGV, as "model minorities" and "ambiguous whites," negotiated provisional acceptances in formerly majority-white neighborhoods in the West SGV by partaking in specific relationships to private property.

"Who's Moving In?" Model Minorities and Ambiguous Whites

In the 1970s, David and Soume Tong's purchase of a home in a North Alhambra neighborhood constituted an exception to prevalent patterns of racial steering, in which Asian Americans were usually taken to "lesser value homes in a different area . . . down closer to the freeway." When the Tongs, who are Chinese American, had initially looked for a house in San Marino (a bastion of old money adjacent to North Alhambra that was then overwhelmingly white), they noted that real estate agents "weren't all that friendly."[49] Ultimately, their entrée into the predominantly white neighborhood in North Alhambra was facilitated by a realtor acquaintance of Soume's who had recommended they look in the area.

Like the Tongs, Mexican Americans Dora and Al Padilla found that their ability to purchase a house in a predominantly white neighborhood occurred through informal channels. According to Dora Padilla, who is now seventy-three, "Alhambra had an unpublished agreement through the realtors. They wouldn't fall out of their chairs to show homes to Latinos. . . . It was prejudiced. There isn't another word for it, it was prejudice." Although at the time, Padilla and her husband didn't "realize that there was that existing, uh, gentleman's agreement among realtors," they found that they were only shown houses that were extremely highly priced, which exceeded their budget. Looking back now, Dora Padilla believes that "the idea was to discourage us." Ultimately the Padillas found their house not through a realtor but after seeing a posted "for sale" sign while driving through the neighborhood on their own and dealing directly with the owner: "The reason we got this house was that the woman here had two children, and she was a widow, and she had to get into a bigger home. And she wanted to sell quick. And I think she just saw the opportunity to sell to us, and didn't do it through a real estate [agency]. She just put up a 'for sale' sign."[50] Monterey Park realtor Sal Montenegro's experiences during this time (the early 1960s) corroborate Padilla's observations: According to Montenegro, some owners simply requested that "property not be shown to Mexicans." Others told Mexican American prospective homebuyers to "go back where you came from." Mexican Americans' ambiguous whiteness constituted an explicit and hierarchical rationale for discrimination: according to one realtor, "If you are light-skinned, we have several homes available, but if you are dark-skinned, don't waste my time."[51]

Even after purchasing their homes, both couples continued to experience conditional terms of acceptance. After the Tongs purchased their house in North Alhambra, Soume, now seventy-nine, described the reaction of the neighbors: "Our neighbors next door . . . asked the neighbor, 'Who's moving in?' They didn't want to say it's an Oriental couple. . . . they [just] said, 'an engineer and a teacher,' so they were really surprised [when we moved in]." The neighbor believed that the Tongs' potentially objectionable racial identities would be mitigated by their middle-class, professional occupations, which proved them to be "good" model minorities. This aligns with the Asian American model minority stereotype, in which Asian Americans, albeit "forever foreign," are provisionally accepted as "honorary whites"[52] as long as they conform to American immigrant narratives of striving for middle-class attainment through hard work and ingenuity.

Similarly, after Dora and Al Padilla moved into their new home in Alhambra, Dora Padilla recounted how their white next-door neighbors, although perhaps initially hostile, seemed to accept them after finding out that her husband coached football at a nearby high school, where he counted their neighbors' nephew as a colleague: "So all [of] a sudden, we were *OK*." Dora Padilla, whose Mexican father was of German and Spanish ancestry, had always been able to pass as white. However, "my husband is obviously very Latino—he looks like a Mexican [chuckles], if you want a stereotype. He's dark-skinned. He doesn't look Italian, he looks Mexican." The Padillas' somewhat ambivalent relationship to their initially white neighborhood—as well as Dora Padilla's ability to selectively "pass" as white—continued to characterize their life in Alhambra over the next decades. For instance, when she decided to run for school board in the late 1970s, a friend who had experience working on local city council campaigns advised her to run with her maiden name, "Swarto"—derived from her father's German heritage—as her middle name. Padilla complied and won the election. Subsequently, "people would run into me, they'd ask, 'so are you a *real* Mexican?'" Padilla describes her response as follows: "After a while, I thought, well, OK, if they're gonna be stupid, asking me questions like that, I can be offhand with them too. And I said, 'Well, I'm not the Pillsbury Dough Boy. I'm real.' [laughs]" While at least in retrospect, Padilla could joke about the "problem" her racial ambiguity presented for white fellow school board members, at home the Padillas worked hard to validate their suburban pedigree by "keeping [up] with the neighborhood" in appearances, particularly through tending their front yard—a principle they passed on to their children.

> People have their attitudes, and if you just go up against them, trying to knock heads . . . you're not going to be successful. You have . . . to educate them. And that's what we did over a period of time. . . . [My husband] goes over there and does yard work at my

daughter's house [across the street]. He's very proud, because he feels that that's something you have to be aware of. He taught our boys. . . . He had a big power mower, he would cut the grass . . . he does everything—the roses, the ivy, all the plants. And he taught them that it's important to have your home looking good. . . . My daughter's husband isn't that great at yard work [laughs], but the same thing is carried over. He's very conscious that even though it's a rental, it [should] look very nice . . . right away he started pruning all kinds of things, just keeping [up] with the neighborhood.

Dora Padilla's ambiguous whiteness won her both trust and suspicion through the years, while her husband's "obvious" Mexicanness was seemingly counterbalanced by his occupation coaching a local school team and his careful cultivation of the house and front yard's appearance to neighborhood standards.

The Tongs and Padillas, as racialized nonwhite bodies, had to either "pass" as white (as Dora Padilla did) or evidence a "proper" relationship with their property as conceived as coextensive with a middle-class, white nuclear-family-based vision of Americanness (to have professional occupations like the Tongs or to "keep [up] with the neighborhood" in appearances, like Al Padilla). In other words, as model minorities and ambiguous whites, their actions and occupations had to be consistent with a spatial imaginary that privileged whiteness—expressed as middle-class social and economic norms and a commitment to maintaining property values—in order to earn the acceptance of their neighbors. The Tongs' and Padillas' detailed retellings of these interactions decades later conveyed their awareness of the conditional status of their acceptance and an enduring sense of difference from their white neighbors.

How this sense of difference translated into action is difficult to generalize. In an immediate sense, strategic uses of whiteness might function simply to facilitate individual gain and looked a lot like complicity. In some cases—and especially as the Asian immigrant and Asian American population increased—Asian Americans and Mexican Americans might be pitted against one another by whites in terms of relative desirability. For instance, in Rosemead in 1993, Milo Alvarez's Mexican American parents were able to purchase a home because of their contingent acceptance as white, in comparison to Asians. When the previous owner, a white woman, complained how Asians were taking over and could buy whatever they liked with cash, the Alvarezes kept silent:

> [T]he lady was a white lady that ended up moving to Tennessee. She refused to sell to Asians, which is the only reason really why my parents were able to afford to move in that neighborhood. She said ... "They think they can come here and buy everything with their money"—"they" meaning Asian Americans, right? So my parents were just, like, quiet. [laughs] And so she took their offer, even though it was a[n] FHA offer, loan thing—they didn't have as much of a down payment—versus a cash offer that was more money, from an Asian American family, because she liked my mom. And it was kind of weird because back when we were growing up, they wouldn't have sold to Mexicans.... I mean, that sentiment would have been reserved for Mexicans. But she for some reason felt like ... it was Asian people she didn't want moving into her place.[53]

The white woman's implicit inclusion of the Alvarezes in her construction of "we" (versus "they," meaning Asian Americans) illustrates how for some whites, the "ambiguously white" status of Mexican Americans stood in desirable contrast to the "honorary white" / "forever foreign" status of Asian Americans.[54] In the context of the West SGV, Mexican Americans were conceived of as relative insiders, more "American" than the "foreign" (and undifferentiated) "Asians."[55] The Asian prospective buyers' purported ability to make a cash offer for a house confirmed their foreignness since it disturbed "American Dream" narratives of poor immigrants working their way up from nothing, unsettling dominant conceptions of legitimate participation in the nation predicated on white, middle-class norms as well as historical narratives built on the experiences of European immigrants.[56]

While it is difficult to interpret the Alvarezes' silence as something other than complicity with anti-Asian racism, the fact that the details of this interaction circulated within the Alvarez family in this way meant that there was, at least, an acute awareness of the ways in which their own acceptance as homebuyers was racially contingent and a careful consideration of the racial, class, and power dynamics in the transaction. Similar to the Tongs and Padillas in the 1960s and 1970s, in the 1990s, in order to purchase their home, the Alvarezes still had to concede to white dictates of who could be American and who could not. In other words, as model minorities and ambiguous whites, all three couples had to make concessions to a white spatial imaginary, in which a moral geography of pure space—predicated on sameness—and the generation of exchange value via property over all else, were the dominant principles of operation.[57] While this could look like and function as complicity with white dominance, it is also clear that these experiences were formative of distinctly nonwhite identifications and, for some, antiracist world views. Taken at face value, the unprecedented ability of large numbers of Asian Americans and Latinas/os to buy homes in the West SGV beginning in the 1950s might be interpreted as racial progress in an integrationist sense. However, the very specific conditions that circumscribed and informed Asian Americans and Mexican Americans' movement into the West SGV also fostered a keen awareness of the pernicious effects of racially exclusive attitudes and practices. In the decades that followed, these experiences would be formative of a distinctive set of goals and expectations regarding property, which residents experienced and articulated as sharply divergent from those of white residents, who fled the area en masse during the same time period.

What Is Produced? Toward a Moral Geography of Differentiated Space

In the 1970s and 1980s, new Asian immigrants—primarily immigrants from Taiwan and Hong Kong, seeking to pursue economic, educational, and professional opportunities and escape political uncertainty—came in rapidly increasing numbers to the West SGV. Taking advantage of both transpacific and local social and economic ethnic networks, they began to transform the commercial as well as residential landscapes of the area, spurring the resistance and animosity of established residents and massive white flight.[58] By 1990, Monterey Park (the site of the most intense battles) became the first majority–Asian American city in the continental United States. During this time of rapid demographic transition, while the white population in Monterey Park dropped precipitously, Asian Americans and Mexican Americans stayed in the area long term at much higher rates than whites and often spurred family members to settle in the area as well. For instance, the Latina/o population increased in the 1970s and declined only slightly in the 1980s. The Japanese American population increased by nearly two-thirds in the 1970s and dropped by about a fifth in the 1980s—a significant decrease but still much lower than the rates of white flight and attrition. In Alhambra, by 1990 the white population had dropped to a quarter of its size in 1970, while the number of Latinas/os more than doubled (Figures 7–9). In short, during this time of rapid social and economic transformation, established Asian American and Latina/o residents, unlike whites, tended to stay, suggesting differing responses, expectations, and stakes in the area. The following stories show some of the dimensions of established Latina/o and Asian American residents' experience of demographic transition in the area during this period and suggest affective as well as practical reasons as to why they chose to stay.

"Nobody Sells Their Home": The Significance of Staying

The sentiment of not selling one's home or moving, tied to expressions of acceptance—albeit sometimes grudging—or difference, is a pervasive theme among Mexican Americans and Asian Americans in the West SGV. "Nobody sells their home," a Mexican American longtime resident of Monterey Park explained, regarding the residents of his block. The man went on to describe how when he first moved there, "[o]nly Anglos could buy houses, but we fought it and could move into these two blocks. There is a Japanese American family at the other end of the block, and they had been here a long time, too."[59] The man's simple statement, "nobody sells their

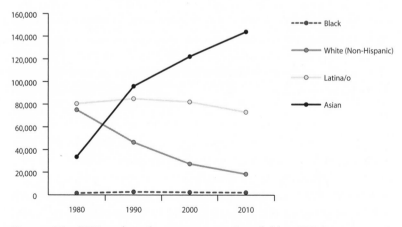

Figure 7. *West SGV population by race, 1980–2010. Compiled from U.S. Census, 1980–2010.*

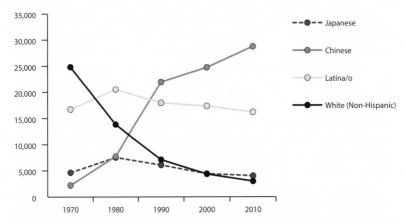

Figure 8. *Ethnic/racial composition of Monterey Park, 1970–2010. Compiled from U.S. Census, 1970–2010.*

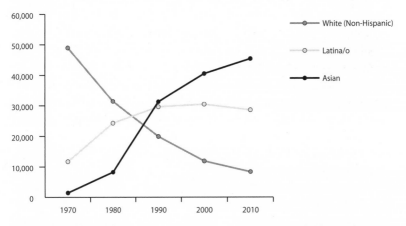

Figure 9. *Ethnic/racial composition of Alhambra, 1970–2010. Compiled from U.S. Census, 1970–2010.*

home," when tied to a recollection of fighting for the right to even live in the neighborhood, evokes a collective, multiracial "we" that implicitly excludes "Anglos" who buy and sell their homes liberally. It is not only a product of shared interethnic histories and spaces but a particular way of making sense of local history and the actions of people in one's community.

Similarly, Bill Gin, a third-generation Chinese American who has lived in Monterey Park since he was ten years old in 1959, believed that "Asians don't move out of the area unless something drastic happens"—a sentiment that was repeated by many of the people I interviewed. Three generations of the Gin family—his parents, himself and his siblings, and most recently, his daughter—owned homes in Monterey Park. He and his family had been in their current house for thirty-two years and explained the following:

> My neighbors were here all that time . . . I notice that. Because even my parents, the only reason they moved was because they wanted a bigger house on top of the hill. So they moved. But that was less than a half a mile move. And then I looked at my aunts and my uncles and everybody else. . . . You notice that they don't move. This neighborhood is a little bit on the old side, but there's enough . . . younger couples moving in [with] their kids. . . . I think they enjoy the area, and moving is basically too much of a hassle. And they have great neighbors—everything's here for them.[60]

In contrast to the multigenerational investments of Asian American families like the Gins, white residents were more likely to move. The children of those who stayed usually did not settle in the area as adults either. Gin remembered "a big shift" in the white population: "[O]ver there it was basically all whites, until the kids grew up and didn't want to live there, and they got older and they just suddenly sold out to the Asian population, and they moved too . . . So there was a big shift." When I asked Gin if he had any idea why the children of white residents did not tend to stay in the area, he replied:

> I think maybe they would feel an oddity right now. They'd be a minority and stuff like that. . . . I mean, they would get along with everybody, it wouldn't be a problem . . . but it's just a matter of everybody having a choice of where they want to live . . . and the [life]styles they want to live. You know, there's a lot of acceptability of mixed marriages here. Even my *mother*, she said, every one of you have to marry Chinese. Twenty years later she modified it. She says, OK, as long as you get married I'm OK, for the girls, but the boys, you gotta marry an Asian [laughing].

Gin's mention of the relative acceptance of interracial marriages, as a response to why whites might have a different relationship to the area, points to not only sheer numbers—being the numerical majority versus a minority—as a factor in people's choices to stay or leave but an atmosphere of tolerance and flexibility.

In national studies, sociologists and demographers have noted disparities between whites and nonwhite groups regarding both neighborhood demographic preferences and underlying motivations. In contrast to metropolitan-level findings, analysis at the neighborhood level has shown that living in integrated, multiethnic neighborhoods corresponds with lower levels of prejudice and competition.[61] Unlike whites, Asians, Latinas/os, and African Americans generally prefer to live in diverse, integrated neighborhoods. Further, among these nonwhite groups, researchers have found that "own-race preference" is not necessarily a sign of ethnocentrism but a reaction to white racism or apprehension of white hostility. In comparison to other racial groups, whites have long shown the highest correlation between negative racial stereotypes and negative attitudes toward neighborhood integration.[62] Indeed, in the West SGV, the reasons some departing white residents gave for leaving clearly evinced nativist, anti-Asian sentiments. For example, former Monterey Park resident Frank Rizzo, interviewed by the *Los Angeles Times* in 1987, expressed disapproval of his new Chinese immigrant neighbors' perceived unwillingness to "give up their traditions and settle into an American way of life." Rizzo commented that when he left, "What I might do is hang a little American flag on my truck and drive through town on my way out and wave goodbye to all my old friends. . . . I'm moving far away from here."[63] For some departing white SGV residents, then, moving was a statement of protest against a foreign invasion. While the earlier-arriving Asian Americans had not threatened residents like Rizzo's need for "an American way of life," the new immigrants—arriving with the capital to transform commercial as well as residential landscapes, and seemingly unwilling or unable to make concessions to a white spatial imaginary—disrupted his sense of an appropriate suburban (racial) order.

Census data for occupational status and income in the West SGV back to 1980 reveals that white residents did have more financial capacity to move than Latinas/os or Asian Americans. For instance, in 1980, a white family's median income was 15 percent higher than a Latina/o family's income, and a white person was 1.6 times more likely to be employed in a managerial or professional occupation. Although Asians'

median family incomes exceeded those of whites and a higher proportion of Asians worked in managerial and professional occupations,
whites still had the highest per capita income of all three groups—
surpassing that of Latinas/os by 40 percent.[64] Nonetheless, even Asian
Americans and Mexican Americans who felt uncomfortable about the
demographic changes in the area still did not express a desire to leave,
though they noted dramatic white flight. As Karen Toguchi put it: "We
were very, very comfortable, until about 20 years ago, maybe? We had
been here for [pause] at least 15 years, and then things started to change.
Chinese people started to come in, and it was like a locust descending
on the land. And next thing we knew . . . it was white flight. I'd never
seen white flight. I read about it in the books and the newspaper, but
to truly be involved in it, it was almost shocking to the system. Literally seeing people run out of this place."[65] Although Toguchi described
the arrival of Chinese immigrants with a dehumanizing metaphor of
an invasion of insects—"it was like a locust descending on the land"—
its effect on her was relatively mild. What stood out to her the most
was not that, but the speed and rate at which white people fled. For the
Toguchis, the conveniences, pleasures, and relatively low cost of living
in Monterey Park ultimately outweighed the discomfort of the demographic changes. However, another factor may have been at play as well.
Karen said she understood that many of those who left—some Chinese
and Japanese Americans, as well as whites—had felt "displaced." Both
of the Toguchis, who grew up in Hawaii, had always been aware of and
interested in the fluidity of culture and identity; perhaps it was harder
to feel displaced if one never had a fixed sense of identity in the first
place.[66]

The rapid departure was noticeable even to a child. Japanese American Romy Uyehara, whose family lived in the same neighborhood as the
Toguchis and was in elementary school in the early eighties, noticed that
her older brother's white friends "kind of just moved away": "I really
noticed it—I noticed that my brother started hanging out with more
Asians—you know, Chinese and Japanese friends, and his white friends
moved away." Romy herself had "a couple white friends" in elementary
school, but they moved away as well, and "pretty much by the end of
eighth grade, most of my friends were Asian. And that just kind of continued on to Alhambra High School." Romy remembers learning about

white flight from her parents during a conversation over dinner one night as a child:

> They were talking about this family moving away, and discussing, "Well, I guess it's that white flight thing." And I remember asking them, what's that supposed to mean? . . . because at that time, I was so young, I thought of flight of being like birds. So I didn't understand, "what do you mean, white flight?" And they explained to me. "You know, sometimes people move out of an area, and in this case it's all the Caucasian white people." So yeah. I remember that. [chuckles]
>
> *So they described it to you kind of as racially motivated?*
>
> Yeah, they did. I mean, my parents didn't delve too deeply into it, they just kind of said, you know, "Sometimes people move away because they don't feel comfortable, or they don't want to live somewhere anymore." . . . But yeah, I kind of got the sense, "Oh, OK, these people moved away because they didn't feel comfortable living here."

Romy's sense of comfort and belonging in the area as a child made it impossible for her to understand people's hostility.

> [E]ven at that age . . . I guess I kind of knew I belonged here. . . . So to me, it was like, well, I don't understand why people would feel uncomfortable that other people are moving in, because . . . I always felt like I belong here. I was born here, I've lived in this house all my life, and it was kind of like, wow, I can't believe people feel so uncomfortable in this place just because *other* people are moving in. I didn't understand that whole idea that people just can't tolerate change, or they just feel uncomfortable with it. . . . I just felt like I wasn't really a part of it.[67]

Tony Gonzalez, a seventy-two-year-old Mexican American, purchased a house in the Monterey Park Hills in 1960. Gonzales, who fought in the Korean War (and met his Korean wife while there), considers

himself an unhyphenated "American" and maintained that location, specifically proximity to his parents in East Los Angeles—and not race or
ethnic composition—was the primary criterion when he and his wife
were looking for a house. When they moved in, their street of around a
dozen homes was about half white and half Japanese American. When
I asked if he ever observed any tension or discomfort in relation to the
mixed neighborhood, he began talking about how whites could be hostile toward Asians—complaining about bad driving and accusing them
of "taking over" or saying, "There goes the neighborhood." Gonzalez's
take on it, however, was that when he moved in initially, "it was more
like I was moving into a Japanese neighborhood, like *I* was the inter-
ruption." Because of his perception from the outset that he was living
in a predominantly Asian neighborhood, Gonzalez was not particularly surprised or disturbed when increasing numbers of ethnic Chinese
began to move in. In response to a question about whether or not his
neighborhood had changed much over the years, he replied, "Yes and
no. It's gone from Japanese and Chinese [to more Chinese]. It's still a
nice, quiet place to live."[68] Although white neighbors over the years felt
comfortable confiding to Gonzalez, who describes his political views as
"terribly conservative" and, with his light skin and blue eyes, can easily
pass for white, Gonzalez did not in fact share their sense of territoriality
and assumptions that the arrival of more Asians represented a disruption in a proper neighborhood balance.[69]

Downhill from where the Toguchis, Uyeharas, and Gonzalezes lived,
Juan Ramirez,[70] forty, recalled the overall diversity of his predominantly
Mexican American neighborhood in the 1970s and early 1980s. His childhood neighbors included Vietnamese, Filipinos, African Americans,
Central Americans, and Chinese. He also remembered how whites had
been quick to leave: "When I was a *real* little kid, there were still some
white people. But they were leaving. I mean . . . they were gone right
away."[71] Just east of Monterey Park in South San Gabriel, Anita Martinez,
thirty-seven, a fifth-generation Mexican American and fourth-generation
Angeleno, recalled that their house, purchased in the late 1970s, was
flanked by a Japanese American family behind, Koreans across the street,
Mexican Americans on one side, and a white family on the other. In keeping with larger patterns throughout the area, the whites eventually moved
away and were replaced by Asians.[72]

Growing Up in a Geography of Differentiated Space

Over time, Asian American and Latina/o residents of the West SGV passed on to their children this different set of meanings and expectations in relation to property. For those who were born into, or moved at an early age, into multiracial neighborhoods in the West SGV, neighborly interethnic coexistence—often expressed as an expectation or acceptance of difference, rather than an expectation of sameness—was all they had known. This expectation of acceptance of difference was primarily expressed in racial/ethnic terms but also occurred in limited ways with regard to class. To some extent, their experiences reflected the fluidity of racial, ethnic, and class distinctions among youth. For some, racial, ethnic, and socioeconomic differences easily traversed at a young age later became harder divisions as they grew older, relegated to distant though cherished memories. For others, however, this fluidity and comfort among difference became a formative and enduring way of living and thinking into adulthood.

Anita Martinez, who now lives in nearby Lincoln Heights—another predominantly Asian and Latina/o neighborhood—recalls for the most part an atmosphere of friendship and acceptance in her South San Gabriel neighborhood, at times actively guided by her parents:

> I can't really remember people being too derogatory or mean. . . .
> I really don't remember there being that much prejudice from
> other Latino kids. The only thing in my neighborhood that people
> would complain about is the smell of food around 5 o'clock. . . . I
> don't know if they were Vietnamese families or whatever, but you
> could smell fish and garlic in the air, and it was really really strong.
> And I know the other kids would be like, "oh, there's that smell
> again!" And then my mom would go, "How do you think *they* feel
> when they smell our chorizo?" . . . She would always try to put it in
> perspective.[73]

Martinez's mother, a teacher who had been active in the Chicano movement, nudged the neighborhood kids not to negatively exoticize their neighbors' food (and by extension, the neighbors themselves) by reminding them that "our chorizo" (a fatty pork sausage common in Mexican cuisine) might elicit the same reaction in others. By likening the smell of "fish and garlic" to the smell of chorizo, Martinez's mother asserted a "moral geography" of differentiated space—an appreciation for diversity and a reminder that everyone had an equal claim to the neighborhood—a lesson her daughter still remembered years later.[74]

Eloy Zarate and Mike Murashige, growing up a few miles north in San Gabriel in the 1970s, both remembered a carefree neighborhood space in which children of diverse ethnicities moved freely in and out of one another's houses. Zarate, now forty, enjoyed a "very mixed" friendship group, including children of Polish and Italian immigrants, Japanese Americans, and Zarate himself, whose parents are Mexican American and Argentinean. Sharing the same community in which nearly everyone was "lower middle class, upper working class" formed a bond of commonality: "We were all *different*, but we were all very similar in how we were in our community . . . I mean, we understood ethnically that we were different . . . there was a label that we understood, that your parents are Japanese or your parents are Polish. But it didn't mean anything past that . . . we didn't see the differences of what that meant, in terms of what you went home to. Because we were also in each others' homes. So what *you* were experiencing, *we* were experiencing."[75] Juan Ramirez, growing up in Monterey Park around the same time, had a similarly nostalgic view of growing up in his neighborhood: "[W]e had a really good time in the neighborhood. A *really* good time. I had a *lot* of friends. . . . There were kids everywhere, so there was always something to do." His best friend was a Central American boy, and he played with a Chinese boy named David. A Filipino family with nine daughters lived nearby—"we [boys] were always there [laughing]"—and the girls' father "was always out there playing with us, because I guess he wanted a son. And so he was out there, you know, on his skateboard—a grown man, he was out there with us."[76]

Many of these stories demonstrate sophisticated understandings about the nuances of socioeconomic hierarchies and the specificity of particular social relations to scale and context—such as relationships that were possible at the neighborhood level but did not translate into other contexts. Mike Murashige recalled being aware that the Chavezes,[77] the Mexican American family who moved in two doors away, were different from the middle-income Mexican American families who already lived on the street or the Mexican American mayor of San Gabriel at the time. Mr. Chavez "sold little Mexican hats at Olvera Street" (a historic tourist destination in downtown Los Angeles), participating in an informal economy that Mike characterized as "not even working class, it's you know . . . kind of that low-rent retail stuff, right." Mike and his younger brother befriended two of the Chavez boys, and the four "hung out a lot," but only in the neighborhood, since the Chavezes attended Catholic school. When they did attend the same high school, Mike and Kiko Chavez[78] would walk to school together or catch a ride with Kiko's father, "sittin' in the back with all the fuckin' sombreros that he sold." But at school, while Mike was increasingly in honors classes, Kiko was "in there with the barrio kids" and had joined a local gang.

> And so he was like, "Dude, at school, so, we don't really talk."
> And I understand that. . . . I thought the same thing. I'd say hi
> to him [at school] and just be like, "hey dude," and walk on. But
> then we'd walk home together. . . . And then when [Kiko] was
> hanging out with them, they'd look at him funny when he talked
> to me. But he was a regular part of my group of [friends]. Even in
> high school, we'd hang out together. And we'd have these ridicu-
> lously hilarious discussions. They didn't seem that at the time,
> but they are now that I think about them. They'd be like, "What
> the fuck are you doing going out of the house with your box-
> ers hanging out?" He's like, "fuckin', that's stylish." . . . We'd have
> these little cultural exchanges. That was the [cholo] style at the
> time. They'd get their sweatpants, like black or gray sweatpants,
> and they'd cut them off, and then they'd have their boxers hang-
> ing low below them.[79]

The neighborhood context, as two kids who grew up practically next door to one another, allowed Mike and Kiko to maintain their friendship and perhaps fostered in the two teenagers an awareness of racial and cultural identities as contextualized performances, as evidenced in their frank discussion of cholo style as "stylish" to one and preposterous to the other—a discussion which, like their friendship, was unlikely outside the permissive and relatively heterogeneous social space of the neighborhood.

For Anita Martinez and her friends, performing racial and cultural identity became a game. As a teenager, Anita became best friends with a

Vietnamese American, Tina, and spent much of her time at Tina's house and with her family: "I was there all the time. . . . I would go to like, the weddings with them and stuff." Anita and Tina became so close that they sometimes played at blurred the boundaries of their identities, bending ethnic lines to "pass" as each other's family:

> [B]ecause she was Vietnamese, she also could get pretty dark dur-
> ing the summer like me, so there would be times when we would
> pretend to be cousins. Or later on, when we got older and I would
> hang out with her, I would go with her to the Vietnamese clubs
> in Santa Ana. And she'd be like, OK, don't tell anybody you're
> Mexican, we're gonna see if you can pass! . . . I'd go to the club,
> I just wouldn't really talk or anything. [laughing] And then she
> would tell everybody that my dad was a Mexican U.S. soldier and
> my mom was Vietnamese. . . . And so we would do that just for
> fun. . . . And then the same thing with her . . . if she started hanging
> out with me a lot . . . people would think she was Mexican . . . she
> doesn't really look *that* Mexican, but she could pass if she wanted
> to. So one time, we did this thing where I used to get my nails done
> at the shop and I'm like, "I think they're talking shit about me, I
> can't tell." She was all, "I'll go with you . . . teach me some words
> in Spanish." So we're pretending to speak Spanish and we're sitting
> there, and she's all, "They *are* talking shit about you." [laughs] And
> then so when we left, she just told them something like, "bye," in
> Vietnamese. And all the ladies are like, "oh my god." [laughing][80]

Anita recalled also playing games of cross-racial passing with anoth-er friend, who was Japanese and white. "She would say, 'Oh, this is my cousin, she's half Japanese too.' When I was younger . . . I could pass for part, maybe half Asian . . . or people would think I was Filipino. . . . If you put that idea in people's mind they'll be like, 'Oh, yeah, I could see that.'" Anita and her friends' games spoke to the porousness of ethnic and racial identities in the area in which they grew up, as well as an early awareness of the socially constructed and somewhat arbitrary nature of such categories.

The fluidity of racial and ethnic boundaries was not seen as positive by everyone, however—particularly adults. Once, Anita recalled, Tina's moth-er told her daughter to "stop acting Mexican." Although Anita believed that

Figure 10. Anita Martinez and her friend Tina, South San Gabriel, 1984. Courtesy of Anita Marie Martinez.

Tina's mother was simply upset by how "wild" the two girls acted together ("We would just goof around like crazy . . . just be rolling on the floor laughing, just doing stupid things") and was not offended by the comment when Tina relayed it to her; however, Anita's father, a former activist in the Chicano movement, was upset by it. Such exchanges show that although, for the most part, young Asian and Latina/o residents of the West SGV developed and practiced a moral geography of differentiated space, normative racial assumptions—more often expressed by adults—nonetheless intruded on and shaped the contours of the regional racial hierarchy. Nonetheless, within this regional hierarchy, Asian American and Latina/o youth were able to develop and assert a multiethnic, multiracial nonwhite identity that fostered a powerful sense of belonging—a feeling that, for many, continued into adulthood.

Troubling Relationships to Property and "Proper" Uses of Space

"What Having a House Represented"

For many people, the nuances of the regional racial hierarchy were learned through observing material and symbolic linkages between property, homeownership, race, class, and location. This was particularly true at the intersections of Monterey Park and East Los Angeles, where in the 1970s, Monterey Park incorporated sections of East Los Angeles, demolishing swaths of working-class residential areas in the process. Juan Ramirez, a teenager in the mid-1980s, remembered feeling like "they wanted to get rid of us." In his mind, "we" meant working-class Mexican Americans, and "they" included "rich Chinese people" as well as white developers: "[M]y neighborhood was going to get demolished. It was a political move by developers. It was categorized as a blighted area. . . . We knew how we were perceived. We knew that our homes were perceived as bringing down property values in Monterey Park."[81] Juan's connection between "how we were perceived" and "our homes" being "perceived as bringing down property values" show his understanding of how perceptions of certain nonwhite bodies and spaces were attached to measures of economic value.[82] In that moment, he saw "rich Chinese people" as complicit with the white developers, articulating a hierarchy of race and class through control of space.

Oscar Ixco, thirty-five, grew up in the low-income Maravilla housing projects, on the boundary of Monterey Park and East Los Angeles—a line that, he recalled, was literally visible on the street. At some point as a child, living in the projects "became something of an embarrassment to me, something I wouldn't share with people." When people asked where he lived, "a lot of times I would say that I lived in Monterey Park, because Monterey Park carried prestige." Ixco, who now works as an assistant project manager in urban redevelopment, is half Mexican and half Salvadorean and has light skin, black hair, and dark eyes. In elementary school, he tested into the gifted program and was sometimes mistaken for Asian up through high school, a slippage he admitted enjoying: "Sometimes it felt like a good thing, because I felt like, wow, you know, I'm not like, looked at in this negative way... I guess thinking about [how] we were poor and where we lived, it kind of felt good to be looked at on that level. And that's why I kind of rode with it for a while." Many of the friends he made in his classes were Asian and white and "better off economically":

> [T]hat fact that they lived in a house? It was just different. Some-
> thing that I didn't have, didn't understand, but liked. . . . I wanted to
> be a part of that, on some level. . . . I remember going through a lot
> of difficulties when I would hang out with them, because I *didn't*
> have the things that they had. Like I remember . . . after school,
> it was so easy for them to go to the store or go to the hamburger
> stand and buy something, and I never had the money to buy any-
> thing, just [had] to sit there and watch. But I guess I was just left
> to be satisfied to be hanging out with them. That was my thinking
> back then, I won't deny it. I realize now that I didn't have to think
> any less of myself because of where I was, but I did at the time.[83]

At the margins of Monterey Park, for Ixco, to be mistaken for Asian was to elicit a respect he ordinarily felt was lacking, in "passing" for a middle-class kid who did well in school and most likely lived in a house that his parents owned, instead of a poor kid from the projects being raised by a single mother, who knew that the onus of improving their family's long-term prospects ("it was up to me to get it to the next level") was all on him.

The symbolic intertwinement of Asianness and homeownership as a badge of middle-class status was powerful among Asian Americans as well. Grace Ahn, a thirty-one-year-old, Korean American social worker, grew up in Alhambra living in rented apartments in which money was tight, while her immigrant parents worked a string of "random," largely blue-collar jobs. She recalled feeling different from her predominantly Chinese American friends, most of whom had parents who were profes-sionals and lived in homes their families owned: "I think the big factor was, they had their own house, and we didn't. . . . That was the biggest difference I noticed between me and my friends." Grace was "a bit embar-rassed" that her family could not afford a house, because of "what having a house represented": "With Koreans," she explained, "part of showing your wealth was having a house. . . . Growing up, that's what I was taught by my folks." For Grace, the symbolism of what having a house meant—that one had "made it" as an immigrant—extended to other Asian American groups as well. She felt, in contrast to her friends, that although her parents were also immigrants, "their immigrant story wasn't similar to my other Asian friends, because I feel like . . . they've kind of made it. Whereas my parents, they didn't really make it. . . . [My friends' parents] had like, professions, and it all goes back to you know, being middle-class, and we weren't really like that." Even though Grace did her best to "keep up" with her friends, she "knew we were kind of different."[84]

Perhaps because she was so conscious of the Asian model minority stereotype's lack of truth in her own life, Grace became extremely sensitive to how she and other Asian Americans—who tended to dominant honors classes and school activities in high school—were perceived by others:

> I was more cautious of how I said things so that the Latino kids
> didn't think we were being prejudiced against them . . . just even
> like, using the right way to identify them . . . you know, is it OK to
> say "chicana" or—you know, things like that, the terminology. I just
> remember being cautious . . . so that I didn't offend other minori-
> ties, because we were such a majority. . . . I didn't want them to
> think of us stereotypically, you know, how Asians are supposed to
> be . . . kind of let 'em be aware that you know, we weren't all
> Chinese . . . because they usually categorized us into one group . . .
> to just kind of show that we weren't all the same. . . . I just feel
> like . . . me personally, I just had to be careful with how I am, so
> that I'm not considered as you know, a typical Asian person.[85]

Grace sought simultaneously to defuse middle-class Asian Americans' relatively privileged status compared to Latinas/os at school (see chapter 2), and interrupt the racial assumptions many Latina/o students held about Asians. Her awareness of the inadequacy of stereotypes and their power to exclude or obscure difference, symbolized by "what having a house represented," inflected her social relationships. Her cautiousness about neither treating other people as homogenous nor letting her own group be treated as homogenous—"to show that we weren't all the same"—served as an attempt to make more room for assertions of difference.

Renting and Owning

At the same time, some residents, particularly immigrant families, produced new meanings regarding what owning a house did or did not mean through diverse uses of space that challenged dominant social and spatial norms.[86] In 2000, the ratio of owner-occupied to rented units in the West SGV averaged 44 percent owner occupied (slightly lower than the 48 percent owner-occupied average of Los Angeles County as a whole) to 53 percent renter occupied. The availability of a mix of units from apartments to town homes to single-family homes translated to flexible uses of space. For example, Paul Pham,[87] an eighteen-year-old whose ethno–Chinese Vietnamese family escaped Khmer Rouge rule in Cambodia via Vietnam and then Los Angeles, lived in a triplex in Alhambra with a combined total of fourteen extended family members nearly all his life, which the family rented for years before saving up enough to purchase it.[88] Traditional narratives of upward mobility feature a young couple or nuclear family that moves "out into the suburbs" in order to buy a home. The experience of the Phams and the stories that follow show that other factors beyond the possibility of homeownership, such as family and community amenities, drew diverse Asian and Latina/o families to the West SGV and that the mix of types of housing made it possible for residents of a variety of income levels to maintain proximity to family members and preferred amenities.

For families at a variety of income levels, renting could be a tactical choice in order to access better opportunities, especially regarding children's education. Siblings Milo and Gina Alvarez's parents chose to rent an apartment in Alhambra for a period of years rather than buy a house in East Los Angeles in order to afford their children better educational opportunities and a quieter environment in which to grow up.[89] Taiwanese American Lisa Sun's[90] parents, who lived in Alhambra, rented an apartment in adjacent South Pasadena solely so their children could attend South Pasadena public schools, which they felt to be superior to the schools in Alhambra.[91] On Dora Padilla's street of single-family homes in Alhambra, the mix of rentals and owner-occupied units made it possible for Padilla's daughter and son-in-law to rent a house across the street. Padilla also described how her Chinese neighbors paved what was previously the backyard to make more parking spaces for their extended family:

[T]his house, it's multiple, from what we can see . . . they took the backyard, had it *all* torn out. Here the former owners had put in a sprinkling system to make it good for selling and everything. And they took it out, all the trees and everything. Everything cemented. They even [put] stripes in, because they'll be as many as eight cars back there.

I see. So you think there's more than one family living there, or—

It's the mother and the father, with I think a couple of sons. I understand from friends telling me . . . in the Chinese tradition, the oldest son has the honor of having the mother and father. And that's the way they pool their resources. One fellow that was a bilingual teacher in the district told me, he says, "That's how they do it. Let the oldest son be successful, everyone pools their money. It's crowded sometimes, but we do it." And I think that's a marvelous tradition, if they can stand each other [laughs].[92]

Padilla clearly observed that the neighbors had disrupted a particular spatial order by "tearing out . . . all the trees and everything," after the previous owners had worked to make the backyard "good for selling." Nonetheless, she made an effort to understand it in light of "the Chinese tradition" and praiseworthy family values.

Grace Ahn first moved to Alhambra when her aunt, who was single and worked as a nurse, purchased a home there. Grace and her parents lived with her aunt for a period of years, before moving into an apartment when other relatives from Korea arrived and took up their place in the house. Thus, in the extended Ahn family, homeownership was not synonymous with furthering the wealth and prospects of a heteronormative nuclear family but instead offered an entry point to the area for extended family members upon immigrating to the United States. Finally, Nancy Do, a twenty-two-year-old child of Vietnamese refugees, described how, growing up in a rented apartment in Monterey Park, she was always surrounded by her "whole family": "You'd walk down the street and—across the street was my grandmother, and up the street were my two cousins. And my aunts lived with my grandmother, and my uncles, you know. So my whole family was there."[93]

Others, following in the footsteps of both white and nonwhite, working-class suburbanites before them, turned their home spaces—both owned and rented—into productive spaces.[94] When Juan Ramirez's father could not make the payments on the Monterey Park house he had purchased from Juan's uncle, rather than sell the house, the Ramirezes moved into the garage and rented the house to another family until "my dad got his feet on the ground and then we moved back into the house."[95] Jinny Hong's[96] mother, a Chinese refugee from Vietnam, took piecework home from local garment factories so she could work and keep an eye on her five young children at the same time. As a young widow faced suddenly with being the sole provider for a household of eight (including her elderly in-laws), she also used their rented home space to find creative solutions, growing vegetables in the yard of their triplex that she then sold to local Asian markets.[97]

Through such creative and flexible uses of both rented and owned space, West SGV Asians and Latinas/os used their home spaces tactically toward diverse goals and, in doing so, actively shaped the everyday landscapes and built environment as well as fellow residents' understandings of suburban spatial norms.

Conclusion: Homeownership, Property, and a New Nonwhite Majority

I never felt, when I was growing up, oh, I wish I was this, or I wish I was that. Because I think we were always the majority where we lived.

—Gina Alvarez

I like being around old men on their bicycles and Chinese people and Mexican people, and I like the fact that there's not a lot of white people out here because they would ruin a lot of things. Gentrification and everything, you know? They would ruin a lot of the things that have already [been] established.

— Nancy Do

When as an adult, thirty-five-year-old Gina Alvarez[98] moved slightly outside of the area and enrolled her two young children in preschools with larger numbers of white children, she quickly realized, "[Y]ou know, the schools over there are good, but . . . when I would look at the ethnicity of it, it's mostly Caucasian, and I didn't want my kids to—because I never grew up like that, being the minority, and I didn't want that for them, you know?" When her older child was ready to go to kindergarten, Alvarez, who is Mexican American, made a choice to "put her in an environment where she's confident in who she is . . . so I moved her to another school where, you know, she is—I wouldn't say the majority, but there's more people that look like her than not." Twenty-two-year-old Vietnamese American Nancy Do[99] felt a similar comfort with the racial mix of the West SGV. She connected her sense of the undesirability of "white people" to "gentrification and everything," linking the particular nexus of racial/ ethnic social relations in the West SGV with class status and relationships to property. White people, as harbingers and symbols of a particular way of relating to space and other people, would be antithetical to what she valued about the area, what had "already [been] established."

Both Alvarez and Do expressed the importance of everyday spatial knowledges to regional racial formation. In the West SGV, despite the heterogeneity of individual experiences, residents were bound together initially by common histories and the ways in which their families were part of broader racialized movements and patterns. What they made of these shared experiences collectively was something distinct—a moral geography of differentiated space that manifested as diverse meanings and uses of suburban space. The sedimentation of history and experience, bound by place, added up to a shared consciousness that was more than the sum of its heterogeneous parts. For many residents, it produced a world view that challenged and opposed whiteness as property. Whatever their professed individual motivations, by choosing to move there and then by staying long term and establishing broad family roots in the area, Asian Americans and Mexican Americans made the West SGV a significant site in the development of a "new polyethnic majority."[100]

Differential racialization via discourse around who is or is not deserving of property—which is then materialized through the housing market— continues through the present, linking notions of whiteness and property. The complexity of these linkages is evident in the West SGV's particular racial mix today, in which lines of identification across racial and ethnic lines shift with circumstances and are often unpredictable. For instance, for the Japanese American man described at the opening of this chapter and others, perceptions of the more recent immigrants range from alternately "locusts" and "damn chinos" to fellow Asians, fellow immigrants, and fellow people of color. Deeply racialized notions of property manifest in established residents' expressions of opposition to what the same man called "McMansions"—a term that in the West SGV as well as elsewhere is often code for the aesthetic tastes of rich Asian immigrants.[101] These immigrants presumably buy their homes with cash and therefore do not conform to the approved immigrant trajectory of starting downtrodden and having to pull oneself up by the bootstraps *before* daring to purchase a piece of the American Dream—a new kind of "yellow peril" expressed through the buying up of all the "bigger homes" and "nicer cars" (as one disgruntled white resident of San Marino put it).[102] For all his complaints about "chinos" and their McMansions, however, the Japanese American man still stayed in the area and near the home that his mother had occupied for so many decades. His presence—and the near total absence of whites—evidences a solidification of differentiated, majority nonwhite suburban space through the years. As Japanese American Lisa Beppu put it, although the community had "changed an awful lot . . . I feel comfortable here."[103]

The development and assertion of a multiethnic, multiracial nonwhite identity points to the social, cultural, and political possibilities we might find in the rapidly increasing number of "majority-minority" suburbs in the United States to challenge the reproduction of white privilege and racially exclusive notions of property—as well as the importance of regional, place-based analysis to uncovering and understanding such sentiments. Shared neighborhoods enabled the development of an inclusionary, distinctively multiracial world view and allowed for the coexistence of apparent contradictions in ways that would be less possible, however, in other central sites of everyday life.

CHAPTER 2

"The Asian and Latino Thing in Schools"

Academic Achievement and Racialized Privilege

I guess in Alhambra you only have a choice—a "choice," and that's in quotations—between Latinos or Asians.

—Nancy Tran,[1] former student, Alhambra High School

[I]n this concert [of reproduction of capitalist relations], one ideological State apparatus certainly has the dominant role, although hardly anyone lends an ear to its music: it is so silent! This is the School.

—Louis Althusser, "Ideology and Ideological State Apparatuses"

IN THE SPRING of 2005, Alhambra High received the Title I Academic Achievement Award, which recognizes schools with low-income student populations that have made progress in closing the achievement gap.[2] Principal Russell Lee-Sung arranged a meeting with student government leaders to announce the good news. One of the students present at the meeting was Robin Zhou, an inquisitive, first-generation Chinese American senior, who began to wonder why this gap—a persistent discrepancy in test scores and grade point averages between Alhambra's Asian American and Latina/o students—existed in the first place. The results of his speculations ran in Robin's monthly school newspaper column, "Nerd Rants," on March 22, 2005. Following the headline, "Latinos Lag behind in Academics," he wrote that "Hispanic students" were not "pulling their weight" and attributed the cause to cultural factors, suggesting that Asian parents "push their children to move toward academic success," while Latino parents "are well-meaning but less active." Zhou also attributed the disparity to what he called a "deliberate segregation" of students into two groups, AP/ honors and regular, beginning in middle school, and closed with a

stern remonstrance for lower-scoring students to take the gap seriously: "Those who casually dismiss their own inabilities that place
them on the bottom end must be forced to understand that those
are not empty numbers, but are indicators of the brightness of their
futures." Even though he stated that he was not "suggesting that brown
people cannot think on the level of white and yellow people" but that
he felt the difference in test scores had to be addressed, the column,
along with a subsequent news article that ran in a local newspaper a
week later, set off what Lee-Sung described as a "firestorm" of controversy among students, teachers, administrators, and parents.[3] The
incident was a flashpoint—a moment of racial formation—that both
revealed and called into question existing regional racial hierarchies
and their sometimes uneasy relationship to national ideologies. It also
illuminated the important role of school, as a key institution of civil
society, in mediating this relationship.

The year Robin wrote his column, Alhambra High was 90 percent
Asian American and Latina/o, with Asian American students making
up 48 percent of the student body, and Latinas/os 41.5 percent.[4] In the
heated dialogue that followed, it became clear that much more was at
stake than raising test scores and grade point averages. In fact, Robin's
column exposed to public scrutiny a socioacademic order dramatically
bifurcated by race. Students, teachers, and administrators' attempts to
resolve the crisis revealed how national ideologies intertwining race,
individualism, and merit deeply shaped participants' ways of making
sense of racial and ethnic hierarchies. Simultaneously, "common sense"
ways of making sense of the existing socioacademic order were elucidated, ruptured, and reproduced. Various participants' struggles to
articulate something different indicated forms of thinking that eluded
hegemonic purview—what Raymond Williams has described as structures of feeling or "meanings and values as they are actually lived and
felt," which are as yet ideologically unthinkable but perched "at the very
edge of semantic availability."[5]

In discussions of family and life histories in the West SGV, high
school frequently emerged as a key period during which social relations
were solidified and established, and achievement in academics and
extracurricular activities often became a marker of one's perceived ability to succeed and prosper. Students' ways of making sense of the social
order were tied intimately with the particular regional context in which

they were growing up—in a majority–Asian American and Latina/o, immigrant, metropolitan suburb in which the alignments of race and privilege were neither fixed nor clear cut. The nuances of the students' reactions to and interpretations of the social order around them speak to the ideologically formative moment in which high school takes place, where societal orders and mores are being taught but have not yet been internalized as common sense, taken-for-granted truths. However, at the same time, as young adults, students have begun to develop regionally based forms of common sense, based on what they see and experience in their own lives, in local and familial contexts. Because of the inevitability of the contradictions and crises that arise at such a moment, high school constitutes a critical site for the study of regional racial formation.

Of all institutions of civil society, school occupies the dominant position in contemporary capitalist societies, as the only institution that has "the obligatory audience of the totality of the children in the capitalist social formation, eight hours a day for five or six days out of seven."[6] Indeed, in the West SGV, while outside of school, interethnic and interracial interactions may happen only unevenly, in the public schools, sustained interethnic and interracial interactions happen every day between students, staff, and administrators. School can inculcate a sense of national culture and ideologies that mold students to enter the working world as productive and loyal citizens. In its capacity as an everyday, "racialized landscape," school concretizes and normalizes "some prescribed social, racial, class, economic, or political order that not only stands for the past and present, but also inescapably embodies power relations that make claims on the future," although its norms are "unconsciously promoted and unrecognized as anything other than 'common sense.'"[7] In other words, because of its central position in civil society, school is uniquely able to normalize stratified groupings under cover of neutrality and egalitarianism. While the effects of such institutions in practice are never uniform or homogenous, looking closely at social dynamics in school allows us to see in sharp relief the ways in which school is fundamental to structuring society along racial and class lines.[8] Concomitantly, school is also a prime locale for the subversion and challenge of hegemonic ideologies; it is both the "stake" and the "site" of ideological racialized, class struggle.[9] Reconfigurations of power can occur, and outcomes are not fixed.

In the regional context of the West SGV, the production of binary discourses of "achievement" at Alhambra High—the racialization of Asian
American academic excellence, along with a concomitant racialization of
Latina/o academic deficiency—shaped students' experiences to such a
degree that it was not merely an explanation for particular outcomes but
productive of a social order that valorized Asian American students at the
expense of "non-Asians." As a result, Asian American students within this
social order often experienced and enacted a distinct form of *racialized
privilege*—in which the particulars are predicated by one's racialization, or
ascribed group identity, by dominant society. To be clear, I am not suggesting that white privilege is not racialized. However, a concept of Asian
American racialized privilege marks a critical shift from thinking about
racial privilege as synonymous with whiteness and argues for increased
recognition of the effects of racial hierarchies from all positions. Grappling
with racialized privilege is necessary and important to understanding how
the dialectic between national ideologies and regional racial norms produces complex meanings and outcomes.

"Our School Does Not Have Very Many White or Black People"

Since the 1980s, students at Alhambra High have been accustomed to
a racial/ethnic mix that is overwhelmingly Asian and Latina/o (most
recently, 45 percent Asian and 47 percent Latina/o).[10] For Gabriela Fernandez, a nineteen-year-old Mexican American whose family had lived
in Alhambra for three generations, since elementary school, the racial/
ethnic mix had "pretty much been like, you know, the Hispanic and the
Asian and that's pretty much all I've ever seen. And sometimes, [a] Caucasian comes in . . . and you're just kind of like, well, OK, you can come and
be my friend too." Gabriela's parents worked as a professional nurse and a
meatcutter, making "good money," as she put it.[11]

Annie Liu, eighteen, whose parents are first-generation immigrants of
Chinese and Chinese-Korean descent, characterized her perception of the
racial/ethnic makeup of the area as a whole:

It's *very* rare you see Caucasian people. . . . Whereas like, if you
drive down the street, you'll see a huge group of Latino kids, or a
huge group of Asian kids hanging out. So I always felt that this area
was more for people who just moved to California from another

country. . . . I don't really know what the appeal of this area is to new immigrants, but if you're looking for a community where you won't feel too, you know, outcasted, I guess this is where it'd be, because you look at the makeup, and it's like, wow, it's mostly Asian and Latino.[12]

Both of Annie's parents attended college prior to immigrating to the United States. Her father worked as a buyer for a department store in Pasadena, while her mother was employed by a Korean airline at LAX.

Twenty-two-year-old Nancy Tran, whose ethno-Chinese parents fled Vietnam after the fall of Saigon, put it this way: "I guess in Alhambra you only have a choice—a 'choice,' and that's in quotations—between Latinos or Asians."[13] Nancy's mother was a clerk for Los Angeles County, while her father worked 2 a.m.-to-noon nightshifts as a machine operator for a manufacturing company.

In eighteen-year-old Paul Pham's view, at Alhambra High, students who were neither Asian nor Latina/o were so uncommon that "we would probably assume that they were either Asian or Hispanic even if they weren't. I think that would be the way we approached them, until they actually told us." For example, he remembered a few Middle Eastern friends "who were assumed to be Hispanic." He continued, "I know that our school does not have very many white or Black people. And when we do see them, we kind of stare for a second, actually. We would actually go, 'hey, we *do* have them here' [laughing]."[14] Paul's family was also ethno–Chinese Vietnamese and escaped Khmer Rouge rule in Cambodia via Vietnam and then Los Angeles. Paul's father worked in an auto body shop, and his mother worked as a seamstress.

Gabriela, Annie, Nancy, and Paul's family histories give a glimpse of the diverse ethnic, transnational, generational, and class contexts in which Alhambra High students lived. Seen in this light, Annie's comment that Alhambra was a place in which new immigrants could be comfortable, where they wouldn't feel "outcasted," and furthermore where they constituted the "norm," expressed a regional ethos in which immigrants and people of color were neither marginal or exceptional (as discussed in the previous chapter). However, the former students' observations, especially Paul's, also suggest a perceived normative, binary aspect to the racial mix of the area. How should we understand the West SGV's apparent Asian American and Latina/o binary, as expressed and experienced by the area's youth? Did it operate with the same destructive tendencies as other racial binaries?[15] What specific dynamics and meanings emerged from this Asian American and Latina/o-dominated socioacademic order?

Producing the "Gap": Alhambra High's Socioacademic Order

Initially, in elementary school and junior high, people who grew up in Alhambra and Monterey Park enjoyed racially and ethnically mixed groups of friends, regardless of the range of their interactions outside of school. By the time they entered high school, however, their social groups tended to become more homogeneous, and they became more conscious of racial and ethnic dynamics. At Alhambra High, this increased separation was influenced by a tracking system and, after tracking was officially discontinued in the late 1990s, by a conspicuous divide between who took honors and AP classes (overwhelmingly Asian American students) and who took "regular" classes (the vast majority of Latina/o students). Because AP and honors classes as well as many extracurricular activities such as social clubs and student government were so predominantly Asian, for many students, especially those categorized as "high-achieving" students, racially segregated social groups were easily perpetuated and naturalized.

In educational circles as well as popular discourse, distinctly racialized socioacademic orders in school are commonly referred to in the language of the "achievement gap," a term that denotes a consistent disparity in grades and/or test scores between one category of students and another. While divisions are sometimes laid out along lines of gender or other identity categories, over time, the term has acquired distinct racial connotations and most often refers to racial disparities.[16] Beginning in the 1960s and 1970s—concurrent with the rise of tremendous struggles over school segregation and desegregation[17]—a considerable amount of popular media and academic research focused on the "achievement gap" between Black and white students. In California, as demographics shifted and white enrollment in public schools declined, attention to the achievement gap focused increasingly on grade and standardized test-score disparities between white and Asian American students on the one hand and Latina/o and Black students on the other.[18]

At Alhambra High, disparities in grades, test scores, and educational outcomes between Asian American and Latina/o students have been treated as a problem by the school and the Alhambra Unified School District (AUSD) as a whole for a number of years. According to Scott Mangrum, AUSD's director of research and evaluation, part of the district's motivation for discontinuing "ability tracking" (in which students are placed into the same "track" for all their courses across the curriculum) had to do with "overtones" of discrimination, since the lowest track, consisting of courses that did not meet standards for state college and university admission, tended to consist of "all minorities" (by which Mangrum, notably, meant non-Asian students—that is Latinas/os). Indeed, students were keenly aware of the ramifications of tracking. Japanese American Adam Saito, who attended Alhambra High in the mid-1980s, believed that curricular tracking influenced social cliques to the degree that "they usually never mixed. They were like traveling on two different planes within the same geographic location." He recalled being almost the only Asian American in the "industrial arts" (shop) class: "all the kids in that class were from Alhambra" (as opposed to the wealthier Monterey Park hills) and "mostly Mexican guys." The class was "known as juvenile hall in our high school, because the juvie unit was in that class."[19] Adam's recollection of the commonly held association of criminality and failure with the predominantly male, Mexican American shop class students demonstrates a broad awareness among students that curricular choices had broader life implications than "just" school.[20]

To make sure more students were eligible for college by eliminating courses that didn't meet standards for admission to California State or the University of California, detracking meant that the lowest track, or "B-level," courses were essentially eliminated, and "A-level" courses became the current "college prep" (or "regular") courses.[21] In the mid- to late 2000s, however, even though strongly racialized patterns among students who took AP/honors versus "regular" courses and differences in college preparedness persisted, Alhambra had reached a point where it compared somewhat favorably to demographically comparable schools at both the district and state level in several respects. In addition to receiving the Title I Academic Achievement Award (in 2005), as of 2007–8, more Latina/o students at Alhambra met state college and university entrance requirements than the district average, and they performed better on the state high school exit exam (CAHSEE) than Latina/o students as a whole in the district, as well as in the state, by around 10 percent.[22] Nonetheless, when Robin Zhou wrote his opinion piece in 2005, public response was such that the "gap" was revealed to be an open wound for which no easy solutions or interpretations could be agreed on. This circumstance was supported and to an extent perpetuated by the specific components of the racialization of academic achievement at Alhambra High.

The Racialization of Academic Achievement

Since the landmark 1954 *Brown v. Board of Education* decision declared racially segregated schooling illegal, a voluminous amount of scholarly literature as well as popular media has been produced on the subject of group discrepancies in academic attainment. In 2002, the passage of the No Child Left Behind Act, with its explicit focus on "closing the achievement gap between high and low performing children, especially minority and non-minority students,"[23] testified to the continued centrality and urgency of the issue on a national level. Two persistent discursive threads have emerged over the years: the pitching of problems and proposal of solutions (1) in terms of generalizations about inherent cultural attributes and (2) vis-à-vis studies of individual motivation and families.[24]

Arguments about "cultural deficiency," which contributed to the pathologization of the Black urban "underclass" by disparaging Black families, were most prevalent in scholarly discourse in the 1960s. More recent academic research in education now takes a multipronged approach, encompassing arguments about the psychological effects of racial stereotypes, "cultural mismatch," curriculum and school structure, and teachers' pedagogical practices.[25] Nonetheless, culturalist and individualist reasoning remains common in education literature and continues to dominate popular discourse. In our contemporary era in which explicit reference to race is taboo, references to culture as an underlying cause for differential outcomes often function as a euphemism for race and continue to reify racial categories and difference as inherent, rather than socially, historically, and relationally constructed. A focus on individual motivation and family dynamics, without attention to larger social and institutional factors, can serve similarly to divert attention from structural and relational factors.[26] Indeed, education scholar Gloria Ladson-Billings suggests that it will take more than diversification in research to shift fundamental thinking on the subject, pointing out that most existing work offers only short-term solutions that treat the symptoms rather than the cause. Ladson-Billings argues instead for reconceptualizing the achievement gap as an "education debt" accrued through the effects of structural inequalities over time (rather than a naturally occurring phenomenon in the present), which can only be paid back through large-scale change.[27]

The racialization of achievement at Alhambra High illustrates how phrases such as *achievement gap* do not merely present a neutral description of facts; they manifest and reproduce ideologies, or ways of making sense of the world. In other words, discourse is not merely representative or explanatory but productive of material conditions and essential to the operation of power.[28] Attaching "common sense" rationales to particular social orders and hierarchies has real effects, ultimately serving to facilitate and justify "who gets what." Indeed, even at the modest scale of Alhambra High, the gap was not merely a problem of some combination of cultural differences, individual motivation, and family environment, but produced by a racialized socioacademic order. "Common sense" arguments involving cultural differences and recourse to the American individualist myth of success served to veil and naturalize fundamentally racial constructions of Asian Americans as high achievers and Latinas/os as academically deficient. These shaped students' experiences to such a degree that they became not merely an explanation for particular outcomes but (re)productive of a social order that valorized Asian American students at the expense of Latinas/os.

"Because I Was Asian, I Pretty Much Had This Path Set for Me"

Popular reasoning behind the commonly held stereotype that Asian Americans excel in education is bound up with the Asian American model minority myth. The stereotype employs two seemingly contradictory lines of reasoning: (1) that valuing education is inherent to an essentialized "Asian" culture and (2) that Asians succeed in school because they work hard, therefore embodying the ideal immigrant, minority group by increasing their capacity to contribute productively to American society. If they can do it, the argument goes, why can't Black people, or Latinas/os, or any other marginalized group? However, the second line of reasoning is actually as essentialist as the first, since it depends on an assumption that the Asian work ethic is attributable, again, to an essentialized Asian culture. At Alhambra High, students, teachers, and administrators frequently expressed such generalized cultural explanations, as the following accounts suggest. When Nancy Tran's family moved from a diverse, generally poor neighborhood in Echo Park to Alhambra when she was in third grade, Nancy observed a difference right away, which she attributed to something "within the Asian community . . . The kids . . . studied a lot more. I think the kids in Alhambra, they just generally work really hard. But it's not true of everyone. Truthfully, I think it's within the Asian community. I think they work a lot harder, maybe because of parental pressure?"[29] Annie Liu counterposed the terms *Asian* and *Western* to describe degrees of commitment to academic achievement. Students in the year following hers, she said, were "even more competitive": some had perfect SAT scores, and all had straight As and were involved in multiple extracurricular activities. "To some extent," she said, they were "even further along than we are—you know, like further 'Asianized' or whatever you want to call it . . . working their butts off to get into a good college." When I asked if she felt that this "Asianized" culture of achievement was generally acknowledged in the area, she said yes, adding, "I mean, whenever I encounter parents who were like, 'oh, as long as they're doing their best,' I think to myself, that's such a Westernized kind of thought, you know?"[30]

Gary Wong, a teacher at Alhambra High who is Chinese American, agreed. It was not wrong, he believed, to say that Asian parents pushed their kids: "They're not satisfied [if] their kids get Bs and Cs. They're satisfied when their kids go to Harvard."[31] Even though Wong, as a teacher, had a detailed understanding of the diverse cultural, economic, and political conditions under which various Asian ethnic groups have immigrated to the United States in the past few decades, nonetheless, like the students I interviewed, he took for granted a shared "Asian" culture undergirding Asian American student success. Any Asian American whose family did not value and push for educational success constituted a deviation from this "cultural script."[32] For instance, Wong asserted that his lack of set college expectations for his own children was "atypical, because my parents were atypical." Because he did not push his sons to go to elite universities, he conceived of himself as deviating from the mandates of "Asian" immigrant culture. Furthermore, he believed that he was this way only because his parents had not performed the usual Asian parental indoctrinations regarding education either. Student Paul Pham had a similar response when asked if he was always expected or encouraged to excel academically. (In his senior year Paul was coeditor in chief of the student newspaper, got top grades in his slate of AP and honors classes, was involved in a biomedical research elective as well as service clubs, and was admitted to Yale and

Harvard, among other elite universities.) Paul answered, "No. Surprisingly not." If he hadn't "achieved" at the level he had, he believed his parents would not have viewed him much differently: "[T]heir expectations of me were not as high as those of other parents—Asian parents." This, to himself and his peers ("my friends tell me this also"), made him "kind of an anomaly, because I achieve, but I'm not pushed to achieve."[33]

For Nancy, Annie, and Paul, as well as their teacher Gary Wong, easy recourse to racialized cultural explanations—referencing a shared Asian culture that implicitly valued education more than other cultures—blocked access to all other explanations. This generalized Asian culture was contrasted against a generalized Western culture, rather than placed in the specific ethnic, racial, and national contexts in which they actually lived. Factors such as a greater amount of social capital or resources derived from "socially patterned associations" on the part of the Asian American students, such as parents' educational attainment and social networks that shared information and facilitated sending students to private tutoring and Chinese language schools, went unacknowledged as contributing factors in the gap.[34]

The effect of such erasures at Alhambra High was an atmosphere in which the brainy, studious Asian student was seen and accepted simply as the truth, showing how racial discourse obscured recognition of substantial social factors and stood in as common sense. In Gabriela Fernandez's opinion, "It was known that the Asian students did a lot better than everybody else. I mean, Asians are smart. Some Hispanics are smart too. But you always see Asians studying, you always see them in the library; they're always reading, they always get As on their tests. So yeah, it was pretty much known around the school that Asians did better in classes than everybody else."[35] This was simply taken for granted; it was, she said, "one of those things that nobody really talked about." In localized common sense, these dynamics seemed so normal that they generally went unremarked. Indeed, the naturalization of a disparity between Asian and Latina/o students even extended beyond the classroom to social relationships. For example, Paul Pham believed that between Asian and Latina/o students "there is sort of a natural barrier. We seem to segregate ourselves naturally, based on race rather than actually acknowledging it." When I pressed him to elaborate, he chose an abstracted second-person phrasing, explaining, "You will tend to ignore the people that do not seem like they have similar backgrounds to you. And not that you would do it on purpose. You wouldn't go, 'oh, he doesn't look like me, I don't want to talk to him.' Not like *that*. It just happens. You don't do it consciously. It's a subconscious kind of action."[36] Although moments before in the same interview, Paul had described how his exclusively Asian American peer group solidified in conjunction with his entry into an honors/AP schedule of courses in high school, the Harvard-bound senior was unable to offer anything but a common sense explanation for what he saw around him on an everyday basis. Any linkages between structural causes and normalized social orders were obscured by his seemingly irrefutable conviction that "it just happens." The degree to which the discrepancy in "achievement" and a concomitant "segregated" social order were seen as "natural" by both Asian and Latina/o students indicated their acceptance as common sense. For Asian Americans, this amounted to a form of privilege predicated on racial terms.

Asian American Racialized Privilege

Much of the available scholarship on Asian Americans has been informed by a post-civil-rights-era inheritance of seeing Asian Americans as an oppressed group that must therefore be inherently resistant and oppositional to hegemonic claims.[37] However, theories of differential racialization such as Claire Jean Kim's work on the "triangulation" of Asian Americans, Laura Pulido's observations on the relationship between racial hierarchy and class position, and Kandice Chuh's theorization of Asian Americans as an "emerging dominant" suggest a more ambivalent view of how Asian Americans fit into U.S. racial schema.[38] Mia Tuan, in her study of third- and fourth-generation Chinese and Japanese Americans, has posited an Asian American experience of "racial privilege," or "the freedom of not having to think about one's racial background . . . the privilege to be considered 'normal,' to have one's race be irrelevant."[39] Tuan concluded that her respondents who grew up in predominantly Asian-American communities enjoyed this privilege "within the context of their neighborhood," consequently suffered fewer injuries (psychological, emotional, and sometimes physical) and were able to develop greater self-confidence than those who grew up in predominantly white communities.[40] Regarding 1.5- and second-generation Asian American professionals, Pensri Ho describes what she calls "class privileged racialized identity," in which an Asian American identity "rooted in class privilege and Pacific Rim experiences"—rather than racial oppression and disenfranchisement—is developed during young adulthood.[41] Deviating from Tuan, Ho locates the beginnings of this particular identity formation in the predominantly white or "racially mixed" suburban communities in which her respondents were raised, arguing that these settings enabled them to "accentuate their meritocratic abilities" over racialized differences.[42] Perhaps most significantly, Ho makes the observation that "*regardless of the source of privilege*—whether achieved as an adult, acquired through parental efforts or *affectation*," class privilege fueled her respondents' "confidence and faith in their abilities to shape their own identities."[43]

Building on Tuan and Ho's observations, I argue that the social dynamics at Alhambra High can be characterized as *racialized privilege*. Rather than the absence (or "irrelevance," in Tuan's words) of racism that the concept of racial privilege implies, racialized privilege foregrounds the centrality of racialized meanings and outcomes—that the circulation of model minority discourse is not merely incidental or external but itself participates in the production and reproduction of privilege. Accordingly, Asian American racialized privilege, in concert with being marked as a model minority, constitutes not a privilege to be considered normal but a privilege to be considered *exceptional* (in comparison to other nonwhite minoritized groups). The prioritization of exceptional, racialized identity collapses racial and class identities into one another and allows for a subsumption of class differences under presumed racial or cultural commonalities. To reiterate: if (white) racial privilege is "the freedom of not having to think about one's racial background . . . the privilege to be considered 'normal,' to have one's race be irrelevant," then (Asian American) racialized privilege is an internalization of privilege accorded to one's ascribed racial identity, which can lead to a conditional freedom of not having to think too deeply about one's racial background, and a limited privilege to be considered exceptional. One's race is not irrelevant but integral. A conception of racialized privilege, like theorizations of white racial privilege, must also take into consideration deep historical contexts, structural forces, and durable material benefits, all of which taken together can ultimately lead to substantial increases in life opportunities as well as insulation from "group-differentiated vulnerabilities to premature death."[44] While a conception of Asian American privilege can never be the same as white privilege, which is based on historical and material legacies of white supremacy that are still enacted and perpetuated on an everyday basis, clearly distinct benefits do accrue from Asian Americans' relatively valorized position in American racial hierarchies at the expense of others.

Under the common umbrella of "Asianness," ethnic, class, and other differences are obscured. For instance, Paul Pham, the ethno–Chinese Vietnamese son of working-class political refugees with few academic expectations for their son, inhabited the same expectations regarding "achievement" as Annie Liu, the Chinese and Korean American daughter of college-educated professionals, whose father mapped out her AP/honors class schedule on an Excel spreadsheet and was deeply disappointed when Annie was not admitted to an Ivy League university. For both Annie and Paul, the subsumption of class and other considerations under racial and cultural expectations meant that "achievement" could become a thing in and of itself, as though to "achieve" itself, albeit with the ultimate achievement of gaining admittance to an elite university, was the goal. Personally, Paul said, he was not "achieving" with the future in mind. "I mean, you might ask someone, why do you want to go to college? 'I want to have a good job, I want to make a lot of money'—that would not be my answer. I don't think I was achieving to get to something, because I don't know what exactly that would be anyway."[45] Annie applied to prestigious colleges "out of loyalty to my parents"; she felt that she had to "try, for them." But when I asked her why she thought this was so important to them, she replied, "I don't *know*. . . . I don't know if it's an American thing, or it's an Asian thing? Because when I talk to my friends in Canada, they're just like, 'there are only a couple universities in Canada'—if you just get into one, you're happy about it. They don't understand the obsession that Americans, or at least Asian Americans, have with Ivy League schools. . . . So I really don't understand what the obsession is about."[46] Because of the racialized character of "achievement" at Alhambra High—the taken-for-granted idea that academic excellence was natural to Asian American students—neither Annie nor Paul felt pressed to explain their drive to achieve in terms beyond generalized racial or cultural explanations. The form of privilege they experienced through their presumed educational life paths as Asian Americans had buffered them so far from having to think deeply about their place and motivations in American society.

Vivian Louie has argued that the "ethnic-cultural narrative" of Asian immigrant academic excellence offered her second-generation Chinese American respondents "a symbolic safe space from the injuries of race." In light of real racial barriers awaiting them in the workplace, if not in school, "the supposed distinctiveness of the Asian immigrant ethos which privileges hard work and, above all, a respect and keen desire for education should be of some utility in offsetting these obstacles."[47] However, at Alhambra High, and in the West San Gabriel Valley (SGV) in general, where Asian Americans are a plurality and often perceived as the majority, anti-Asian discrimination was not as pervasive as elsewhere; in turn, the rationale behind embracing the ethnic-cultural narrative for high-achieving Asian American students was harder to discern.[48] When pressed, both Anne and Paul admitted that they did not have a highly developed understanding of their motivations and goals as "high-achieving" students. To Paul, his academic success seemed quite detached from his family's immigrant, refugee, and working-class background. As a result of conversation with her Canadian friends, Annie was able to sense that the "obsession . . . with Ivy League schools" might have something to do with the particular history and position of Asians in America, but this was not yet something about which she had thought deeply. Lia Chen, who attended Alhambra High in the early 1990s and was an honors student as well as senior class president before going on to attend college at Penn State, summed up the general rationale at work: "Because I was a good student, and because I was Asian, I pretty much had this path set for me."[49]

"I Always Felt That Outsiderness"

For Mexican American as well as Asian American students, cultural explanations played prominently in the debate over the achievement gap. However, while Asian culture was valorized—at least in the context of pursuing academic success—what was construed as Mexican or Latina/o culture (often used interchangeably) was stigmatized. While Asian culture was characterized as studious and hardworking, Mexican American students suffered from a "systematic undervaluing of people and things Mexican."[50] Like all processes of racial formation, these racial discourses around achievement were fundamentally relational. This became apparent in the categorical use of the term *non-Asian*, which often functioned as a euphemism for Latina/o. For instance, Annie Liu reported that students who were in sports "have a lot more interaction with non-Asians," while the more "bookish, nerdy activities" such as newspaper, included "a very limited amount of non-Asians." The "rule" for Latina/o students—to *not* excel and progress academically—formed a warped, reverse mirror image of prevalent characterizations of Asian American achievement. Just as deviation from high academic achievement was considered anomalous for Asian students, interlinked discourses dictated that among Latina/o students, to deviate from the rule of low achievement was to be an exception. While for Asian American students, high expectations generally buttressed their self-images and minimized barriers to academic continuation, for Latina/o students, breaking out of low expectations often proved to be a constantly demoralizing, uphill battle, often causing them to "disidentify"—or detach their measures of self-worth—from academics from an early age.[51]

Unlike the Asian American students with whom I spoke, few of whom mentioned any problems with staff or administration, all the Latina/o students and nearly all the teachers and administrators had stories of Latina/o students who were openly discouraged from reaching more ambitious goals. For example, Gabriela Fernandez described her counselor, a Latina/o woman who was widely known to favor Asian students because "they don't talk back to her" and "they get really high grades." Gabriela felt this counselor disliked her and Latina/o students in general: "Other Hispanic students that I talked to that had her were kind of like, why is she like that?" As a result, Gabriela "avoided going to the counselor at all costs. Which is probably the reason why I didn't get to go exactly to a university like I wanted to because I just didn't want to talk to her."[52] When I asked teacher and student activities advisor Matt Ramos about experiences like Gabriela's, Ramos, who feels that many of his Mexican American students regard him as a mentor, acknowledged, "We have discouraging counselors—you know, they have them everywhere. . . . I've heard students say, 'This counselor's ruined my life. They have *ruined* my life.'"[53] Principal Lee-Sung recounted an incident in which a hesitant Latina student was persuaded by her counselor to take a higher-level math class, but when the student went to the class, "first thing the teacher says is, 'What are *you* doing here? You don't belong in this class'. . . . Just shot her down, just like that." This had everything to do with expectations, he said, adding, "I would bet that [in] that same scenario, [if] an Asian kid walked in with that slip to be in that class, he [the teacher] wouldn't have said that."[54] Student Perla Trejo found that in her AP classes, teachers seemed to expect less from Latina/o students than from Asian American students. "When we answer a question wrong, they say, 'It's OK. You're trying really hard.' It's like, OK, but what's the answer?"[55]

Paul Pham related a similar pattern of expectations among students: if "a person with a completely different background" joined a class or activity that was "mostly Asian," "that person would actually receive a lot of attention—positive attention," simply for showing up at something conceived to be out of the ordinary for a Latina/o.[56] Although Paul interpreted this to have a positive meaning, a more troubling interpretation, in accordance with Claude Steele's concept of disidentification, would be the following: if someone who was "different" (i.e., non-Asian) joined an AP class or a challenging extracurricular activity, she would be greeted with surprise and praise for exceeding expectations of low achievement. Devalued with the stigma of low expectations from the outset, the student would grow increasingly likely to disengage with academics, unless this pattern was interrupted by mentors or other factors that recognized and nurtured her abilities and potential.

Alan Fernandez's account of his academic experiences growing up in Alhambra shows the difficulty of breaking polarized expectations of Latina/o versus Asian students. Alan was told in kindergarten that he "was going to be mentally slow"; from then on, he felt that he constantly had to prove himself to teachers who did not believe in his ability to do well in school. He recalled an instance in sixth grade when his math teacher, a Japanese American woman, would not put him in an advanced class until he consistently turned his homework in early (and correctly)—"and she would be like, really angry, checking it." Although of course we can't really know the motivations of Alan's teacher, the mere fact of her anger—the oddity of it, under the ostensibly heartening circumstances of a student making extra efforts to be placed in a more challenging class—suggests that she perceived his efforts as a transgression of accepted boundaries, perhaps rupturing her sense of (racial) order. By the time he got to high school, Alan was usually the only Mexican American in AP and honors classes populated predominantly by Asian American students and felt that teachers stereotyped both him and Asian American students, in a binary of high and low achievement: "I definitely felt like in the classroom, [the teachers] favored the Asian American students. It was like they stereotyped them, in a way: these are going to be the smart kids. And then . . . they'd look at me like, what are you doing here? I always felt that outsiderness."[57]

Alan also recalled two incidents that occurred with close friends, who were Asian American. First, in his senior year of high school, when he was admitted to Berkeley and UCLA, "some of my friends were like, oh, I wish I was Mexican, 'cause I could have gotten into Berkeley or UCLA." He remembered with annoyance one friend in particular who had made such comments: Howard, a relatively wealthy Asian American boy from the Monterey Park hills with only mediocre grades, who on several occasions had paid Alan to write his papers for him because he was "too lazy" to do them himself. Howard's professed belief that he too could have gotten into Berkeley or UCLA if he was "Mexican" perpetuated stereotypes of Mexican Americans as inherently academically deficient, indicating that he believed Alan could only have gained admittance under special circumstances.[58] The second incident involved Alan's best friend, who was Chinese American: "When we graduated from eighth grade, he wrote in my yearbook that I was . . . the only smart Mexican he knew, or the smartest Mexican he knew. And I kind of felt like, that sucks, you know, why would he say that? And then I thought about it, and I was like, well, I was one of the few in the class." The friend's comment, as well as Alan's reaction, highlights the difficulty of separating what appears to be everyday material reality from ideological racial "truths" and the degree to which the regional Asian-Latina/o scholastic-racial order had already been ingrained in the two boys by the close of junior high. Alan's experience, as well as the accounts of other former students, suggests that by high school, both Asian and Latina/o students were conditioned to expect bifurcated groupings, separating academically excelling Asians from low- or average-performing Latinas/os. In high school, Latina/o students who attempted to cross the line were often met with surprise, outright hostility, or more subtle forms of disapproval, most devastatingly from teachers and counselors.[59]

Like many schools in the area, until recently Alhambra High had a large concentration of "veteran," predominantly white teachers who exerted a great influence on the school culture.[60] However, as we have seen, racist cultural assumptions and behaviors were not merely the provenance of white teachers. They had more to do with an institutionalized culture, shaped by prevailing national ideologies of race, in which Asian American and Latina/o students experienced differentially racialized patterns of relationships to schooling. This illustrates, as Angela Valenzuela puts it, the ways in which "[a]cademic success and failure are . . . products of schooling rather than . . . something that young people do."[61] Nonetheless, essentialist views were difficult to dislodge, even for those who were critical of institutionalized practices. For example, in contrast to his observations of the obstacles faced by Mexican American students, teacher and activities advisor Matt Ramos offered the opinion that "high-achieving Asian American students" were simply "a different breed altogether." He went on to describe their intensely ambitious approach to learning and high expectations of themselves and others. Ramos, living and teaching in the particular contexts of his area, implied that these dynamics and characteristics were not only regional but racial in nature: you could talk to any activities advisor who worked in the West SGV, he said, "from Keppel to Arcadia to San Marino to Schurr [names of area high schools with similar populations of students] to . . . you name it, and they will all tell you the same thing about how these students are."[62]

School, as a key engine of inculcating dominant national ideologies, constituted the setting in which a regional socioacademic order tied intimately to comparative racial constructions of Asian Americans and Latinas/os in the United States took shape strongly and was internalized not only by its young subjects but by their mentors and peers.

The Column Controversy

Until the spring of 2005, however, most of these dynamics went unspoken and generally unacknowledged in any public or community discourse. In the furor that followed the publication of Robin Zhou's column, however, the "common sense" notions supporting the existing socioacademic order were simultaneously elucidated, ruptured, and reproduced. The heated dialogue concerning language, race, and the irreducibility of lived experience to racialized generalizations suggested that many participants sensed that Robin's column was not only symptomatic of the racialized socioacademic order but also a struggle over, and opportunity to shift, discourse[63]—to challenge prevailing common sense and concomitant configurations of power.

"Don't Turn This into a Racial War"

Perhaps no one understood this better than Principal Lee-Sung. In his opinion, the language in which the conflict was depicted was absolutely crucial to the way in which it unfolded. He believed that what might otherwise have been "a very positive thing, a healthy discussion," was derailed by the way in which local newspaper reporter Cindy Chang portrayed the situation in an article published in the *Pasadena Star-News* a little more than a week after Robin's column. "Latinos object to being called laggards," the front-page subheadline proclaimed. Chang opened with a description of how the column had led to an "uproar" on campus. In the second and third paragraphs, she highlighted how Robin had been "threatened with bodily harm by other students," how a teacher had denounced the article as racist, and that "opinions have generally converged along racial lines, with Asian students agreeing with the gist of the piece and Latinos questioning whether it should have been printed at all."[64] Lee-Sung believed that Chang's focus and choice of words "inflamed the situation. . . . There were a couple quotes on there that really focused on the racial part, the racial tensions. I'm here at the school, and I'm talking to the kids and staff, and you know what, I don't see that. Yes, people are angry about it, but don't turn this into a racial war. Because sure, that's what's going to get the headlines and get picked up on the AP Wire. . . . I was so upset that that's the way the article was written. So it made matters worse."[65] In the thick of the situation, "talking to the kids and staff," Lee-Sung refused to recognize the conflict in the racialized terms in which it was cast by the *Star-News* reporter.

In part, the principal may simply have been fulfilling his obligation as an administrator to defuse conflict. However, his response to the situation also showed a complex understanding of the world in which he lived and worked that precluded its reduction to a formula of racial conflict by mainstream press. Indeed, Lee-Sung knew from his own life the nuances of the region's particular class, racial, and ethnic mix as they pertained to attitudes about education. Raised in neighboring Monterey Park, where he still lived as an adult at the time of the column controversy, he was the child of a Mexican Chinese father who had grown up poor in Texas and a Chinese mother from a wealthy family in China. His father "was very encouraging about what [grades] I got. If I tried my best, that would be fine." But his mother was more demanding: "If I came home with all As and a B, she'd question me. 'What's the problem?'" However, Lee-Sung asserted that while his parents "communicated in different ways," "they both valued education."[66]

As a result of his personal history in the area and his lifelong navigation of Asian and Latina/o identities, Lee-Sung felt that "pretty much my beliefs my entire life" fed into how he handled the situation; he was, he felt, "the ideal person to be in the middle of this whole controversy." As principal and both Asian and Latino, he was always keenly aware of how his appearance and ethnic identities influenced his interactions with parents as well as students. For instance, various parents' comfort and ability to identify with him were often inflected by what they either assumed or knew about his ethnic/racial background:

> Because I appear to be more Asian than Hispanic . . . I've had Asian people come up to me and say things to me [laughing]—"all those Mexicans and blah blah blah" [in disparaging tone]. . . . Sometimes I will say "I'm Mexican also, you know . . . what you're saying is not true"—kind of balance out their opinions. But yeah, they'll confide in me sometimes and say some things that uh, they think it's safe to say, because they think I'm just Asian. . . . What's nice is that once people do realize that I'm Mexican also, a lot of the Mexican parents feel very comfortable talking to me too.[67]

Still, despite feeling that such patterns of identification were "just part of human nature" (that "people will tend to be more comfortable with people that look like then, that [have] the same ethnic background"), he consistently refused to generalize the response to Robin's article as split among racial lines or even primarily racial in nature, maintaining instead that "[t]here is no simple response to this," and that it really was "not along racial lines":

> When this article happened, it was amazing. I had people who supported the article and said, "You know what? He's right on. And good for him! He's the only one courageous enough to say it like it is." And I had Caucasian people, Asian people, even Hispanic people saying "Right on!" you know? [laughing] And on the other side, who were saying, "He's racist, he should be disciplined . . . he should get his butt kicked". . . . It was mostly Hispanic, but there were Asians, there were Caucasian people who sided on that end. So it really was amazing that it was not clearly down racial lines.[68]

Lee-Sung, whose own life reflected so well the complexities and particularities of the area's class, racial, and ethnic mix, knew himself that there was no "simple response" to the achievement gap—that the problem was not reducible to racialized generalizations. What seemed "amazing" to him, perhaps, was that at moments, the community response reflected this complexity as well. Similarly, even though he affirmed that there were "underlying feelings that had not come up" previous to the publication of Robin's article, he was careful to distinguish these from the usual tropes of interracial conflict inevitably resulting in violence. "Did we see any kind of racial problems? No, we didn't. It wasn't like there was tension, people beating each other up just because of their ethnicity. . . . It wasn't a situation that I was concerned that there was gonna be this riot, OK. I never, ever felt that way. There were students that actually wanted to beat up Robin. They were angry at *him*. But it wasn't like the Hispanics were getting together and saying, 'Now we're gonna go beat up Asian people in general.'" Lee-Sung's distinction between the kind of tension that might lead to generalized racial violence and the kind of tension that might lead to personal animosities and heated debate might travel a fine line, but it is essential to understanding how at a regional level, members of racialized groups produce subtle forms of coexistence that cannot be assimilated by dominant racial discourses. The principal, at the center of the controversy, illustrated this, even as he skillfully managed what amounted to a full-blown crisis for the school.

"Why Didn't We Just Work Harder?": Narratives of Individual Merit and Immigrant Success

As in racialized discourses of achievement in general, perhaps the most difficult ideological strands to extricate from the column controversy were interlinked narratives of individual merit and immigrant success. Immigrant success narratives, such as the model minority myth, are somewhat contradictory. Although they often rest on essentialist precepts about race and culture, they are also anchored by core "American" principles of individualism and the Protestant work ethic—that anyone can succeed in democratic, capitalist America, if they only work hard enough. In Alhambra, these easily available narratives often made it difficult for students to articulate anything but individualist explanations that discounted structural or institutional factors. The comments of Crystal Tchan, a junior at the time, encapsulated in many ways the pitfalls of individualist thinking vis-à-vis issues of structural racism: "It's clearly an antiracist article; in a sense, I think it should be motivating for Hispanics."[69] Tchan's belief that the article was "antiracist" was linked to her sentiment that "it should be motivating for Hispanics." That is, racism could be solved if only individuals could be "motivated" to prove it wrong.

In another instance, Principal Lee-Sung described a Latino senior who had transferred from another high school, where he was failing all his classes, to Alhambra. "He says, 'Alhambra is a so much better school . . . so all of a sudden I got my act together.' He said, 'I got my act together. I didn't need my parents or anybody else to tell me.' And he says, 'Now I'm going to graduate, I'm going to go to college . . . but it was all me. . . . One day I just decided you know what, I'm going to start doing my homework, I'm going to start showing up to class.' And he turned his whole life around."[70] Regarding the turmoil over Robin's column, the senior said, "Don't blame our parents, don't blame our culture. Blame us." The student's comments point to the difficulty of making sense of the multiple cultural, historical-structural, and individual factors at play. In Lee-Sung's account, even while acknowledging that Alhambra was "a so much better school," the student still attributed his improved motivation solely to individual factors: "[A]ll of a sudden, *I* got my act together."

In a comment sheet generated from a meeting between Lee-Sung and a number of students, the same student elaborated in his own words: "Academic progress has nothing to do with culture. . . . I believe that a positive attitude can lead to confidence and personal achievement. And it's also wrong to blame parents who work hard to give their children a better life. It's the student's fault for doing poorly. Hispanics have the ability and potential to succeed just as well as other races. Confidence, support, attitude, and environment all have an impact on achieving success.'"[71] Even though this student's abrupt academic turnaround happened immediately after transferring to a "much better" school, he still believed that it was the "student's fault for doing poorly." His own experience could have supported a slight modification to his statement—that, indeed, "Hispanics have the ability and potential to succeed just as well as other races, [yet] confidence, support, attitude, and environment all have an impact on achieving success." However, his attachment to narratives of individual culpability seemed to place this larger-scale analysis just out of reach.

Even those who were offended by the column had trouble breaking free of such narratives. For instance, although Gabriela Fernandez was one of the most vocal students protesting the assertions in Robin's

column, she nonetheless believed that everyone had the ability to succeed: "It's all about you . . . and your mind-set. . . . These kids [who]
just want to slack off and have fun in high school—what excuse do they
have? There really isn't an excuse to not get an education, to not better
yourself." Further, reflecting on student protests against Robin's column
in which "Hispanics . . . joined together and wore brown shirts," she
felt that it would have been more effective to "work harder" to prove
that Robin's charges were wrong, rather than uniting on grounds of racism: "I mean, I guess it was a way to unite, but now thinking back on
it, it's kind of like, *well*, why didn't we just work harder to prove that
that was wrong, instead of just wearing shirts for a day and thinking
that that's going to solve everything?"[72] Gabriela and others' attempts
to articulate the problem at hand underline the difficulty of disentan-
gling historical legacies of structural racism from dominant ideologies.
Through the absence of any reference to inequalities in the structure of
institutions themselves, they illustrate how the perception of school as a
neutral environment, "purged of ideology," is actually key to its effective-
ness in purveying and inculcating ideology.[73] Students at various levels
were encouraged or discouraged to "succeed" in ways that served the
existing social order, yet these patterns were veiled and cast as individual successes and failures. In fact, the ideology of success depended on
the individualization of failure—and, more deviously, via implicating an
individual's family background in order to attribute the causes of failure
to racial and "cultural" factors.

"I'm Mexican, and I'm Lazy": Practices of Disidentification

One of the most insidious attributes of U.S. racial discourse is its inability
to include or account for experiences that fall outside a dynamic of conflict versus assimilation. This is linked to an obsessive focus on singular,
essential identities rather than a more fluid understanding of *identification* as a process of multiple alliances that shift with context. Performance
studies scholar José Esteban Muñoz has further theorized *disidentification*
as an act of refusal of dominant narratives.[74] In contrast to Steele's concept
of disidentification discussed earlier in this chapter, Muñoz characterizes
disidentification as a shifting set of practices that, while avoiding fixed
tendencies or outcomes, consistently subvert dominant narratives, often
through direct acknowledgment and engagement with racial discourses.

In his analysis of queer-of-color cultural production, Muñoz employs Althusser's "ideology cop fable" (in which identification occurs through an act of interpellation, or being hailed), putting forth a "working definition" of queer as the following: "[P]eople who have failed to turn around to the 'Hey, you there!' interpellating call of heteronormativity."[75] Muñoz argues that the artists and performers of which he writes perform disidentifications in their work, moving *through* racialized stereotypes and narratives in order to subvert them in the end.

Indeed, throughout my interviews, I noticed a quiet but consistent refusal on the part of many of my respondents (such as Lee-Sung, in the previous discussion) to agree with the thrust of questions I phrased, somewhat disingenuously, in the language of racialized conflict. As in Muñoz, in the context of regional racial formation, *disidentification* refers to the ways in which people employ racialized stereotypes and narratives yet come out somewhere unexpected at the other end—a set of practices that expresses and reproduces specific, local knowledges that contradict hegemonic norms. For example, reacting to Robin's column, Gabriela Fernandez noted the irony of a member of one minoritized group using racial generalizations to chastise another: "I mean, I can't just go into a predominantly Asian area and say insurance rates are high because Asians are bad drivers. I can't *do* that. So he can't come into Hispanic territory and say, your parents don't care about your education, that's why your test scores are low. It's the same thing. You have to *live* that life in order to say that you know what's going on with it."[76] By recognizing that "you have to live that life in order to say that you know what's going on with it," she gestured to the inadequacy of normative discourses in describing the particularity and complexity of everyday life in Alhambra as she knew it. She also grappled with the references to racial stereotypes in the column, eventually subverting their meaning in a way that suited her world view:

> Who is this *guy*, just making assumptions? . . . Trying to assume that, you know, all Hispanic families have ten kids and are working three jobs and don't care about their children's education? And like, maybe that was true in Mexico for his nanny, but not *here*. I mean, you could still have that ten-people family with the mom working three jobs. But at the same time, if she *is* working three jobs, you can see that she's trying to make a life for her family. Is

that necessarily a bad thing? So that article kind of really rallied a
lot of Hispanics together to say no, that's not the way it is.[77]

Gabriela recognized and was offended by the implied racial-economic
stereotypes but then backtracked to suggest, in effect, "So what?" Even
if they were superficially "true," they did not mean what racial discourses
intimated them to mean.

In a similar vein, sophomore Robert Himenez told the *Moor*, "Most of
[the article] is true. I'm Mexican, and I'm lazy. But [the author] shouldn't
have blamed it on our parents and ancestors."[78] Himenez, after making the
surprise move of admitting the personal "truth" of the racial stereotype,
then blocked discursive access to pathologizing the family unit, which,
as Althusser has observed, forms the key pairing with school in dissemi-
nating hegemonic ideologies in institutions of civil society. Without the
ability to generalize via the supposedly neutral institutions of school and
family, racial discourse loses its power.

Conclusion

As of 2008, three years after the controversy over Robin's column, probably
the most significant change at Alhambra High was the implementation of
open enrollment for honors and AP classes.[79] In the previous system, students had to apply for honors and AP classes, with qualifying grades, test
scores, teacher recommendations, and in some cases a specialized exam.
In the debate over open enrollment, as in the debate over the achievement
gap, the rhetoric of individualism and equal opportunity figured strongly.
It was used both in support of and against it, with a circular reasoning that
recalled conservative and liberal debates over "color-blind" admissions
policies in the 1990s. To "high-achieving" former students Paul Pham
and Annie Liu, opposition to open enrollment seemed universal among
their friends, classmates, and teachers. Paul explained that he personally
was against it, because it would "water down the quality of the students . . .
you would not have students who actually met some prerequisites, or have
shown some sort of merit that would allow them to be into the class."[80]
Annie expressed the following:

> [J]ust because you open the enrollment doesn't mean that there's
> going to be a flood of non-Asians who want to enter AP. I think if

you really wanted to take the class, you would have filled out the application. It's not such a difficult process . . . to start with. . . . If they [Latinos] really wanted to do it, they would just go out and fill out the application and ask the teacher for details. . . . I don't think that was what was holding them back. It was just, if they don't want to take it, they're not going to take it. That's what I felt.[81]

Although Annie agreed in theory that "it's good to give people a chance," like Paul, her belief that the previous system could not be held at fault because it was based on individual achievement prevailed. While Paul and Annie upheld the view that open enrollment would undercut the institution's ability to uphold an equitable system of rewards based on individual merit, teacher Matt Ramos believed that it was the only way to be truly equitable: "If they want to take it, I don't think any student should be denied access to it. Let them prove themselves. If they're failing the class, well, they're failing the class . . . if they can do it, let them prove it."

However, the one thing they all seemed to agree on is that open enrollment was unlikely to effect the desired changes. In Ramos's words, "this open access thing looks better on paper, I think, than it will prove to be any sort of positive result. . . . It's just like saying, 'OK, we're going to go ahead and leave this plate of cheese out for all the mice who are full,' and 'let's see what happens.' I mean, it may be open, but how many of them are going to go in there and do anything?"[82] They all seemed to sense, even if they could not acknowledge it as such, that without any substantive acknowledgment of historical and structural effects on educational equity, real change was unlikely. In the context of Alhambra High, the particular regional demographics—a lower-middle-class to middle-class, multiracial, and majority nonwhite space—might have yielded opportunities to reconfigure commonly accepted racial and class dynamics. Instead, "color-blind" liberal ideologies of individualism and merit, in concert with immigrant success narratives such as the model minority myth, proved impossible to disentangle. Racialized "cultural" discourses of academic achievement and deficiency justified and perpetuated an experience of racialized privilege for Asian American students, continually reproducing a bifurcated school experience for Asian American students in comparison to their Latina/o peers. Yet the controversy over Robin Zhou's column also forced students, staff, and administration to confront socially constructed hierarchies that had previously been accepted as simple common sense. It left a lingering sense of unease, exposing the fissures between normative racial discourse and more nuanced, regionally based ways of knowing. Even if ideology supporting the reproduction of dominant racial hierarchies remained powerful, the incident showed that at a regional level these racial logics were not forgone conclusions but would be observed and challenged.

Around the same time, nearby, in another civic institution, the Boy Scouts of America, another teenager was also challenging the regionally accepted racial order—with equally complex and revealing consequences.

· CHAPTER 3 ·

"Just Like Any Other Boy"?

Race and the San Gabriel Valley Boy Scouts of America

[E]very culture that's in that Troop right now, every different kind of culture that we have in Troop [252], is learning the same values.

—Joe Castillo, assistant scoutmaster, Troop 252[1]

He was always the lone milk dud . . .

—Marie Johnson, mother of Shawn Smith[2]

BOY SCOUT TROOP 252 was chartered in 1922, when the West San Gabriel Valley (SGV) municipality that hosted it was a newly incorporated, semirural town on the outskirts of Los Angeles—still decades away from becoming the even sprawl of strip malls, faux-Mediterranean townhomes, and aging 1950s subdivisions it is today. A 1928 photograph of the troop depicts fourteen white-looking adolescent boys and two men clustered around a Rose Bowl float decorated with an American flag made of flowers. The boys are solemn-faced, their hands raised crisply to their foreheads in the scout salute.[3] Fast-forward eighty years to a Troop 252 meeting in July 2008: Dozens of adolescent boys in dark green T-shirts adorned with the Boy Scouts of America's (BSA) fleur-de-lis logo and khakis move energetically in the parking lot and up the stairs of a large, Methodist church. Parents—mostly mothers—cluster in small groups, chatting amiably. A handful of men—assistant scoutmasters, most of them fathers of boys in the troop, also wearing the green BSA shirts— seem to be leading the enterprise, pointing moving currents of boys in various directions or standing back with their arms crossed surveying the scene. A little later, the meeting is under way. Boys sit on one side, leaving irregular gaps between themselves for slouching in the pews, and mothers on the other, gathered in conversational groups of two or three. It might be any BSA meeting anywhere in the United States—except that nearly all the boys and parents present are Asian American or Latina/o and conversations can be heard in Spanish, Cantonese, Vietnamese, and Mandarin, as well as English. Scoutmaster Bob Lee estimates that, similar to the racial-ethnic makeup of its surrounding area, the troop is about two-thirds Asian and the remaining one-third mostly Latino, with some white and white-Latino scouts as well. "We like to refer to three of them as token whites," Lee joked.[4]

In the spring of 2007, Shawn Smith became the first African American Eagle Scout in the eighty-five-year history of Troop 252. His achievement of the highest rank a scout can earn was the subject of extensive articles in the local *Pasadena Star-News*, the African American paper *The Sentinel*, and others. His mother, Marie Johnson, sent out press releases and custom-printed invitations to Shawn's Eagle Court ceremony with the return address labeled, "First African American Eagle Scout." The ceremony, which took place at the Asian American church that sponsors the troop, lasted over three hours. Shawn was feted by a long list of officials, including the head of the regional BSA council, a deacon from a church in nearby Pasadena, a representative of the National Guard, and local congresswoman Hilda Solis. During the ceremony, a significant portion of the audience responded to the speeches with emphatic vocal affirmations, following the norms of Black church services. Afterward, guests were treated to a soul food banquet and a live jazz band. Johnson had hired assistants to decorate the banquet room: "We had cloth tablecloths. . . . It was just old-school elegant."[5]

However, fewer than half of the troop's assistant scoutmasters attended. According to Shawn, for an Eagle Court, usually nearly all of them would attend. While two of the assistant scoutmasters I interviewed recalled that there may have been a scheduling conflict that prevented some of the others from attending, Scoutmaster Bob Lee attributed the low attendance to something else: some "didn't feel it was going to be appropriate, the way it was gonna come out." According to Lee, they felt that the ceremony, which he described as "a different type of Eagle Court that no one has ever seen," overemphasized Shawn's status as the first African American Eagle Scout in the troop, when it should have simply focused on "the boy and his accomplishments. If you read the newspaper beforehand and everything else . . . sometimes you felt that hey, this is not going to be for me. . . .

They felt it wasn't a scouting-type deal. . . . It just wasn't the Boy Scout way, or anything that we were used to, basically."[6]

Lee's statements raise significant questions: in the minds of scouts, leadership, and parents of Troop 252, what constituted "a scouting-type deal" or the "Boy Scout way"? Why did one scout's Eagle Court ceremony cause so much consternation and discomfort within the troop, and what was the nature of that discomfort? In fact, the Eagle Court of Honor ceremony was the culmination of not only Shawn's many years in the troop but also a long path informed by the regional racial and ethnic dynamics of Troop 252, in which Shawn was the only African American among more than fifty primarily Asian and Latino counterparts. Shawn's elaborate, much-publicized Eagle Court of Honor was preceded by several newspaper articles framing his achievement in clearly racial terms yet omitting any mention that the troop as a whole was predominantly nonwhite. The treatment of the majority Asian American and Latino troop as racially invisible or "neutral" (a role historically reserved for whites), coupled with the treatment of African American identity as hypervisible or exceptional, speaks to the particular racial formation at play in this part of the West SGV. The emphasis on race in Shawn's advancement to Eagle Scout both constituted a rupture in the principles of the BSA as understood and expressed by its local proponents and exposed complex racial dynamics operating within the troop. How the episode was perceived externally as well as experienced and understood internally also showed how Blackness and whiteness remained important to structuring racial formation and identity, even in the West SGV's overwhelmingly Asian American and Latina/o context.

In the following analysis, the experiences of Troop 252 affiliates show another instance in which, as in schools, racial ideologies are produced, perpetuated, and subverted not just in explicitly political contexts but through the civic institutions that guide people's everyday lives. This doesn't merely occur in settings involving whites and nonwhites but also plays out in "majority-minority" contexts. Historically, American civic institutions have played an important role in fostering immigrant involvement in public life, mostly toward the end of assimilating white ethnics for the purposes of political participation. More recently, scholars have begun to analyze the role of a wide array of civic institutions, such as community organizations, ethnic voluntary associations, and ethnic churches, in mobilizing nonwhite immigrants to participate in civic life.[7]

The BSA has long been an influential national organization that openly espouses frontier ideals, patriotism, good citizenship, and heteronormative masculinity[8]—attributes historically interwoven with the production of racial and other social hierarchies in the United States. A look at the history of racial minorities and scouting, however, in combination with an analysis of its meaning in the lives of members of Troop 252, calls into question how supposedly hegemonic civic institutions such as the BSA actually operate in people's lives. The ways in which the diverse members and leaders of Troop 252 reacted to and made sense of Shawn's progress in the troop had much to do with their beliefs about the United States, such as the roles of egalitarianism, individualism, and hard work in ensuring equal access to the "American Dream," as well as their own place in the nation as racialized ethnic minorities. The nuances of their individual experiences show not only the difficulty of escaping the overdetermined meanings of race in the United States but also the ways that latent counterhegemonic possibilities of meaning-making operate at a regional level in people's daily lives.

Racial/Ethnic Minorities and the BSA

The BSA began in 1910 as an offshoot of British scouting. Its British founder, Lord Robert Baden-Powell, had been an army general who led campaigns in Africa and India. Baden-Powell intended Boy Scouts to be a program to give boys training inspired by colonial frontier practices and mythologies, which would make them into men able and willing to defend the waning British Empire.[9] In the United States, scouting was similarly defined from the outset by "frontier" ideals of expansion, conquest, and the appropriation of conquered native peoples' cultures by whites.[10] From the beginning, in Britain as well as in the United States, scouting also had a Progressive Era emphasis on "uplifting" the working poor and reforming delinquents via the teaching of discipline and middle-class values such as moral uprightness and good citizenship. Gradually, the BSA narrative was consolidated around the principles of "scouts, pioneers, patriotism, and service," with some incorporation of "Indian" aspects, and encased in a militaristic structure.[11] In lieu of the vanished frontier, the BSA viewed wilderness as good for boys, especially the urban poor or immigrants, to develop the "hardiness" they needed to be true Americans.[12] Patriotism was enshrined as the BSA's most important defining value. As expressed by BSA founder Dan Beard, "[W]hen you go to camp this summer, see that you are under a patriotic American camp director. He may possibly be of foreign birth or parentage, but he MUST BE A PATRIOTIC AMERICAN. No others have the right to guide and instruct American youth."[13] This combination of patriotism, moral development, and physical hardiness was distilled into the scout oath:

> On my honor I will do my best
> To do my duty to God and my country
> and to obey the Scout Law;
> To help other people at all times;
> To keep myself physically strong,
> mentally awake, and morally straight.[14]

These precepts still structure BSA activities today. Troops take regular hiking and camping trips in which wilderness survival skills are taught, and scouts engage in community service and earn merit badges through the cultivation of specialized skills and knowledge. For participants who subscribe to the organization's expressed values, Boy Scouts is not merely a recreational organization but a way of life that represents certain ideals. Members of Troop 252 spoke often of how scouting built "character" and taught boys valuable leadership skills that made them mature into men. Often built into such views, particularly when combined with a strong sense of patriotism, was a belief in the purported color-blindness of the American Dream—that anyone can succeed with a bit of ingenuity and a lot of hard work and that those who don't have only themselves to blame for it (also discussed previously in chapter 2). If this "myth of success"[15] is true, the logic goes, then race doesn't matter; if it ever did, that unfortunate period of time is past and everyone stands on equal ground now.

Indeed, the official contemporary image of the scout as an abstract figure of boyhood and nationhood that transcends divisions of race, ethnicity, and class (although never gender or sexuality[16]) presumes one unified national culture. This notion of Americanness—based on the "frontier" ideas mentioned previously—is predicated on ideologies of racial succession and white "manifest destiny." Just as Blackness has been an "essential precondition" for American whiteness, constructions of American nationhood such as those employed in the BSA have depended on contradictory relationships to Indianness epitomized by the notion of "noble savagery," in which Indianness is both the "impetus and precondition for . . . assembling . . . an ultimately unassemblable [*sic*] American identity."[17] "American" identity is also frequently suffused with ideas of liberal individualism. However, national political and cultural institutions, in direct contradiction to the creed of individual liberty for all, have in fact been integral to structuring inequality by intertwining definitions of citizenship with race from the outset. Like citizenship, race, "the marker of personhood and subpersonhood," has functioned as a category of "inclusion within or exclusion from the . . . polity."[18] Since liberal citizenship has been predicated on racial difference—constituting a fundamental contradiction—even as citizens, racialized groups such as Asian Americans have a "differential relationship" to national institutions.[19] As such, when Asians or members of racialized minority groups become "abstract citizens" of the state—for example, symbolically, by donning a Boy Scout uniform—the act does more than just erase individual particularities. Such an act, according to Lisa Lowe, actively negates history, suggesting that equal freedoms can in fact be fully achieved through immigrant "naturalization." This supports the fiction of "American liberal democracy as a terrain to which all citizens have equal access and in which all are equally represented . . . a narrative that denies the establishment of citizenship out of unequal relationships between dominant white citizens and subordinated racialized noncitizens and women."[20]

"A Lot of Us Were Ashamed of Our Parents and Our Culture"

A moment broadcast on national television in 2003 illustrates how the historical negation described by Lowe occurs in the context of racial minorities and the Boy Scouts. Gary Locke, then governor of Washington, had been chosen by the Democratic Party to deliver its response to the president's annual State of the Union address. After Locke's speech was aired, news anchor Tom Brokaw, in his recap, listed Locke's political offices and added two more details: "Gary Locke . . . Yale-educated, Eagle Scout." According to Eagle Scout chronicler Alvin Townley, this statement "told America volumes about Gary Locke"; upon hearing that he was an Eagle Scout, "viewers in every household would immediately recognize something rare and admirable about Washington's governor."[21] The listing of Locke's Boy Scout credentials suggested to television viewers that, despite Locke's Asian background, he could be considered an "abstract citizen"; having donned the Boy Scout uniform as an adolescent served to symbolically foreground his status as a citizen—his *Americanness*—over his Asianness.[22]

In fact, Locke's status as a racialized minority was not peripheral or irrelevant but central to his experience as a scout. Locke remembered his troop, an all-Chinese troop affiliated with Seattle's First Chinese Baptist Church, as a source of solace in contrast to school, where teachers disparaged immigrant Asian children's backgrounds and constantly impressed on them the ways in which they must assimilate into (white) American culture. Since many of the adults and children in the troop were recent immigrants, meetings were conducted half in English and half in Chinese, and the scouts wore neckerchiefs embroidered with Chinese characters. As Locke remembers it, "A lot of us were somewhat embarrassed or ashamed of our parents and our culture. . . . That's why Scouting was even more important. Here, I had a surrogate family and kids I could relate to. We also had adults who tried to instill in us some pride in our culture while at the same time helping us to understand American society."[23] However, in the national symbolic registers of what being a Boy Scout is commonly understood to mean (i.e., assimilation into a presumably white, middle-class polity), the fact that, for Locke, one of the main functions of scouting had been to affirm his ethnoracial identity within a racist mainstream society, were effectively erased.

This delicate balancing act of cultivating pride and patriotism while feeling "embarrassed or ashamed" in larger "American society," as Locke put it, has been shared by a large number of nonwhite scouts in ethnically based troops that began organizing almost immediately after the founding of the BSA in 1910. As an organization, harkening back to its Progressive Era origins, the BSA has consistently made efforts to promote scouting across lines of race and class, beginning with the establishment of its "Inter-Racial Service" in 1926 to promote scouting among nonwhites. In 1961, the Inter-Racial Service was replaced by the Urban Relationships Service and the Inner-City Rural Program in 1965, targeting both inner-city and poor rural areas.[24] The first Black Boy Scout troop was founded in North Carolina in 1911, only a year after scouting began in the United States as a whole. By 1926, there were 248 all-Black troops. Although Black scouts had to contend with segregation, poor funding, discrimination, and sometimes vigilante opposition, the troops, many of which were based in Black churches, often served to build a sense of individual and community pride. As a writer for the African American Registry put it, for individual scouts, becoming an Eagle Scout meant that they could be "no longer just 'Boy'"—treated by whites as less than a man and constantly subjected to a subordinate position—but an Eagle Scout. Although many troops slowly integrated after the Civil Rights Act, some remained segregated by choice: "[i]f they had made it this far under such extreme oppression, why should they happily submit themselves to white churches and social clubs?"[25]

Beginning in the 1930s, Japanese American Boy Scout troops flourished in Southern California and other parts of the West, and Boy Scout troops were active in all ten World War II Japanese American detention camps.[26] One of the oldest and most well known, Koyasan Troop 379, based in Los Angeles's Little Tokyo, was founded in 1931 by Buddhist Reverend Taido Kitagawa to serve "as a way to help Japanese American children armor themselves against the anti-Japanese rhetoric of the early Depression."[27] Troop 379 still operates out of Little Tokyo today.

As these examples illustrate, scouting in racial/ethnic minority communities has often functioned not as one might think—to encourage assimilation into mainstream white society—but as a means for youth to "armor" themselves against racist sentiments, to assert worlds of their own in which becoming white, or closer to white, was not necessarily the goal. For these communities, participating in scouting served not only as an avenue through which marginalized adolescents sought to assert themselves as legitimate American citizens but as a means to build individual and community pride. Ethnic churches and temples often served as foundations for troops that stood at a slight distance from American civil society at large, simultaneously asserting their place in it but also maintaining a separate sphere of activities through which the pride and legitimacy systematically denied to them as subordinately racialized subjects could be developed and nurtured.

Nonetheless, despite this history of organizational flexibility and openness, as one might guess, the experiences of ethnic-minority scouts were not all flags and roses. Two stories regarding Japanese American scouts during World War II, one real and one fictionalized, suggest some of the grimmer dimensions in which this was so. In these examples, at a crucial historical moment, the fallacy of the BSA's egalitarian and individualist creed was exposed in an exercise of power by the racial state.[28] The first instance involves American politician Norman Mineta, a long-time California congressman who successfully championed redress for interned Japanese American in the Civil Liberties Act of 1988 and has most recently served as U.S. Secretary of Transportation in the George W. Bush administration. When soldiers came to the Mineta family home in San Jose in 1942 to "evacuate" them to the camps, eleven-year-old Mineta was wearing his Cub Scout uniform and carrying a baseball, bat, and glove. But the uniform was no protection against the grim chain of events; a U.S. Army MP confiscated Mineta's bat "as a potential lethal weapon" before allowing the boy to board the train.[29] Eve Bunting's children's book, *So Far from the Sea*, offers a fictional echo of Mineta's experience. In the book, set in the present day, a young Japanese American girl named Laura Iwasaki visits Manzanar with her family. The main purpose of the visit is to pay respects to her grandfather, who died there while incarcerated during the World War II internment of Japanese Americans. Laura has brought her father's yellow Cub Scout scarf to leave as a kind of offering, and her younger brother wants to know why. Standing at the barren memorial, Laura's father answers, his "voice coming from some remembering place": "When they came for us, my father said to me, 'Koharu! Put on your Cub Scout uniform. That way they will know you are a true American and they will not take you.' I put it on. But they took me anyway. They took all of us."[30] At these two crucial moments in Mineta's and the fictional Iwasakis' lives, the ability of Japanese Americans, as racial subjects, to become abstract citizens (in Lowe's terms) was shown to be selectively dictated by a racial state.

Both of these dynamics—the flexibility of the meanings and functions of the institution of Boy Scouts in individual lives, as well as its racially inscribed limits—were also important in the contemporary experiences of members of Troop 252.

"Vale La Pena": Marketing the BSA

The existence and enthusiasm of specific African American and Asian American troops notwithstanding, however, in general the BSA has consistently had to make extra efforts to attract nonwhite participants. While the BSA is often perceived as a public, civic institution, it is nonetheless a private organization that adheres to conservative social values (recently, most conspicuously spelled out in its adamant refusal to admit openly gay members). By its own admission, the BSA is perceived by many Asian Americans, Latinas/os, and African Americans as overwhelmingly and unwelcomingly white.[31] However, as a private organization in a country whose youth are becoming increasingly nonwhite, the BSA must maintain its capitalist imperative to appeal to the greatest number of boys and parents as possible. Since 1998, the Scoutreach division (the present-day incarnation of the BSA's earlier minority recruitment programs) has focused on developing relationships and promoting scouting among African Americans, Latina/os, Asian Americans, and rural communities (including Native American communities).[32] The BSA has focused much of these efforts on recruiting Latinas/os: as of 2009, Latinas/os constituted 15 percent of the U.S. population but accounted for only around 3 percent of the BSA's membership. As Rick Cronk, then the BSA's immediate past president, put it, "We're either going to figure out how we can be the most exciting and dynamic organization of Hispanic youth, or we're going out of business."[33] The BSA established a "Hispanic emphasis" in the 1990s, launched a Spanish-language marketing campaign in 2002 (with the central slogan, "Vale la pena" ["It's worth it"]), and in 2004, established the Soccer and Scouting Program specifically to appeal to Latina/o youth and families.

In 2006, the BSA conducted nationwide focus groups with African American, Latina/o, and Asian American parents and youth in order to better understand perceptions of scouting among ethnic-minority parents and children. While the resulting report maintains that those surveyed generally had a positive impression of scouting, the BSA also found that "many see a Scout as a white or Anglo person who is not comfortable with people from diverse backgrounds" and that in general parents "lack an emotional connection with Scouting."[34] For parents and youth in racial-minority groups, the traditional symbolic connotations of the Boy Scout uniform were not ones they wanted to embody or felt their kids would want to embody. Parents believed their kids would not want to wear the uniforms, and all groups of youth agreed it was outdated—African American youth in particular suggested that the uniform should be optional. All groups of parents surveyed agreed that they "do not see a Scout as someone their child would hang out with." Their children concurred, mentioning to researchers that they "do not see others like themselves in Scouting," "do not have friends who are Scouts," and that "Scouts are not someone they can see themselves hanging out with." Further, African American and Latina/o youth also "[did] not think Scouts are comfortable with their racial/ethnic group." Asian American and Latina/o parents also expressed concern about language barriers and that their children would "[lose] their cultural heritage."[35] In addition, specifically regarding "Hispanic/Latino" families, the two main obstacles cited by BSA executives were the perceptions that "scouting is for wealthy families," and that scouting was not "a household experience shared by most Hispanic Americans / Latinos."[36]

The report's recommendations to address these concerns fall among racial lines: "When addressing African American parents emphasize the values reinforced through Scouting and *faith-based partnerships*. When addressing Hispanic/Latino parents emphasize the values reinforced through Scouting and *building family bonds*. When addressing Asian American parents emphasize the *educational benefits* of Scouting, *the merit badges*, and the *activities that can help their children in future careers*."[37] Even though both the findings and the recommendations are presented as arising in a straightforward manner from the focus groups, the lack of correspondence between the expressed concerns (at least those expressed as having to do with race) and the "solutions" (culturally specific target marketing) is striking. The failure of 2002's "Vale la pena" campaign showed that basing marketing tactics on racialized cultural stereotypes was not effective. In fact, the slogan was "neither culturally resonant nor especially rousing," nor did it explain to Spanish-speaking parents "*what* was worth it." While some Spanish-language fliers highlighted "ideals, like reverence and obedience, embedded in the Scout Oath," these completely omitted the organization's main goals of producing "good citizens and leaders": "While those are nice values that are consistent with the Latino community, if a parent reads that, they still don't know what the Boy Scouts of America is," said one market strategist.[38]

In August 2008, an "emerging markets" department was established for "diversity purposes,"[39] suggesting that the organization, in keeping with a larger "retreat from race" in American society, was moving away from explicitly racial/ethnic language.[40] The delicate navigation between fundamentally conservative values and the need for constant expansion has been aided by a considerable amount of flexibility built into the organizational structure that allows for the continuance of ethnic-based units. Indeed, the large degree of autonomy exercised by individual troops (albeit within carefully delimited parameters) allows for quite a bit of variation in terms of troop composition and interests, as the following discussion of the BSA's San Gabriel Valley Council illustrates.

"What You Build on That Bedrock Is Up to You"

In the San Gabriel Valley Council, Senior District Executive Jack Pan maintained that scouting participation simply mirrored regional demographics: "[I]f you look at the census, you can pretty much predict what Scouting's going to look like."[41] Participation in the BSA's three programs, Cub Scouts, Boy Scouts, and Venture Crew, grew by about a third in the San Gabriel Valley Council between 2002 and 2006.[42] Troop 252 is one of more than 350 units that make up the San Gabriel Valley Council.[43] Altogether, 35,000 youth participate in the BSA in the council. The Mission Amigos District encompasses 96 units within the four cities of San Gabriel, Rosemead, Monterey Park, and Alhambra, and involves 2,200 youth and around 700 adult volunteers. The troops in the Mission Amigos District of the San Gabriel Valley Council, which covers Monterey Park, Alhambra, San Gabriel, and Rosemead, are correspondingly majority Asian American and Latino.

In these multiethnic, multiracial troops, the role of race and ethnicity was perhaps less clearly defined than in single-race or single-ethnicity troops. As Pan put it, "Our bedrock, our foundation, is character education and outdoor learning. *How*, what you build on that bedrock, is up to you." Similarly, longtime SGV scoutmaster Bob Matsumoto, who is Japanese American and leads a historically Japanese American troop, told me that "each scout troop has its own identity and personality. So . . . if a boy and their family come into a unit and they're not happy . . . or if they just don't feel comfortable— there's a spot for them in the scouting organization if they want to be there."[44] When I asked District Executive Pan if he believed Boy Scouts still offered members of ethnic-minority groups a way to develop their racial pride and identity, as it had in the past, he said, "sure"—but was careful to generalize ethnicity as just one way of "social identification":

> We're very social animals, like it or not, and oftentimes we flock together towards those of similar backgrounds, and sometimes that background is an ethnic background, sometimes it's educational background, sometimes it's an economic background. So there are different ways of flocking together. One of those, yeah, sure, is certainly an ethnic one.
>
> We do have a number of units that are predominantly Asian or predominantly Hispanic, or predominantly African American. And

I think the identity there, it *is* helpful. It does instill a certain sense of self to these kids, and particularly for early or new immigrants to this country. That's another avenue that we've really approached, in that you know, just because you're a recent immigrant, doesn't mean scouting's not for you. Because a lot of people felt like you have to be in the United States for several generations before you join scouting, which is not true. And units like that provide an avenue for new immigrants who may not have a full grasp of the English language to join and be able to participate, because somebody else there speaks their language, whether it be Spanish, Cantonese, Mandarin, whatever it is.

Will we ever preach segregation? Of course not. Of *course* not. Will we ever recommend that you set up a unit exclusively for one group or another? Of *course* not. But like you mentioned, sometimes the importance of fitting in is very, very important for adolescents. . . . And one of the tabs, or bookmarks, of fitting in, fortunately or unfortunately, is race and ethnicity. So that is an important factor, oftentimes.[45]

Pan's answer, as an official representative of the BSA, is a skillful piece of spin, in keeping with the BSA's organizational history and philosophy. (And indeed, Pan was a self-professed "professional Boy Scout"; although he was never actually a scout himself, he had a degree from Harvard's Kennedy School and had worked as a political consultant—which according to Pan is "a nice way of saying spin doctor"—previous to working for the BSA.[46]) Even as Pan appeared to validate my query, he redirected the lines of the conversation so we were talking not about race and historical, structural racism, but about "new immigrants," language, participation, and "like you mentioned . . . the importance of fitting in" (which was not actually what I said or meant). Finally he emphasized that just *one* way of "fitting in, fortunately or unfortunately, is race and ethnicity." Shifting the terms of the conversation to immigration and assimilation and adolescent desires to "fit in"—and away from race, as a socially produced category of difference with material effects—squares neatly with "American Dream" ideology, in which each individual has the same capacity to succeed if only she works hard. At the same time, while he was careful to say that the BSA would never "preach segregation," Pan affirmed the continuing large degree of autonomy exercised by individual troops in terms of recruitment and focus.

Dynamics of Race and Ethnicity in Troop 252

How did this institutional history and philosophy work on the ground in Troop 252? Over its first eighty-five years, the troop's enrollment seemed to have roughly paralleled the demographics of the area. At its founding, twelve boys with Anglo/European surnames were enrolled, and Anglo/European-surnamed scoutmasters led the troop every year at least until the early 1970s, when the BSA stopped listing the name of the scoutmaster on the charters. A March 8, 1972, letter from the BSA's San Gabriel Valley Council to a Japanese American reverend, expressing appreciation for sponsoring the troop, signaled the arrival of an institutionalized Japanese American presence in the area. In 1996, when Lee, a third-generation Chinese American, became scoutmaster, there were twelve boys in the troop; as of 2008, over the twelve-year span of his leadership so far, the troop had more than quadrupled in size, usually hovering around fifty-five but peaking at nearly eighty boys one recent year. The troop also had an unusually high number of assistant scoutmasters compared to other troops of its size—a ratio of approximately one assistant scoutmaster for every four boys. This indicated not only Lee's collaborative leadership style but also a high degree of parental involvement. Troop 252, like many other troops across the SGV, had become majority Asian American in recent years. The Asian American members were generally a mix of later-generation Chinese Americans and Japanese Americans, more recent ethnic Chinese immigrants, and kids with mixed backgrounds (both interethnic and interracial). The Latinos in the troop were mostly Mexican American, but at least one was of Cuban descent and several came from mixed Mexican and white (Anglo) families. As Assistant Scoutmaster Joe Castillo saw it, primarily "we have four cultures in there . . . Anglo, Chinese, Japanese, and Latino."[47]

"My Group Is Pretty Well Mixed"

"My group is pretty well mixed," said Scoutmaster Bob Lee, "and they all work towards one goal . . . and it's pretty good to see. A lot of other troops—they're maybe all Asian, or they're all Hispanics."[48] Assistant Scoutmaster Gary Wong agreed: "You would say we are *uniquely* . . . one of the few multiethnic troops in the area. . . . Most troops are predominantly Asian or Hispanic, or whatever."[49] Since the troop's traditions were not, and never had been, defined along ethnic lines, the role of race and ethnicity in parents', scouts', and leadership's experiences was not easy to pinpoint. In addition, since nearly all my respondents grew up in the Los Angeles area, many of them had lived all their lives in contexts where majority-minority, multiethnic groupings were the norm, and thus they had nothing else to which to compare it. For instance, Assistant Scoutmaster Castillo, a third-generation Mexican American, participated as an adolescent in the 1960s in a multiethnic troop that simply mirrored his East Los Angeles neighborhood: "Every kid on the block . . . belonged to Boy Scouts. . . . We had everybody in it, every race that you could think of. We had Jewish, Black, Chinese, Latinos, Italians. . . . Every kind of race and language was spoken at [those] meeting[s]." Correspondingly, in Castillo's view, "I can't think of any troop in Southern California that's all one culture. I think it would be totally impossible."[50]

The normalcy of such scenarios for many Southern Californians made it difficult for some to "see" race and ethnicity at all. For instance, Assistant Scoutmaster Gary Wong felt that *because* Troop 252's mix was so multiethnic, he never gave much thought to the significance of its racial/ethnic composition. "I don't really think about it because we've had such a multiethnic troop. . . . Because unless you consciously think about race, I don't see—you know. . . . I see kids as, 'Is he rowdy? Is he a good citizen?' That's what I look at. . . . I don't see them as, 'He's a white kid, he's a Black kid'—they're just kids."[51] Even for Wong's son, David, whose grandfather and great-uncle on his Japanese American mother's side had become Eagle Scouts in Little Tokyo's Koyasan troop decades earlier, his decision to become a scout was not motivated by a desire to continue family or ethnic-community tradition: "[T]he person who actually got me into Boy Scouts was not one of my grandparents, but this friend of mine from [school], an African American boy . . . one of my good friends. And he kept telling me, 'You've gotta come to Boy Scouts.' [I said] 'Oh, no no no. I'm too busy. I'm taking swimming and I'm taking piano.' And I was in basketball at the time. So when I quit basketball, he said, 'Well, you gotta'—so I went, and that was it."[52]

"A Doorway to the White Experience"

Like David, no one else I interviewed mentioned the racial-ethnic composition of Troop 252 as either a draw or deterrent; no one had initially searched, for example, for a Mexican or Japanese or Chinese American–based troop. However, this is not to say that culturally or racially inflected considerations were unimportant to Troop 252 members' motivations to participate in scouting. Conceptions of scouting activities as stereotypically white—or at least *not* "Mexican" or "Asian"—were quite prevalent. Asian American parents and troop leaders tended to characterize scouting as providing activities that were not typically available to Asians. When I asked Scoutmaster Lee if he felt there were any aspects of scouting that Asian Americans responded to in particular, he responded, "I think they [Asian Americans] want more out of life than what they've got, what they had when they were a child. It's probably because the parents were saying, you gotta go to school, you gotta do this, and you'll get a good job. Marry a[n] . . . Asian, nothing else—that's what they do [laughs]—so that's the way they look at it. And so now they want more for their child besides sitting at home." In Lee's opinion, Asian Americans "get overboard on education" and are "not well-rounded." "That's where the Boy Scouts are good, because they give you another alternative, to do other things. Instead of sitting there doing your video games. Because that's what most of the parents say—'they're playing too much video games.' Okay, send 'em over and we'll get them out. . . . So they learn a little bit about everything."[53] In the scoutmaster's analysis, Asian Americans joined scouting in order to find out how to be less stereotypically Asian, "to do other things" besides "going overboard on education," and raise their children in ways they themselves wish they had been raised.

Mexican Americans were more direct about characterizing scouting as a stereotypically white activity. Mexican American parent Mary Hernandez, who worked as a literacy coach in local public schools, recalled her nonwhite coworkers' distaste when she mentioned her family's involvement in scouting: "When you say 'Boy Scout,' you picture a white kid. You don't usually picture an Asian kid or a Latino kid, or an African American kid. Because you know, that's not the stereotypical picture of a Boy Scout." As a counterargument, Hernandez evoked the little-known flexibility and diversity of the organization. "[A]t the same time, they have to see that . . . we have evolved as a country, where you know, kids can do anything. . . . I think that they need to realize that . . . every troop is different, even within Boy Scouts."[54] Assistant Scoutmaster Walter Ruiz, a first-generation Mexican American, was the most outspoken in his blunt description of the BSA as fundamentally a "white, paramilitary organization." However, Ruiz did not see this as a problem but rather as a desirable characteristic, admitting that he "kind of like[d] that paramilitary thing," and that he saw scouting as a "doorway to the white experience" for his kids, in that it offered them new experiences and hence a greater capacity to "do something really special for themselves":

> One of the things my wife and I say is that our kids get an Anglo experience . . . because they're in scouting. When you look at your typical Hispanic, like from . . . my upbringing in a predominantly Hispanic area, you don't *go* camping. You don't go fishing . . . you don't do community projects . . . you don't do this, you don't do that. Those are what [rich] white boys [do] . . . and for us, being in the lower class, "rich" is middle class. That's the perspective *I* grew up with. So. I'll be honest with you. Scouting to me? is one way I can give my children the Anglo experience.
>
> Because [brief pause] what governs scouting? The scout book. Okay. Who started scouting? Sir Baden Powell—Anglo, British guy. And if you look at the leadership in Virginia, they're all Anglo. If you look at the values in the scout book, they're really Anglo values. They're not the Hispanic experience. They're not the Asian experience, or the African American experience. It's the *white* experience. You know, pioneering, frontiering, orienteering . . . using buck knives, and making bridges out of rope. And the Indian lore—those are all *white* experiences. So for me, scouting is a doorway to the white experience for my children . . . that's what it is.
>
> I can give my kids the Mexican experience, that's no problem. We'll go to the park and I'll drink beers with my buddies and make 'em run around with a soccer ball, and we'll eat carne asada—the Mexican experience, I can do that with my eyes closed. It's the white experience that I want . . . for my children.[55]

That the presumption of one unified national culture in the BSA was from the outset defined by conquest and appropriation of subjugated cultures by whites ("pioneering, frontiering . . . Indian lore") was not lost on Ruiz. But for him, this assessment did not lead to an oppositional political outlook but functioned rather as a pragmatic position. When I pressed him on what he meant by the "white" or "Anglo" experience, he explained that what he meant was having the time and the money to do the kinds of activities scouts did (although, clearly, this also included a devaluation of stereotypically "Mexican" culture as unable to furnish success in "American" terms). For him, scouting being "a doorway into the white experience" meant that his kids would have "a platform . . . to succeed" and have a wider range of choices in the world than he had had growing up in a poor, predominantly Latina/o neighborhood in Los Angeles. The more "Anglo" experiences his children had, the more their chances for social and economic mobility increased: "[Y]ou start to put pieces together, and you start to decide where you want to be. And *that's* what I want my kids to do. I want them to decide where they wanna be." For Ruiz, then, "race" functioned as a set of practices and performances that lead to particular opportunities and entitlements. Once one was "successful," having achieved the trappings of stereotypically white social and economic status, "you can be whoever you want to be at that point."

"I Don't Want No Chinese Food": Reactions to the Asian American Majority

An additional dynamic in Troop 252 requires comment: a sense in the troop—as in the region as a whole—of an increasing "Asian" majority. Twenty-year-old Jesse Boden, an Eagle Scout from Troop 252 who is half white and half Latino, recalled that as more Asian Americans joined the troop, he felt that there was "a shift in consciousness, maybe, toward that group" and that his friendship group, which included Shawn Smith and a couple other Latino boys, "were kind of pushed aside a little bit." He noticed especially that Shawn and "a couple other [Latino] kids," when working to advance within the troop, "wouldn't get any attention" or would experience what he felt were "unnecessary hindrances." As a result, "it would take them forever to advance. It was just little things like that . . . that kind of made one sit back and think . . . what's going on here *really*?" He wondered, "how the fact that the troop has become predominantly Asian might've played into any instance of prejudice or discrimination that my friends might have experienced . . . I'm being completely honest here. . . . I mean, you can almost follow it . . . down from a chain of events, [and] you almost have to conclude that that that's probably what happened. [pause] Where it happened and how it happened, I don't know, but I can't help but wonder about it." I pressed him to say more about this, asking him why an increase in the number of Asian Americans in the troop led to discrimination by troop leaders. He replied:

> [A]ll it is, is a simple change in demographics. There's just . . . more Asian people coming from wherever to live in these areas. And it just so happens that as a result of that, there's this kind of indirect experience of, you know, prejudice. . . . In any situation, in any group where there's a visible majority, and there is just that shift of power . . . there's just that shift of focus and people are affected by that. It doesn't just have to be with an increase in Asian American population. . . . It's just any increase of one group, I think, results in that sort of struggle, you know?[56]

Jesse vacillated between "human nature" explanations—that any group becoming a "visible" majority would "naturally" shift the balance of power toward some and away from others—and an awareness of a long history of racial discrimination in the United States (in his words, "Considering the history of prejudice and discrimination towards minorities in this country anyway, how can one not almost assume that that would be the cause?"). Interestingly, although Jesse's mother was Mexican American and he identified as Latino, within the troop he was read as white, since his white father was an assistant scoutmaster and he did not have a Hispanic last name. Perhaps because of Jesse's particular racial status within the troop, he was able to observe these dynamics somewhat from a distance, without animosity or, it seemed, direct effect to him. He was a secret Latino—read and treated as white but observing things with the acuity of someone who identified as a person of color. In the end, he preferred not to draw conclusions—or at least not to share them with me, only repeating that he "can't help but wonder" about it.

Some of the Latino assistant scoutmasters felt tested by the majority Asian American leadership as well, at moments. Although Joe Castillo did not think that "they" (the Asian American leadership) were "harder on me because I'm a Latino," he added, "I think I've already proved myself," suggesting that the sense of acceptance he felt had not been a given. Walter Ruiz recounted an incident where he almost resigned as assistant scoutmaster, fairly convinced that he had been excluded from invitation to a community event by the other scoutmasters because of his ethnicity.

To their credit, they didn't just let it stand like that. [Gary Wong] sought me out, and we talked about my misperceptions of what I thought was a slight because I was Hispanic and they're Chinese, or Asian. And after I got over myself, and then I started realizing that I'm really the one that's putting a lot of emphasis on certain things, and I'm looking for ghosts where there aren't any ghosts— once I got over that, and kind of relaxed and just saw my assistant scoutmaster comrades as just that, just people who are here with their kids 'cause they want something good for their kids, and not saying like "oh, they're Chinese, they're Japanese, I'm the only Mexican around"—once I got over that, then I haven't had a problem anymore.[57]

While Castillo and Ruiz both made their peace with the troop's mix, there were still moments in which the accepted order of things was revealed, if only by a desire to rupture it: According to Castillo, when his older son was preparing for his Eagle Court ceremony, he told his father, "Dad, I don't want no Chinese food. I want Mexican food, and I want mariachis."

Patriotism: "The Heart and Soul of the Organization"

Asian American and Latino members of Troop 252 all agreed, however, on the importance of patriotism to the troop and to their participation in Boy Scouts in general. For them, Boy Scouts was not merely a recreational organization but a way of life that represented certain ideals. For instance, Walter Ruiz's ability to reconcile white privilege with a staunch belief in the "American Dream"—that everyone has the chance to "do something really special for themselves," regardless of racial/ethnic background— was intimately tied to his fervent sense of patriotism:

I'm the guy that goes to the Dodger Stadium and when the Star Spangled Banner is played, I get goose bumps and I get a tear in my eye. . . . I don't agree with everything this country does—well, [everything] its leaders do, but I love this country. I love the flag. The flag to me is the embodiment of opportunity, of ability. You know . . . one of the greatest words and ugliest words in the English language is "potential." And this country gives you the opportunity to realize potential. . . . I think the flag is a symbol of that, and I feel *very* strongly about the flag. . . . And [pauses] I know I'm a Mexican [chuckles]. I know I'm just a permanent resident of this country, but in my heart . . . I believe the red, white, and blue. I mean, that flag *means* something to me.[58]

Even as a noncitizen, Ruiz believed fervently in what he felt being American represented, embodied in the flag as a symbol of "opportunity," "ability," and "potential."

To Jesse Boden, the "heart and soul of the organization" was "the patriotism and the respect and appreciation for the fact that you live in this country, and . . . everything that's wonderful about it." Echoing the principles of the scout oath as well as what many others told me, he said, "It's about your god . . . what you believe in, in terms of . . . a higher power; it's about your family, and it's about your country. . . . It's about having those sensibilities and being aware of all of that."[59] Troop participants' attitudes toward patriotism are significant not only because it is a central tenet of the organization but also because of patriotism's relationship to conceptions of race and citizenship. How a person sees herself and people like her in relation to the nation defines how she sees others—what being a good citizen means and, by extension, who is and who is not deserving of citizenship.[60]

Still, everyone acknowledged that there was a wide spectrum of engagement with these principles within the troop. Scoutmaster Lee told me that he believed that some of the "new immigrants or some of the parents" did not "really fully understand duty to God and country" and that he sometimes got the feeling that many of the boys did not know what it meant either. But while Lee accepted the much more open definition of "duty to God" that the BSA has adopted in recent years, he still held that duty to country was important, "because you're here."[61] For all the internal diversity within troops, as Castillo put it, "every different kind of culture that we have in Troop [252] is learning the same values."[62] Most of these BSA values, as espoused by the troop leadership, were in keeping with heteronormative, prototypically "American" ideals. They were grounded by a patriotic notion of color-blind individualism—that in this country anyone could succeed if they worked hard enough. Conversely, if one did not succeed, it was ultimately one's own fault.

"First African American Eagle Scout"

In 1989, Marie Johnson, who was then twenty-eight years old, moved to the West SGV with her one-year-old baby Shawn, first living with her mother, then finding an apartment around the corner when Shawn was around five years old. Johnson's mother had raised her and two sisters as a single mother in a poor, predominantly African American neighborhood in South Los Angeles, and Johnson recalled summers "stuck right there in L.A., just right on the street." In comparison, she and her mother enjoyed the "fresh," "brand new" apartments they found in the West SGV, the "well lit," "wide" streets, and the greater sense of safety they felt as women coming in and out of their apartments at night. The location was convenient to where she worked as a probation officer in Eastlake. From the beginning, Johnson saw being in their new area as a move "outside of the box" that few people made: "To grow up and then come out, and just to see this part of town . . . It's like [Shawn] and his scouting . . . he's the first African American in eighty years [to become an Eagle Scout in Troop 252], and you're . . . this close to L.A.? . . . People don't venture outside of the box." Their apartment complex was racially diverse, with a mix of Latinas/os, whites, and Asians, but only one other African American tenant. For the most part, it was comfortable, although Johnson initially felt racially stereotyped by their next door neighbors: "Until they got to know us . . . they just seemed a little snobbish. . . . It's like the stigma follows you. You enter into another area, and . . . they have to kind of like, as they say, 'peep us out'—you know, try to observe us and see if we're going to bring trouble to the area."[63]

Shawn's friends were Asian and Hispanic, reflecting the mix around him at home and in school. Growing up, he felt "there weren't any racial cliques ever" and that in high school, "everybody was friends with everybody." Nonetheless, being the only African American kid in mostly Asian and Latina/o settings nearly all the time took a toll. "I had a lot of insecurity when I was little. Because of course, when you're different from other people, you start looking at yourself like, what's wrong with me, why am I like this? You kind of want to fit in and be the same, but [brief pause] as I was growing up, I just started realizing there's nothing I can do to change it. I'm stuck—there's nothing I can do. I'm not going to complain about it, I'm going to make the best of it." When I asked Shawn what he meant by being "stuck," he elaborated, "I felt like I was stuck in a way. . . . I didn't *want* to change my skin color . . . I wanted people to look past that and see me for me. But of course they didn't do it. So I was just kind of like, 'OK, whatever . . . who cares? If you don't like it, just get off my back and leave me alone, and stop talking smack, you know?'"[64] Despite the bitterness of such feelings, Shawn still maintained that he was not discriminated against by his peers—that it was just "typical" school bullying. When I asked if he wished he had grown up in a different place or a different community, he answered that although he wished sometimes that he could have gone to a different school just to have a new experience, "I didn't want to move. . . . I wouldn't want to change [where I grew up] . . . to me it was fun. I liked it a lot." Both Shawn and his mother's experiences show a very different relationship to living in the West SGV than Asian Americans and Latinas/os, most of whom adapted readily to the predominantly Asian and Latina/o mix even if they had not grown up in the area and were able to derive a sense of comfort from it. As much as Shawn liked where he grew up and was used to it, they were unavoidably, as his mother put it, "outside of the box."

Johnson was determined for Shawn to make use of the opportunities he had in the West SGV, many of which she believed he would not have had if they had stayed in South Los Angeles. When Shawn was in elementary school, he brought home a flyer announcing the formation of a Cub Scout Pack at his school. At the time, "my mom was having me try all these new things—sports . . . arts and crafts, YMCA, all this other stuff—she had me do *everything*, I'm telling you, believe me . . . She was like, 'Did you want to become a Cub Scout?' And I was like, 'Yeah, sure.'" Johnson herself had been a Girl Scout for a period of time as a child but had to stop because of limited finances; nonetheless, she appreciated that her mother, who raised her and her two sisters alone, had given them "a taste of it." At a certain point, Shawn considered quitting scouting and raised the subject with his mother. As Johnson recalls it, she said, "'OK fine,' [but] we're not quitters in this family. You're going to quit, you're going to talk to the . . . cubmaster or scoutmaster, and you're going to tell them yourself [laughing]." Shawn decided to keep with it, and finally, just before his eighteenth birthday in the spring of 2007, he became an Eagle Scout.

"Youth Beats the Odds"

As with the controversy over the achievement gap at Alhambra High, trouble began with a newspaper article. Several local newspapers ran stories on Shawn's achievement of the Eagle rank. Shawn's story made the front page of a well-known African American paper based in Los Angeles. Another local paper ran a long profile focusing on Marie Johnson's challenges and successes as a single mother. However, for the leadership of Troop 252, one article in particular, published in a local SGV newspaper a month before Shawn's Eagle Court, stood out.[65] This was the paper they and people they knew were most likely to read. But further, while all the articles lauded Shawn for being the first African American Eagle Scout in Troop 252 and presented the troop's overall racial/ethnic makeup only as a neutral, unspecified backdrop, this was the only article that suggested Shawn may have faced specific difficulties in the troop on account of his race. The central focus was on how Shawn had "beaten the odds" to achieve his rank. While the other articles kept to a more personal angle, limiting their interviews to Shawn, his mother and grandmother, and Troop 252 affiliates, this article quoted the president of the local NAACP, who stated that the reason they were most proud of the accomplishment was because Shawn came from an area where there were not many African Americans. Finally, Shawn told the reporter that he had wondered at times if he had singled out for disciplinary action because of his race and that "[a] lot of adults there didn't know how to handle my type of culture." With these statements, he directly contradicted the professed egalitarianism and "color-blind" approach of the troop leadership—that, in Scoutmaster Lee's words, "we treat every kid the same no matter what."

Of the three assistant scoutmasters I spoke with in addition to Scoutmaster Lee—one of whom was Chinese American, and two Mexican American—two agreed that Shawn had nothing to complain about and that he had been treated no differently from any other boy. Everyone acknowledged that Shawn's path to achieving his Eagle rank had been difficult, but most felt that that had been Shawn's doing and that, in fact, much of the leadership should be thanked for continuing to hold him to a higher standard and helping along the way. It became clear, however, through some respondents' linkages of professed color blindness to charges of "playing the race card" and "Black entitlement," that in fact, racial discourses were not at all irrelevant but an integral part of the conflict over Shawn's Eagle Court.

"All the Boys Are the Same": Discourses of Color Blindness

The dominant racial discourse of the post–civil rights era is "color-blind": it operates without explicit reference to race and explains present-day "racial inequality as the outcome of nonracial dynamics."[66] Color-blind discourse functions as "a veil that hides the American racial order from view, protecting it from challenge."[67] It is based on liberal individualist beliefs, which prescribe a focus on individual prejudice, success, and failure, and rules out systematic analysis. Three key elements of color-blind discourse are important to our discussion here: First, color-blind discourse is naturalized, professing that patterns such as racial segregation or racist sentiments are in some way part of human nature or "just the way things are." Second, it is culturally racist. Deriving from "culture of poverty" explanations of the 1960s, racially essentialist sentiments are expressed through observations about culture, usually as explanations of social inequality. Third, color-blind discourse is teleological, suggesting that though racism may have been part of the American past, it is over now—or soon will be. This allows for the dismissal of present-day racial inequality as minor or nonexistent compared to the past—or anomalous.[68] As Claire Jean Kim has pointed out, however, color-blind discourse actually perpetuates racial power. Because overt references to racial differences are taboo, it "obscur[es] the operation of racial power, protecting it from challenge, and permitting ongoing racialization via racially coded methods."[69] Persistent patterns of racial inequality and privilege are attributed to individual failure and success, and "the most egregious efforts at racial classification" become "permissible . . . as long as they are . . . expressed in cultural rather than explicitly racial terms."[70]

In my discussions of Shawn's experiences with troop leadership, these characterizations of color-blind discourse proved apt. Espousals of color blindness were often interwoven with euphemistic references to "culture" and sometimes even frankly racial statements. At the same time, in keeping with the norms of color-blind discourse, much of the leadership operated under the assumption that to even mention race was "racist." In a typical explanation, Scoutmaster Lee argued that even if "we don't understand the culture of the boy . . . we treat every kid the same no matter what."[71] Assistant Scoutmaster Gary Wong was perhaps the most overt proponent of color-blind discourse in the troop. Wong is a second-generation Chinese American, who was raised in an "all-Black neighborhood" in San Francisco in which his parents ran a laundry and was deeply influenced by the idealism of the civil rights movement when he attended UC Berkeley in the early 1970s. "We treat every kid like a kid, we don't treat 'em as a white kid, Black kid, Yellow kid. . . . I felt it was . . . a misstatement, that there could not be a Black Eagle Scout out of our troop. You understand?

That we were so *not* color-blind to keep a kid from achieving." Wong was considerably more emphatic when I brought up the question of whether or not Shawn Smith had been treated any differently than any other boy, as the newspaper articles suggested. "Well, it was like, the inference was it was such a hard road, made so much harder for him because he was Black. No. You know what? He was a knucklehead, that's why it was harder. He was a turkey. And we disciplined him in the same way that we would have disciplined any other knucklehead. In fact, we didn't—we don't say hey, [Shawn's] Black, we say, [Shawn's] a knucklehead."[72] Both Wong and Lee seemed to feel the implication that the troop leadership was not color-blind as a personal affront. Lee explained that the reason "we were not too happy with . . . the way he talked to the press about it" was because Shawn had made them look "not human at all, that we didn't understand him culturally." The way Lee refers to humanity in this context is telling: that to be accused (at least by implication) of being racist is to be dehumanized. This turns on its head the historical "invention of race"[73] as a discourse that divides into hierarchical categories which groups are accorded full humanity and which groups are not. In Lee's formulation, to be human was the capacity to see and treat everyone as human. The charge of "making us look . . . not human" can be read then as referring to racial injury—that, for Lee, what was at stake was not merely being perceived to be not a racist but something affectively sharper and unresolved.

Indeed, the fact that almost all the leadership of Troop 252 were ethnic minorities who had had to contend with the salience of race in their own lives made their responses to Shawn's foregrounding of race even more fraught. For instance, Karen Lee, Bob Lee's wife, who had been actively involved in the troop's parent committee for years, related Shawn's experience as the only African American boy in the troop to her own experiences growing up in a Los Angeles neighborhood in the 1950s and 1960s: "It is difficult . . . if you're the only—that type of ethnic group within a larger ethnic group. . . . We were the only Chinese family at that time in the area, that had gone to that school. So it was just kind of like, they didn't treat me like a very—how would you say—human-type person. You know, like, they would play with my hair, and stuff like that. . . . I was a curiosity. So I could kind of understand where he [Shawn] was coming from, because it's awkward when you're the isolated one."[74]

However, she drew the conclusion that in such an experience, "you *think* everybody is against you, but they're not." In her opinion, "we

supported [Shawn] *totally*." Karen believed this so strongly that in a conversation she, Bob Lee, and I had regarding an incident that occurred
during one of the troop's camping outings, Karen literally could not
even *see* the possibility of overt or even implied prejudice toward Shawn.

WC: *Did any of the parents ever have problems with having a Black
    kid in the troop or anything like that?*
BL: Yes, yes.
KL: They did? [in a surprised tone]
BL: Yeah. We had one parent . . . the parent was Hispanic and
    it was just a boy about a year into our troop, and the mother
    found out that [Shawn] was his bunkmate. . . . And so she
    came up right away and plucked him out of there, and never
    came back to our troop.
WC: *Wow.*
KL: Oh, that one at [camp name]? That was strange.
BL:. . . You know, it's not like any of the boys was going to do any-
    thing. But I guess the perception of what a Black kid is . . . you
    got too much stuff in the papers . . . you know, the bad ones are
    not doing things right, and they're always in the paper. So that's
    what she thought of him. And I said, what's wrong with him?
    There's nothing wrong. [But] she pulled [her son] out.
KL: [skeptically] No, she was just insecure, period, with letting her
    son go camping.
BL: Well, that too, but the kicker really was that there was a big
    Black kid. You know how big [Shawn] is.
WC: *Did she express that openly?*
BL: Yeah, she did. She really did. [brief pause] So I said, "OK. But
    you know, he's not that type of kid. He's actually a steady, nice
    guy, real teddy bear."
KL: He's made some good friends in the troop.
BL: Yeah, he has. . . . That's the only incident I can think of.
KL: I didn't even know . . . I didn't even know that was the
    incident.[75]

In this exchange, both Karen's skepticism and Bob's insistence stand out.
Karen much preferred to believe that the mother in question's "insecurity"
about letting her son go camping was the primary motivation—although,

initially, when Bob first brought up the incident, she does recall that it was "strange." If not for Bob Lee's detailed memory and insistence that the mother's motivation was due primarily to racism, the story would likely have been brushed aside. Karen Lee's skepticism points to how difficult it was for some members of the troop leadership to even admit the possibility that race could have been a factor in how people behaved in Troop 252. Bob Lee, as scoutmaster, was able to astutely observe the racist dynamics in play in the incident but nevertheless held to the line that the troop leadership never treated Shawn any differently than any other boy.

Indeed, the scoutmaster's adamant downplaying of any racial significance to Shawn's experiences in the troop, much less his achievement of the Eagle rank, was clear to others as well. Parent Mary Hernandez recalled an exchange between her son and Scoutmaster Lee sometime not long after Shawn's Eagle Court:

> [M]y son came home from the meeting that day . . . and he said, "Did you know that [Shawn] was the first African American to get his Eagle [in Troop 252]. . . ." And I said, "Really? . . . I didn't know that. I can't *believe* that that's true. . . ." I was shocked. . . . I thought they must have got it wrong or something . . . I said, "are you *sure* you guys heard right?" . . . He said, "Yeah, because I asked Mr. [Lee]" . . . and Mr. [Lee] said to him, "Now that doesn't matter. What matters is that he's your brother just like everybody else here." So he kind of got the impression that he was deemphasizing the color issue.[76]

To Hernandez and her son, the fact that there had never before been an African American Eagle Scout in the troop was surprising and worthy of notice: "I thought, hm, that's interesting. . . . If I was him [Scoutmaster Lee], I would have been really proud. . . . I think if I was the leader I would have been making a big deal of it, because I think it merits it." However, she was quickly able to rationalize the scoutmaster and others' attitudes by employing the troop's prevailing color-blind logic that "all the boys are the same": "If they weren't that happy, the only thing I could imagine [is] because they do really stress that all the boys are the same. That you know, 'Why should we make a big deal out of this boy making it, and this boy over here is doing it too, and this boy over here is doing it too?'"

Discourses of color blindness easily shifted into accusations that Shawn had "played the race card." Gary Wong, for one, believed that if Shawn had never "played the race card," the discussion would never even have come up.

> I don't think there was ever a reference to ethnicity, or a racial slur, or any of that stuff, with him. . . . I mean, until that issue came up with him being the first Black Eagle Scout . . . we just [thought of him as] "[Shawn]". That's it. I mean, not, "hey, that Black kid over there, that's [Shawn]. He's our Black kid. He's our lone Black"— you know what I'm saying? We didn't point him out. . . .

> *And do you remember any incidents where parents or anybody else—*

> No.

> *—brought up race?*

> Not at all, not at all. Until . . . the race card was played. Up to that point, I don't think we ever even thought about that.[77]

In Wong's account, he seemed to offer as proof of lack of racism the fact that in his experience, there was never "a reference to ethnicity, or a racial slur, or any of that stuff." The implied relationship between these two acts (of referring to race or ethnicity and committing a racial slur) feeds into the logic of color-blind discourse—that if racism is relegated to unfortunate events of the past that no longer have any substantial bearing on the present, to even acknowledge race is to be in some sense racist.

Tracing the phrase "playing the race card" back to the 1995 O. J. Simpson murder trial, in which prosecutor Christopher Darden charged that police detective Mark Fuhrman's evident racism was irrelevant to the case, Linda Williams argues that "behind this statement stands a moral assertion that within American jurisprudence—and indeed in many other areas of contemporary American popular culture—race should be unmentionable . . . the very accusation of playing the race card has now become a way of disqualifying the attempt to discuss past and present racial injury."[78] The Simpson trial reference, as well as a host of other contemporary examples, suggests that although the race-card charge has certainly been applied to other groups of racial minorities, it is associated especially with discussions of race and racism by or about Black people.[79] Like color-blind discourse more generally, this association traces its roots back to the first decades after the civil rights movement, when "underclass" and "culture of poverty" discourses blamed continuing inequality on the supposed failings of individual Black people and their families. As Claire Jean Kim has pointed out, within a color-blind framework, underclass discourse operates in tandem with its reverse mirror image—the model minority myth. Both perpetuate racial claims under cover of "culture," with the implication that model minorities (such as Asian Americans) are good "Protestant ethnics" that make good on the American Dream, while the underclass (i.e., Black people) fall down on the job.[80] This binary pits racial minorities against one another while leaving undisturbed a power structure that privileges whiteness.

The idea that those who "play the race card" are trying to circumvent legitimate channels to get something they didn't actually earn—an offense to a central tenet of the American Protestant work ethic—feeds into an idea of "Black entitlement," or a view that African Americans are the primary and undeserving beneficiaries of ameliorative programs such as affirmative action.[81] Assistant Scoutmaster Walter Ruiz's perspective on Shawn was typical of this rationale:

My opinion is that [pause] he felt entitled to being an Eagle Scout, and he felt that we should do more to funnel him through. And I think that the fact that the troop maintained their standards, and . . . treated him equally, as they would any other Eagle applicant, spoke volumes of the integrity of the troop. And the fact that he managed to finally get his act together, and do the things he had to do, showed that he had the ability to do them, all along. . . . So, do I think it's unfortunate he made those comments? It shows that he didn't really learn everything he should have learned out of the experience. In my opinion, there's a part of him that didn't understand the reason why he was being held to the high standard that we hold *every* Eagle applicant to. He obviously felt singled out and excluded, and maybe used the race card as kind of a shield, instead of being a little more introspective and looking at his part in the deal.[82]

Scoutmaster Lee had a response along similar lines. Lee described an "us" (the troop leadership—that is, non-Black people) in opposition to a "them" (Black people), in an interpretation of the events that ultimately led to the same conclusion: Shawn and his family were acting with an undue sense of entitlement.

> It was not a good thing, because . . . you know, we're a little bit more conservative, and they have another view of things. How would you say it—Black entitlement, or something like that? [A] "woe is me" attitude . . . His family or him was lock-step into what the Black culture of the paper and everything else has said. . . . It's strange because . . . generally you don't get any politicians coming out to a Eagle Court, but because he's the first Black American to get his Eagle from our [troop], you've got um, [Congresswoman] Hilda Solis coming out. And then you have another politician too that came out too. You don't get those people coming out unless they want to pander to that particular type of group.[83]

Individual actions and perspectives, however, are inevitably complex and often contradictory. At the same time that Lee complained of "Black entitlement," at other moments, concerning Shawn, he showed a deep understanding of the effects of racially coded sentiments expressed by others and acted to counter them as best as he could.

The purpose of my analysis of troop leaders' statements is not to point fingers at individuals but to show how despite their protestations that Shawn was "just like any other boy," they could not help but speak about Shawn in racialized ways. In fact this is precisely why dominant racial ideology is so effective. It does not so much as establish "ideological uniformity" (hence the seemingly contradictory statements and emotions expressed by many in this chapter) but "provid[es] the frames to organize difference."[84] For example, while Bob and Karen Lee characterized some of the Chinese American boys in the troop as having "absent fathers," Bob Lee maintained that Shawn came from a "broken home." Even when Shawn did not fulfill stereotypically "Black" tropes, he was nonetheless measured against them: Walter Ruiz, for one, held that Shawn could not have been discriminated against was because he was not a "*real* Black kid." Growing up in a working-class neighborhood in Los Angeles, Ruiz said, he had grown up with "real Black kids":

[Shawn] was not a *real* Black kid. [Shawn] was a middle-class Black kid, in a middle-class, bedroom community. . . . He was not a *ghetto* Black kid . . . he was not a gangbanger. He was not a dumb kid. . . . He was just a kid that was going to [name omitted] High, that dressed like every other kid that went to [name omitted] High. . . . He didn't come off as an urban Black—you know, a gangster, a ghetto Black kid. He was just a normal kid that happened to be Black, just like any other scout in the troop. So . . . I don't think that anyone looked at him like that. I know *I* didn't. . . . Because it's not about our perception of him, it's the way he carries himself? And he doesn't carry himself like that. He was . . . OK, first of all, not into sports. So you couldn't look at him as a "Black athlete" . . . he was great at our skits, and our things of that nature. He was very kind of art-centered . . . and had a great speaking voice. He had a good, sharp wit. So you know, he wasn't a *Black kid* when you think of "Black kid." You think of what you see on the videos and things like that. He wasn't like that. So I don't think anyone treated him like that.[85]

The associations Ruiz had about "real Black kids" ("urban," "gangbanger," "ghetto," "Black athlete," "what you see on the videos") and also about the qualities Shawn had that, by implication, "real Black kids" did *not* ("middle-class," "not dumb," "not into sports," "artistic," "great speaking voice," "a good, sharp wit"), in their near perfect recitation of Black "underclass" tropes, showed the difficulty of opting out of dominant racial expectations.

"Don't They Know It's Not Just Asians . . . That Scouting Touches Everybody?"

Within the atmosphere of general disapproval among troop leadership regarding Shawn's handling of his advancement to Eagle, one assistant scoutmaster, and some of the Latino boys in the troop, disagreed strongly. Joe Castillo's account of Shawn's experiences in the troop was strikingly different from the others'. He believed that in fact Shawn "*was* held to a different standard, and they were somewhat harder on him. And whether [it was because] he was Black, I don't know. You know, I'm going to lean towards that and say probably?" Of all the leadership, with the possible exception of Bob Lee, Castillo knew Shawn the best. Shawn had been a Cub Scout in the pack of which Castillo was cubmaster and had essentially grown up with one of Castillo's sons. In addition, Marie Johnson and Castillo's late wife had been very close. To Castillo, they were "like family. Coming from a Latino, that's a big thing. There isn't a thing I wouldn't do for [Marie] and [Shawn]."[86]

In contrast to the other assistant scoutmasters, none of whom recalled any instances of discrimination toward Shawn, Castillo recalled an incident in which some parents did not want their children to share a tent with Shawn. Though similar to the incident that Bob Lee mentioned, this one involved Asian parents instead of a Latina mother. "I heard it from parents, 'I don't want my son sleeping with [Shawn]—he's Black—in a tent. . . . They were Asian parents. . . . And they were new parents in the troop, who I guess [had] never seen a Black person before, or never seen a Black person in the troop, which is more where I'm gonna tend to lean." According to Castillo, the issue was discussed not only among parents but also among the leadership:

> And some of the Asian parents that heard that got very upset with those parents who said that. In fact, I know for a fact two parents went up to that family or families and said, "you know . . . [Shawn] has been in scouting for, you know, five years here and then four years with Mr. [Castillo]. So this gentleman has *nine* years of scouting. My son has slept in a tent with this man . . . and so has [the son of] that mother over there [and] that mother over there. . . ." These two parents were kind of very upset at those three parents who made that comment. So when I heard that, I was like, wow, man, where have these parents been?

And they expressed that in a public setting?

> Yes. And so the leadership was like, "Where have these parents been? Have they been hiding in the garage or what? Don't they know that it's just not Asians, you know, that scouting touches everybody?"

Although Castillo was careful to point out that other Asian parents had stepped up to counter the parents who expressed racist sentiments, his comment that perhaps the new parents had "never seen a Black person before" and his phrasing of the question, "'Don't they know it's just not Asians . . . that scouting touches everybody?'" suggest a tension in the troop, as discussed previously, regarding the troop's recent shift to an Asian American majority. With Joe Castillo and at least two of the Latino scouts more sympathetic to Shawn's account of his experience in the troop (one of Castillo's sons, and Shawn's good friend Jesse Boden), Latinos in the troop were sometimes triangulated between the Asian American majority and Shawn's position as the lone African American. As mentioned earlier, Jesse Boden had felt that when more Asian Americans joined the troop, he felt that there was "a shift in consciousness, maybe, toward that group" and that his friendship group, which included Shawn and a couple other Latino boys, "were kind of pushed aside a little bit."[87]

At moments when Shawn felt that he was being treated unfairly, Jesse said, he and Shawn would have long conversations. After making attempts to make Shawn see it differently, Jesse would reluctantly conclude that probably there was a racial aspect to what Shawn had experienced, and the two of them would wonder, "Are we really part of an organization that would do this?" Jesse put the problem succinctly:

> Boy Scouts is supposed to stand for . . . a unity . . . a sense of com-
> munity, a sense of loyalty to your family and to your friends. . . .
> It was never a question of race or ethnicity or any of that. It was
> always just one big group. . . . We were—Boy Scouts was supposed
> to represent this diverse, multicultural society that we live in. You
> were supposed to promote that message [that] everyone has the
> same opportunity, everyone can do this, everyone can be this,
> everyone can get to the rank of Eagle Scout . . . everyone has that
> opportunity.
>
> But it [Shawn's experiences] just sort of like [brief pause] flew
> in the face of all of that. It was like, well, *really*? . . . Is that really
> the truth? *Does* everyone have the same opportunity, you know?
> Is everyone treated equally and fairly? It just raised those kinds
> of questions. . . . It just contradicted what we thought we were
> standing—what we stood for.

For much of the leadership of Troop 252, Shawn's open discussion of racial dynamics in the troop constituted an affront, a rupture that contradicted deeply cherished beliefs of egalitarianism and individualism that had been nurtured in the institution of scouting. For scouts like Jesse Boden, it raised questions and contradictions in the nature of the organization itself.

Conclusion

"[Boy Scouts] taught me *so* much," Shawn told me, with apparent sincerity. It was the fall after his Eagle Court. He had graduated from high school and Troop 252 and was taking courses at a local community college to get an associate's degree, as well as working as a cashier at large retail store. He still lived in the West SGV with his mother. He had learned, he said, "how to deal with different people, different situations, how to be a leader. It taught me all of that stuff and . . . you know, that's why I'm not really upset about the situations I was put in. Because that's what's gonna happen in life—why not learn it at an early age? That's how I looked at it. I was like, fine, this is what I'm gonna be dealing with in life? I'm ready, you know? . . . Nothing surprises me, you know, from what they were doing. So it was just basically—it was like a little mini world."[88]

In marked contrast to the troop leadership, and even to his close friend Jesse Boden, Shawn expressed no surprise about the ways he felt he had been treated differently from the other boys, showing quite different expectations of the institution—indeed a different world view. He was aware of the troop leadership's consternation over what he had told reporters: "[O]f course they all get mad at me about it," Shawn said. "[T]hey always tell me, you know, 'why would you say something like that?'" But Gary Wong had spoken with him directly about it, and even though they disagreed, Shawn claimed, "he's a good guy." He still spoke affectionately of Scoutmaster Lee: "Mr. [Lee]—he means well. I can say I know Mr. [Lee]. I can talk to him about anything. I talked to him about some things, some issues I was having before. . . . He means well, and—and you know, he's just not like everybody else to me. That's why he's in the position that he's in. That's why he's the scoutmaster." The following January, Shawn regrouped with Troop 252 to march in the Pasadena Rose Bowl parade. "When I saw him interact with the boys, the ones that graduated out with him . . . they were just wonderful," said Karen Lee. "I wish that news reporter could see them now, you know, write an article about them doing the Rose Parade together." Time had tempered Bob Lee's reaction to the events as well: "We've moved on, we understand . . . OK fine, we just move on and that's it."[89]

For its key players, the moment had passed. Nonetheless, Shawn's public naming of race as a factor in his Boy Scout experience challenged the troop leadership and BSA's prevailing assertions of "color blindness" and individualism—that every boy was, or could be, treated exactly the same, opening up a space of uncertainty. The episode showed that although Troop 252, like the West SGV as a whole, constituted a majority-Asian American and Latina/o space, as a national institution, it was still integrally shaped by prevailing national racial binaries of Black and white. Even in a context in which Asian Americans and Latinas/os were considered the norm, scouting still functioned as a "doorway to the white experience," in which Blackness was marked as hypervisible or exceptional. The rhetoric of color blindness masked the alternative histories and possibilities of scouting for racialized minorities, yet consistently marked Shawn, a Black person, as a representative of Blackness—as the noncooperative Other in a teleological narrative of national racial progress.

Certainly, although during the course of my interviews, distinguishing a "real from a fancied injury" became increasingly difficult,[90] the ways in which diverse members and leadership of Troop 252 reacted to and made sense of Shawn's progress in the troop also had much to do with their beliefs about America and about their own place in it as racial minorities. For Troop 252 participants who believed in a certain vision of America and its national institutions, in which race could be irrelevant, Shawn Smith's refusal to "pass" as an "abstract citizen" ultimately showed the lingering impossibility of doing so as a nonwhite national subject. The fuss over Shawn's achievement of Eagle rank harkened back to the experiences of fictionalized and real scouts Koharu Iwasaki and Norman Mineta at an earlier historical moment ("I put on my uniform. But they took me away anyway. They took all of us"). It suggested that to put on a uniform was still not enough in a circle of abstract citizenship that had perhaps expanded but was still shaped and delimited by race.

In this West SGV Boy Scout troop, while many Asian Americans and Latinas/os were highly self-reflexive regarding racial dynamics in other parts of their lives, their belief in the principles of the institution of scouting—particularly its liberal-individualist and nationalist dimensions—prompted them to deny the validity of race as a salient factor in one scout's experience. As Eduardo Bonilla-Silva reminds us, although all groups have the capacity to develop racial (and, I would argue, regional) frameworks, "the frameworks of the dominant race tend to become the master frameworks on which *all* racial actors ground (for or against) their ideological positions."[91] In this case, adherence to color-blind interpretations did not allow for race to be acknowledged as a valid social fact. Even to name race was to go against the principles of the organization and—as most of them saw it—of the nation itself. As we have seen, however, "color-blind" American Dream discourse, like strategic uses of whiteness, only *provisionally* and *temporarily* positions Asians and Latinas/os as neutral or normative. Marking Blackness as hypervisible or exceptional in comparison to other nonwhite groups and treating race and racism as the anomalous problems of individuals erases the history of a nation that has been fundamentally shaped by systematic exclusion from whiteness. In the end such viewpoints continue to veil and reproduce white social, political, and economic dominance.

Indeed, local struggles over civic power, landscapes, and belonging—to which we will turn next—expose some of the ways whites continue to dominate the racial hierarchy and hold decisive power in this majority-nonwhite region, as well as emergent challenges to this dominance.

CHAPTER 4

Diversity on Main Street

Civic Landscapes and Historical Geographies of Race

*What you see here is kind of an area that's always been in transition . . .
you have incorporated cities that have an idea of an identity. And they
never realized that they didn't have one until all these Asians started
coming in.*

—Interview with Eloy Zarate, April 18, 2007

*The most frequently asked question in San Gabriel these days is not
"Where's the mission?" but "Where's a good Chinese restaurant?"*

—Stephanie Chavez, "New Look Reflects
an Old Pattern," *Los Angeles Times*, July 25, 2004

DRIVING NORTH TOWARD Alhambra's Main Street on Garfield Boulevard in the summer of 2006, soon enough you would see a banner
featuring a sedate blond white woman with blue eyes and black-rimmed
glasses (Figure 11). She was a prominent face of Alhambra City Council's
"diversity" campaign, a face that, unlike the vast majority of Alhambra's
population, looked neither Latina/o nor Asian. In the early twenty-first-
century United States, how should we read such a scene, in which a young
white woman is touted as an official representative of diversity? The banner encapsulated a particular set of struggles over race and ethnicity in the
civic landscapes of the West SGV as a whole, in which the question of lingering white social, political, and economic dominance loomed over Asian
American and Latina/o pasts and presents, in ardently contested bids for
the future. In the late 2000s, the West San Gabriel Valley (SGV) found
itself caught between varying bids for civic identities with particular material and ideological ramifications: two branding campaigns (Alhambra's
diversity campaign and San Gabriel's "Golden Mile") put forth specific

discourses of race, ethnicity, and culture, and in doing so, illuminated and reinforced larger racial, geographic, and ideological divides. A third episode, also in San Gabriel, in which a grassroots organization called Friends of La Laguna dedicated itself to saving a local park from redevelopment, offered a third possibility—an appeal to shared immigrant pasts in the forging of a suburban utopia.

The two branding campaigns contrasted significantly: "Diversity" on Main Street embraced pluralist multicultural discourses of the nation, while the "Golden Mile" proposal sought to showcase the transformation of a central thoroughfare by ethnic Chinese capital and immigration. However, both deployed discourses of race—in particular, of diversity—in attempts to actualize specific visions and claims to place, identity, and history. Miriam Greenberg defines civic branding as a "marketing-led strategy of economic development" that is both visual and material, in that it combines intensive "place marketing" with neoliberal political and economic development and restructuring.[1] While branding is fundamentally concerned with representation, these representations have material effects because they are intimately tied to economic development and restructuring and so privilege "certain social classes, economic sectors, and geographic regions over others."[2] Therefore civic branding often plays an important role in erasing complex polyethnic pasts and presents, as well as histories of struggle and inequality. Indeed, the Alhambra city-led diversity campaign's articulation of "decontextualized multiculturalism"[3] served to justify retroactively the expulsion of small businesses—many of which were owned by ethnic Chinese immigrants—to make way for national chains and businesses with more "mainstream" (implicitly middle class and white) appeal.

San Gabriel's Golden Mile branding campaign, backed by a newly elected Taiwanese American city council member, also sought to utilize discourses of diversity but met with stiff resistance from other city officials whose opposition was informed by assumptions of Asian inassimilability and the exclusion of Asian space and bodies from the polity. The San Gabriel situation was further complicated by local elites' highly contrasting relationship to what Carey McWilliams called a "Spanish fantasy heritage," referring to the nurturing of Southern California whites' claims to place via a fabricated European lineage.[4] Each episode illustrates the inseparability of such branding campaigns with larger-scale regional and national spatial imaginaries and ideologies, even

Figure 11. *The city of Alhambra's 2006 diversity campaign featured a banner of a white woman, among other faces. Photograph by the author.*

as they also represent the neoliberal privatization of public spaces as spaces of consumption.[5] The actions as well as perceptions of leadership associated with these episodes—including two recently elected Asian American city council members—also signal the complexities of translating individual into public identities within the context of long-standing racial, class, and geographical divides. These dynamics were rooted in a recent regional past characterized by striking disparities between who lived in the area (predominantly Asian Americans and

Latinas/os) and who made decisions regarding civic space (primarily white elites).

In contrast to these constricted and uneven power dynamics, the grassroots organization Friends of La Laguna, while consciously engaged with similar issues, offered a much different vision of the area's identity: as inclusive, determined by a multiethnic and multiracial community, and centering immigrant pasts. Their ability to instantiate their vision in the landscape through the preservation of a local park points to hopeful emergent alternatives to heavily polarized racial and class geographies. A close examination and comparison of these three episodes show how struggles over race, geography, and history are intertwined in the contemporary identities of places and integral to the shaping of civic landscapes. Each episode also revealed a confluence of particular spatial configurations within the West SGV with larger-scale ideologies. Chinatown typologies of race and space were still salient, through discourses of Chinese "takeover" or "invasion." In the West SGV, such struggles over "Chinese" (usually used interchangeably with "Asian") space should also be put in conversation with ambiguous constructions of Mexican Americans as both more and less American than Asians. Historically, Mexicans have been simultaneously erased from the Southern California landscape (along with indigenous peoples) and fetishized via a Spanish fantasy past. In the West SGV, Asian space and Spanish/ Mexican space were triangulated vis-à-vis whites: in municipal politics white elites were able to dictate the terms of belonging, often validating Spanish space as central to the identity of the area (though firmly relegated to the past), while continuing to treat Asian space as perpetually foreign.[6] While in other local contexts, such as school, we have seen how Asian Americans benefited from their model-minority status relative to Latinas/os, in these power structures, in which white elites were still actively present, Asians and Asian space were seen as a foreign threat. In contrast, the ability of the Europeanized Spanish/Mexican past to be claimed by whites was crucial to its continued legitimization in space. Asians and Asian space functioned as the constitutive outside to a spatialized, multicultural identity whose terms of inclusion were dictated by whites. If Asian Americans were not wholly excluded, they were figured alongside whites and Latinas/os as interchangeable parts of a diverse potpourri in a "flattened," consumerist multiculturalism.[7] Within these dynamics, with the important exception of the campaign to save the park, West SGV Latinas/os were either effectively silent or allied their interests with Anglo/white interests.

Eurocentric conceptions of areas of Chinese settlement as separate and autonomous foreign spaces date back at least to the eighteenth century, when a class of diasporic Chinese merchants began to establish themselves globally in interstitial spaces created by European imperialism.[8] The eventual abstraction of these historically grounded conceptions into (racial) common sense gave them a normative quality, leading to the conjectural leap that Chinese or Asian spaces *should* operate autonomously, neither requiring nor being worthy of partaking in public resources. The spaces produced and reproduced by such ideas and discourses are most obvious in the numerous urban Chinatowns in the United States and Canada. For example, geographer Kay Anderson documents how Vancouver's Chinatown became a "physical manifestation" of Western ideas of "Chineseness"—in large part due to state practices.[9] In Anderson's words, "Chinatown accrued a certain field of meaning that became the justification for recurring rounds of government practice in the ongoing construction of both the place and the racial category." Chinatowns are therefore a "western landscape type," shaped and produced by racial ideologies and state practices in Western societies, rather than any straightforward expression of Chinese culture or practices.[10]

Although patterns of immigrant Chinese settlement in the United States have shifted over time, from the dispersed settlement of laborers and merchants to central urban Chinatowns to ethnoburbs such as the SGV,[11] the racial ideologies that inform discourses around Chinese race and place have remained remarkably the same. Nineteenth-century Chinese settlements were considered to be unsanitary, morally aberrant sources of contagion both in public health and territorial senses because of their purported tendency to spread and "contaminate" larger and larger amounts of space if left unchecked.[12] In early twenty-first-century multiethnic suburbs with a significant immigrant Chinese presence such as the West SGV, struggles over the landscape are still racially coded in terms of values and territory. For instance (as mentioned in chapter 2), public discourse around McMansions or "monster homes"—a practice associated with wealthy ethnic Chinese immigrants of tearing down a newly purchased house in order to build a larger house, usually resulting in significant reduction of yard space—is one way in which Asian immigrants are depicted as being unable to conform to American values and ideals. Such practices render them unfit as neighbors and, by extension, as members of American civil society.[13] In short, places coded as Chinese or Asian, like the nineteenth- and twentieth-century Chinatowns before them, continue to be seen either as threats encroaching on implicitly white, American suburban space or as autonomous foreign spaces that serve particular functions but are not to exceed their prescribed bounds. The prescription and negotiation of these bounds is a conflictual process, with both symbolic and material consequences.

In California and the American Southwest as a whole, struggles over Chinese or Asian space should be discussed alongside the erasure of Mexican and indigenous pasts and presents from the landscape. In Southern California, the fabrication of a Spanish fantasy past was key to the establishment of a newly arrived Anglo American power elite in the late nineteenth and early twentieth centuries.[14] By ensconcing Spanish architectural references in the landscape and placing the Spanish Franciscan missions in a mythicized narrative of European racial succession, Anglo Americans relegated Native Americans and the Spanish to the past in order to legitimize national narratives of manifest destiny and frontier colonialism. Indigenous Californians— who under successive Spanish, Mexican, and American rule suffered the genocide of the vast majority of their people by the close of the nineteenth century due to direct violence, contagious diseases, forced labor, and natal alienation—were reduced to naturally vanishing, picturesque figures in a sentimentalized history.[15] Mexicans were rendered as both invisible laborers and hypervisible, threatening foreigners. Throughout the twentieth century, discriminatory spatial and economic practices buttressed by such ideologies contributed to both the "barrioization" and dispersal of Los Angeles's Mexican American population—for instance, through practices of urban renewal and freeway building.[16] Partially in response to such practices, Chicana/o activists and scholars in the 1960s Chicano movement and since have placed issues of history and representation, particularly in civic landscapes, at the forefront of contemporary struggles for social, political, and economic equality.[17]

However, in predominantly middle-class suburban settings such as the West SGV, the role of ethnic and political identifications for Mexican Americans may not be as clear-cut, as a brief consideration of Latinas/os and Asian Americans in West SGV politics suggests. In the 1980s and 1990s, the West SGV's adjacency to East Los Angeles—namely, in Monterey Park—gave rise to multiracial Asian American and Latina/o political formations that launched the careers of notable Asian American and Latina/o politicians such as Judy Chu, Mike Eng, and Hilda Solis, and mounted successful campaigns for redistricting.[18] Asian American and Latina/o politicians had begun to serve in Monterey Park City Council as early as the 1960s and 1970s, and in 1984, Lily Lee Chen, a Chinese immigrant from Taiwan, became the mayor of Monterey Park and the first Chinese American mayor in the mainland United States.[19] In the rest of the West SGV, however, Asian American and Latina/o representation remained uneven. In San Gabriel, Alhambra, and Rosemead, although Asians constituted a plurality by 2000, no Asian Americans were elected to city council until 2003, 2004, and 2005, respectively.[20] In contrast, Latinas/os were able to secure a steady presence in local city councils in San Gabriel, Rosemead, and Alhambra, dating back to the 1970s and early 1980s. In the early 1990s, sociologist Jose Calderón found that Latinas/os who held city council and city administrative positions in Monterey Park typically placed more emphasis on middle-class identifications rather than race or ethnicity: "They saw themselves as part of a middle-class community and a middle-class culture, holding political positions that were fluid, ambivalent, and middle-of-the-road."[21] The loss of Spanish language—institutionally and culturally enforced beginning with the parents of most Mexican Americans of this generation[22]—as well as social mobility into an integrated, suburban, middle-class community "motivated them to see themselves as 'Americans like everybody else.'" In addition, most identified as "Hispanic" (rather than "Latina/o" or "Chicana/o"), believing that this term was "politically safer" and "more acceptable to the mainstream."[23] Many prided themselves on "not making waves"—ostensibly in contrast to later-arriving Asian immigrants.[24]

However, the ability of middle-income Mexican Americans to assimilate into the West SGV suburbs—and into an implicitly white American norm—remained imperfect and uneven. In San Gabriel and Rosemead, Spanish-surnamed officials rarely occupied more than one city council seat at a time, which suggested that they were not able to expand their constituency beyond a fixed voter base. It appeared that whatever officials might claim, ethnoracial identification—whether for or against

them—happened nonetheless among West SGV voters.[25] In the late 1990s
and 2000s in Alhambra, an explosion of racially tinged conflict between
two newly elected Latino council members and an "old guard" white faction ruptured the West SGV Latina/o paradigm of deemphasizing race
and "not making waves."[26] The old guard's eventual reassertion of control
over the council, which included along the way the endorsement and election of Alhambra's first two Asian American council members, illustrated
complex racial and class alignments at play and the white elite's continuing
control over city politics.[27]

The role of Asian American council members in helping to preserve
Alhambra's old guard merits some discussion. Political observers agreed
that for aspiring Asian American politicians in the area, attaining the
acceptance and approval of old-boy, mainstream, white organizations
was not optional. According to the head of a locally based Asian American political action committee, previous to Japanese American Gary
Yamauchi's election (in 2004), "[i]n Alhambra you haven't been able
to elect an Asian because of the old boys—a small group of old-timers
that controls the city. Not one of them is Asian. To overcome that, there
are no shortcuts. You have to develop relationships with these people,
become one of them."[28] In his analysis of political change in Monterey
Park, Leland Saito concurs that, at least initially, Asian Americans and
Latinas/os who ran successfully for office tended to build their campaigns as outgrowths of a white power structure that included the Lions
and Kiwanis Clubs and the Monterey Park Democratic Club.[29] Indeed,
Yamauchi, in addition to building relationships with the "old-guard" city
council members, had previously served as Rotary Club and Chamber
of Commerce presidents. Chinese American Stephen Sham, elected
in 2006, followed Yamauchi's lead, also serving as president of both
organizations.[30]

In sum, in the 2000s, with the possible exception of Monterey Park,[31]
race remained "a largely unspoken but constant theme" in the West SGV's
municipal politics, with important consequences for differing groups'
claims to public space and civic identities.[32] The uneven representation of
Asian Americans and Latinas/os—and the fact that the terms by which
those who did attain public office were still heavily controlled by whites—
was a strong factor in how each of the following episodes, as spatialized
moments of racial formation, would play out.

"Diversity" on Main Street

Alhambra's Main Street runs for approximately three miles from Alhambra's western boundary with El Sereno (part of the city of Los Angeles) to its eastern boundary with San Gabriel (Figure 12). From the west, it travels through industrial buildings, box stores, and car dealerships until it reaches the city's downtown—a stretch of six blocks centered between Atlantic and Garfield Boulevards, dotted with restaurants, stores, a few clubs, a large mixed-use condominium complex, and two movie theaters, most of which have turned over or been newly built in Alhambra's push for "redevelopment" since the late 1990s. In 2003, in the wake of Alhambra's intensive multiyear redevelopment initiative—involving over $30 million in city and federal redevelopment funds, the

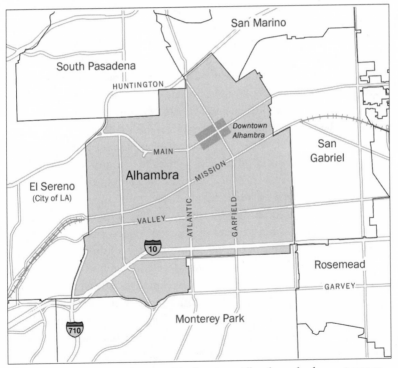

Figure 12. Map showing the location of the downtown Alhambra redevelopment zone on Main Street. Map by Julienne Gard and John Emerson.

ejection of dozens of existing businesses, and the opening of over forty new businesses—the merchants of the Downtown Alhambra Business Association (DABA) were ready to solidify the identity of Alhambra's reconstituted Main Street. The work was initially contracted to a high-profile design firm in Santa Monica. DABA asked Gregory Thomas, the head of the firm, "to give the area one alluring brand image." Thomas interviewed about twenty business owners and civic officials and noted that "the same word—diversity—came up over and over again in his interviews." Thomas also drew inspiration for a "Mosaic on Main" theme from mosaic tiles decorating the new Edwards movie theater plaza. "With the colors all working together, a mosaic reflects the quality of the restaurants and the shopping, and the diversity of the people, which is what makes Alhambra unique," Thomas told the *Pasadena Star-News*. The merchants' association spent $28,000 on the branding effort in 2003 and had budgeted an additional $30,000 for 2004.[33] The four faces, meant to represent Alhambra's diversity on banners hung on and around Main Street in subsequent years, were selected from stock photographs and meant to match the area's demographics:[34] a young, blond, and blue-eyed white woman; a middle-aged Asian American man; a young, olive-skinned woman with light freckles and dark hair (labeled as Latina); and an older, blond white woman (Figures 13a–d).

Municipal celebrations of diversity or multiculturalism are often, as various scholars have pointed out, a flawed panacea in their "reification of decontextualized ethnicity."[35] In such pluralist expressions of multiculturalism—of a "mosaic" "with all the colors working together" (in Thomas's words)—distinct racial, ethnic, and immigrant groups are leveled and presented as "equally 'other.'"[36] Official multiculturalist narratives that suppress tension and opposition suggest that the American Dream has already been or will imminently be fulfilled—that multiculturalism has already been achieved and "is defined simply by the coexistence and juxtaposition of greater numbers of diverse groups."[37] With their celebratory tone, multiculturalist narratives allow us to gloss over structured inequalities, conflicts, and heterogeneity among different racial, ethnic, and immigrant groups.[38] Indeed, in their presentation, Alhambra's diversity banners implied equivalence without specificity and presented white as just another ethnicity—one of a rainbow of ethnic options.[39] Race was reduced to individuals of various ethnic provenances and different kinds of consumption, as suggested by a banner that was also titled "Diversity" but, instead of faces, featured an image

Figure 13a–e. *Alhambra's diversity and Mosaic on Main campaign featured stock images of faces that were meant to be representative of the city's demographics as well as a colorful plate of salad. Photographs courtesy of Gregory Thomas Associates (GTA), David LaCava (designer) and Gregory Thomas (principal / creative director).*

of a colorful plate of salad (Figure 13e). In such a "festive public deployment of race and ethnicity," cultural differences are celebrated largely as commodities available for possession to an implicitly white Anglo public.[40] The diversity and mosaic themes, with their implications of egalitarian multicultural harmony, belied two important aspects of Alhambra's Main Street: First, the celebratory multicultural version of Main Street, rather than simply reflecting the municipality's diverse population, had been produced via concerted efforts by city officials to excise particular types of small businesses—many of which were ethnic-Chinese and immigrant owned—to make room for national chains with "mainstream," implicitly white, appeal. Second, Main Street was and remains contested terrain, a key dividing line in the racial geography of Alhambra.

North–South / East–West Divides

Even before redevelopment, Main Street had long served as a line between established white residents and the growing Asian immigrant population in Alhambra. As local historian Susie Ling, a forty-eight-year-old ethnic-Chinese immigrant who grew up in the Philippines and has lived in the area since the 1980s, described it, "Valley [Boulevard] was all Asian, and then Main Street was all white. . . . [T]here was at one point a JC Penneys on Main. . . . All the service people were white. The Ralphs, the supermarket, was white. . . . Today Ralphs has some Asian foods, right? No [not then]! . . . if we wanted Asian stuff, we would go to the other side of town."[41] Generally, as Ling's comments suggest, whites have lived in the north and Asian Americans in the south. Mexican Americans have clustered in the west but are more dispersed throughout than Asians and whites. In fact, the Main Street divide in Alhambra was part of a broader north–south racial-ethnic divide in the SGV. Ling has traced this separation back to the late nineteenth and early twentieth centuries, when landed wealth and more racially restrictive strictures characterized the areas north of Huntington and railroad depot towns and smaller-scale orchards, farms, and vineyards lay to the south.[42] Accordingly, most nonwhites living north of Huntington during this period were servants and laborers. South of Huntington, some nonwhite groups were more able to carve out modest niches, such as Japanese truck-gardening families (of which the San Gabriel census counted more than eighty in 1920) and Mexican and Mexican American farm workers living in "semiautonomous" camps or colonias in and around El Monte.[43] These boundaries were policed and enforced, first with official codes and white vigilante violence and then by real estate agents in the 1950s through the 1970s, as Mexican Americans and Asian Americans began to settle in the bedroom communities that sprouted along newly constructed freeways (chapter 1). The north–south divide, while increasingly porous, is still generally true today, whether residents name the dividing north–south line as Huntington Drive, Main Street, Valley Boulevard, or the railroad tracks along Mission Road (Figure 14).

In recent decades, this racial and geographical divide has manifested through more subtle struggles in the civic landscape as well as in local politics. In the 1980s and 1990s, numerous racially coded struggles occurred in Monterey Park over growth, commercial development, and signage.[44] For instance, in a protracted struggle over the architectural design of the Atlantic Square shopping center, a group of established white and Latina/o established residents banded together to affirm non-Asian culture.[45] In

Figure 14. Map showing major east–west thoroughfares in the West SGV that also serve as racial dividing lines. Map by Julienne Gard and John Emerson.

one public hearing, a young white man active in a citizens' group advocating for "a strong local definition" to the shopping center asked, "What's the theme? Things have changed so fast that our roots are blurred. We have to go back to the history of the town"—meaning European, not Asian, roots.[46] Planners first evoked Southern California's Mexican past, suggesting a Mexican architectural theme that was eventually "whitened," becoming Spanish and, finally, vaguely "Mediterranean." Saito notes that the wide acceptance of Mediterranean style as somehow more American than Mexican or Asian styles also played a role in the struggles in Monterey Park over business signs written in Chinese and other visual markers of Chinese culture.[47]

Similarly, during the push for redevelopment on Alhambra's Main Street, Susie Ling remembered that at "that corner where the Applebee's is now, they had this huge sign that said, 'Wanted: American restaurant' . . . I drove by every day. And I was like, well, screw you."[48] Ling's understanding of the word "American" on the sign as unequivocally anti-Asian taps into local memory of a large sign placed at a gas station and printed onto car bumper stickers in Monterey Park in the mid-1980s that read, "Will the last American to leave Monterey Park please bring the flag?"[49] The slogan

Figure 15. *Multilingual strip mall signage in Alhambra. Photograph by the author, 2012.*

was widely understood to be as an expression of nativist hostility against incoming Asian immigrants and Asian-owned businesses and is still vividly engraved in the minds of long-term Asian American and Latina/o residents today. The "Wanted: American restaurant" sign on Main Street, read in the context of local history as an expression of nativism via consumer desires, as well as the idea that restaurants serving Chinese food, and by extension ethnic Chinese people themselves, could not themselves be American suggested that the struggles that began in Monterey Park of the 1980s and 1990s were not over.

These residential divides were and are also political divides in the eyes of both voters and political candidates. In a recent state assembly election, Ling voted against a candidate who lived north of Huntington: "I knew that I wanted the guy to be south of Huntington. I'm not alone in this. . . . That line of Huntington is very clear." A Hong Kong–born, local city council member described his experience walking door to door in neighborhoods north of Main Street during a recent campaign for election: "I went up north, one sentiment that I got from the [white] residents there is—some of them expressed strongly, some of them not, but you can see from their facial expression—one person in particular says, you know, 'you guys [are] Chinese invaders.' You know, 'they took Monterey Park, they took Valley Boulevard, they now come to Main Street—when [are] you guys going to stop?'"[50] In this exchange, the white resident depicted Main Street as the last stronghold of territory that had not yet been "taken" by "Chinese invaders" in their northward sweep. The city council member described what he felt was the general attitude of such north-of-Main residents: "[W]hen I send my propagandas, my brochures, out to the voters—especially up north—they see the Chinese family [and think], 'to hell with you. I don't know you, I'm not going to vote for you'" (although he was careful to qualify that residents, on an individual level, might be won over by his assimilationist stances, "once they understand who you are," and count him as an exception to the rule). Latinas/os, in the vision of the resident the council member encountered, were also excluded from the "pure" space of Americanness north of Main. He recounted that during the course of the same conversation, when he mentioned that "we have a lot of Hispanics" in the area, the resident immediately responded in a negative tone, "Yeah, those Hispanics!" When the council member replied, "You know what? I'm a first-generation immigrant too," the resident was quick to say, "Oh, no no no no, you're American. You're OK." Although the person had just vented to the council member about "you . . . Chinese invaders," he or she was quick to award him honorary American status relative to other immigrants and Hispanics in general, simultaneously constructing the council member as an exception and asserting white domination and privilege in the ease with which he or she assigned racial and national identities to others.

Clearly, Main Street was never a neutral territory—a blank slate on which a harmonious multicultural future could be drawn.

Redevelopment: "No Guts, No Glory"

To understand the context out of which the diversity campaign grew, one must begin by going back several decades. The central stretch of Alhambra's Main Street was declared officially "blighted" in 1972. City officials used this designation to secure redevelopment funds and U.S. Department of Housing and Urban Development (HUD) monies. During the 1970s and 1980s, vacancy rates continued to increase to the point that, by the early 1990s, according to city manager Julio Fuentes, "you could have shot a missile down Main Street and not hit anyone."[51] In 1994, Fuentes was hired to take a more aggressive approach to redevelopment.[52] With the motto "No guts, no glory" scrawled across the whiteboard in his office, Fuentes and other city officials set about remaking Main Street. Between 1994 and 2006, the city spent more than $30 million (drawn primarily from HUD grants and redevelopment-area tax increments) on public improvements to attract commercial development, including land acquisition, tenant relocation, façade improvements, and the building of three new parking structures.[53] A large portion of the efforts were concentrated on a stretch of Main Street that measures not quite one mile long, between Almansor and Fifth Streets. City officials spearheading the efforts acted in an explicitly entrepreneurial manner, acting "like real estate brokers, scouting out . . . sites for new businesses that fit their vision for Main Street."[54] As Fuentes put it, "we thought: 'Why don't we try to become developers ourselves?'"[55]

By 2002, forty new businesses and a plaza anchored by a fourteen-screen movie theater complex had opened.[56] When some national chains were initially hesitant to move into Alhambra—due, some city officials thought, to chain representatives' belief that these businesses would not be popular with Asian residents—the city provided extra incentives. For instance, after the national restaurant chain Tony Roma's refused several overtures, the city bought an eight-thousand-square-foot building for over $1 million for Tony Roma's to lease, and spent $350,000 on upgrades.[57] The redevelopment agency gave Edwards Theatres a 43,000-square-foot parcel and $1.2 million from a HUD loan for the Renaissance Plaza movie theater. Alhambra was also the first city in the state to give Starbucks a "tenant improvement allowance," using $136,000 of HUD money.[58] Although the city used eminent domain only twice during this period of time, some existing business owners and tenants complained about favoritism toward new businesses and "high-pressure tactics." In 1998, several immigrant-owned small businesses, including a bakery, a wig shop, dental office, liquor store, and Vietnamese restaurant, were told to move or face eminent domain proceedings in order to make way for the Edwards movie theater complex, which would feature national chain restaurants Johnny Rockets, Panda Express, and Applebee's.[59] Arthur Wong, who owned one of the buildings the city wanted to raze, complained that the city's "vision" was nothing more than to turn Main Street into "a yuppie thing"—excluding, at least implicitly, immigrant-owned small businesses. Bryan Kan, the son of the owner of a restaurant supply business who sued the city during condemnation proceedings, described how the lump sum for which his father eventually settled for still represented a loss of what the family had hoped would be their monthly retirement income. Their family business was replaced by a national smoothie franchise and two small shops and counted by city officials as a redevelopment success story. To Kan, however, it was a misuse of eminent domain: "Normally, you use eminent domain for a public use, but not to bring in a juice stand."[60]

Although the dynamics at play in the redevelopment of downtown Alhambra can be explained in part by broader shifts in the neoliberalization of urban development,[61] many Chinese Americans felt that redevelopment had a racial cast, perhaps in part because, as already discussed, there was no Asian American representation on city council until 2004—long after the Main Street redevelopment juggernaut had been set in motion. Specifically, according to an Asian American city council member (and developer by profession) in a neighboring city, some believed that eminent domain had been exercised disproportionately "to drive away a lot of the Chinese-owned businesses, or properties that were held by Chinese Americans, and they were handed over to developers . . . with a huge advantage."[62]

Mosaic on Main

In 2007, the "diversity" banners on and around Main began to be replaced by "mosaic" banners. The new banners did not feature any faces but just the words "live," "dine," "shop," and "work," counterposed against a tiled mosaic pattern. According to Sharon Gibbs, business outreach director of the Alhambra Chamber of Commerce, at some point DABA realized its initial branding scheme was too ambitious and contracted with the chamber to take over the promotion, which was considerably reduced in scale. Gibbs inherited the promotional materials that had been developed by Gregory Thomas Associates. Based on Thomas's designs, the chamber produced the new "mosaic" banners to replace the fraying "diversity" banners.[63] In early 2009, the Chamber of Commerce also produced a downtown shopping guide and map, which featured five faces (real Alhambra residents this time, photographed on Main Street, according to Gibbs). The single, isolated faces were interspersed with the words "live, work, dine, shop, play." In descending order by the size of the image, they were: an older man and a middle-aged man, who might be white or light-skinned Latinos; a young Asian American woman; and two young Latina-looking women. Although these faces were more reflective of Alhambra's residents than the earlier diversity banners, in their selection and relative size, they nevertheless affirmed a white, male-dominated, and heteronormative hierarchy. White(-ish) males figured most prominently, and darker-skinned Latinas and Asians appeared secondarily and only as friendly looking young women who were attractive in stereotypically feminine ways. Thus, despite being more "authentic" in presenting actual residents of Alhambra, the Alhambra Downtown Shopping Guide still presented a vision of pluralist multiculturalism via consumption (dine, shop, play), in which white male dominance remained unchallenged.

In describing the mosaic theme, DABA evoked the city of Alhambra's namesake, a centuries-old palace and fortress in Granada, Spain:

> Alhambra's roots harken back to a beautiful palace in Spain where arts and culture flourished, a crossroads of culture and commerce, and a destination for shopping, dining and entertainment.

> Mirroring the mix of cultures and art of that palace in Granada, The Alhambra Mosaic On Main—a mosaic of tastes, sights and sound for a myriad of customers uniting to form a beautiful scene. It is the perfect metaphor for the Main Street Alhambra's unique offering and cultural diversity.
>
> When considering a day or evening of entertainment, dining, cinema, music, dancing or shopping, consider the unparalleled eclectic mix of The Alhambra Mosaic on Main.[64]

In fact, the reference to the Spanish Alhambra is more fitting than city officials might have intended.[65] The Kingdom of Granada was one of the last strongholds of Muslim Iberian rule by the time of its defeat by Christian Spain in the late fifteenth century. Subsequently Granada's Muslim and Jewish occupants were expelled, forced to convert to Christianity, or killed. The Spanish cooptation of its ruling edifice and the Alhambra's contemporary representation as a cultural crossroads for tourist consumption obliquely parallels the exclusion of Mexican, indigenous, Mexican American, and Chinese immigrant histories from Southern California civic landscapes—also histories of conquest and exploitation as well as of resistance. Nonetheless, small hints—for instance, the minor grammatical imperfections in the Mosaic on Main text, including article and singular- versus- plural errors common to many English speakers whose first language is Chinese ("It is the perfect metaphor for the Main Street Alhambra's unique *offering*")—nonetheless indicate a persistent immigrant presence that cannot be excised from municipal narratives. Such disjuncts suggest that official multiculturalist discourses such as Alhambra's diversity and Mosaic on Main campaigns might, as Lisa Lowe has argued, "ultimately emphasize, rather than domesticate" contradictions and irresolution within various narratives.[66] The uncovering of such dissonances may serve as a first step toward calling attention to the processes by which systemic inequalities are literally built into, and then continually reproduced by, civic landscapes, economies, and geographies.

Valley Boulevard: San Gabriel's Golden Mile

"The City with a Mission"

Like its neighbor Alhambra, San Gabriel is divided internally north to south, with the north holding larger numbers of wealthier, long-term white residents and the south home to a more heterogeneous mix of working-class to middle-income Asian Americans and Mexican Americans. Symbolically, the "historic Mission District," where city hall and other municipal buildings are located, anchors the north, while San Gabriel's portion of Valley Boulevard looms large in the south. The question of civic identity in San Gabriel is complicated by the fact that it is home to Mission San Gabriel, the first of the Spanish missions in California and a key signifier of California's Spanish fantasy past. The official city slogan is "the city with a mission." The Mission Playhouse adjacent to the mission (now the San Gabriel Civic Auditorium) originally housed the Mission Play, a cultural phenomenon that engraved visions of a mythicized mission past onto the hearts and minds of thousands of predominantly Anglo American California residents and tourists in the early twentieth century.[67] Middle-class Mexican Americans with long family histories in the area (some of whom are descended from elite, landowning Californio families) are selectively incorporated into the San Gabriel social and political elite. The presence of a significant working-class Mexican American population as well as recent local activism that seeks to highlight San Gabriel's Chicana/o history adds to the mix of Californio, Mexican American, and Chicana/o identities.

As in Alhambra, San Gabriel residents often described such racial and political dynamics in spatial terms. Mike Murashige, whose Japanese American family had lived in San Gabriel since the 1920s, described the train tracks just below Las Tunas Boulevard, around Mission Road, as "a hard barrier" between a working-class, Mexican American barrio ringed by industrial corridors and "everything else." He also described how "a lot of people" noted the differences between the two zip codes in San Gabriel.[68] Indeed, in 2000, an average resident of the northern zip code reported a median household income almost 50 percent higher than her southern zip code counterpart and a per capita income almost 75 percent higher.[69] She was much more likely to own a home, and home values were much higher, on average, than those of homes in the southern zip code.[70] Finally, she was three times more likely to be white.[71] San Gabriel city council member Albert Huang did not realize until he became a city official the degree of "the polarization of the city, the north versus the south." He characterized the political power in the north as dominated by mostly white, wealthy residents, as well as some Latinas/os, who had lived in San Gabriel for a long time. "It's kind of weird, because people say, you're very diverse. To the north, you're mostly Caucasian, to the middle part, you're mostly Latino, south, you're Latino and Asian. That's not diverse."[72] San Gabriel residents like activist and history professor Eloy Zarate, who is Argentinean and Mexican American, had heard people say that the "Asian" population was "taking over," "spilling over" northward, from Monterey Park. Some felt that "Monterey Park wants to take over San Gabriel."[73] It was in this divided racial and geographical context, in 2007, that council member Huang, a 1.5-generation Taiwanese American and the sole Asian American on the council, decided to put forth a proposal.

The Proposal

The Golden Mile will serve as one of Southern California's most vibrant shopping, dining and entertainment destination districts with emphasis on its rich heritage and well influenced Asian and fusion cultures. . . . The essence of the Golden Mile is defined by the pursuit of the American Dream and the symbol of the Golden Opportunity. The corridor is an economic phenomenon without any financial assistance from the government.

—Albert Huang, "Golden Mile Summary" (draft), 2009

In May 2006, when Albert Huang was thirty, he was selected by the San Gabriel City Council, whose members are elected at large, to replace Chi Mui. Mui, an immigrant from Hong Kong, had been elected as the first Asian American city council member in San Gabriel's history in 2003. He was a well-loved public official known for bridging language and cultural gaps and for being an activist in Los Angeles's Chinatown for over twenty years. Mui had become San Gabriel's first Asian American mayor only two months earlier, before passing away from liver cancer at the age of fifty-three.[74] Huang, a developer and San Gabriel planning commissioner, was chosen unanimously from a slate of three candidates, all Asian American men.[75] Huang considered Mui a mentor and came into office determined to honor the older man's legacy, particularly Mui's habit of referring to San Gabriel's vibrant, commercial stretch of Valley Boulevard as the "Golden Mile." According to Huang, Mui emphasized the retail and business opportunities that offered a "golden opportunity" to immigrants and that the "essence of the Golden Mile" was "the pursuit of the American Dream."[76] "It is bitter that it had to happen under

Figure 16. Map showing the locations of the proposed Golden Mile on Valley Boulevard and Vincent Lugo Park in San Gabriel. Map by Julienne Gard and John Emerson.

these circumstances, but sweet in that I'll be able to complete some things that Mui was not able to complete," Huang stated in the days after his appointment.[77]

In March 2007, Huang transitioned into a new four-year term as councilman, without opposition. That spring, he began in earnest to push forward the Golden Mile concept. Like Alhambra's diversity campaign, Huang's Golden Mile plan would use banner-based advertising branding to market the city's approximately one-mile stretch of Valley Boulevard to both visitors and locals. Emblematic of the character of San Gabriel's section of Valley Boulevard is San Gabriel Square, a huge complex of pan-Asian restaurants and stores dubbed by mainstream English-language media as "The Great Mall of China" and the "Chinese Disneyland."[78] San Gabriel Square is anchored by a department store that caters to Chinese-speaking clientele and 99 Ranch Market, the largest Asian American supermarket chain in the United States and Canada (founded by a Taiwanese expatriate). It also features restaurants like the thousand-seat Sam Woo Seafood Restaurant. Initially funded by a Taiwanese commercial bank and private investors, San Gabriel Square is indicative of how coethnic local, regional, and transnational flows of capital have shaped the contemporary development of the West SGV.[79] Indeed, according to city planner Mark Gallatin, "Valley Boulevard has been the economic engine for the city of San Gabriel for the past decades."[80] By the mid-2000s, San Gabriel Square alone provided as much sales-tax revenue to the city of San Gabriel as some of the other commercial streets "along their entire length."[81]

Huang envisioned the Golden Mile as a "destination district" "with emphasis on its rich heritage and . . . Asian and fusion cultures."[82] He likened the "Golden Mile" concept to "Old Pasadena, Third Street Promenade—these places have a name that draws people there": "when you have something that works . . . you have to still go back and promote it."[83] However, the plan ran into opposition from other city council members almost immediately. In Huang's view, when he presented the initiative to the chamber of commerce and other city officials, he encountered opposition that was clearly expressed in racial terms. In May 2007, he described the proposal's reception:

> Some major concerns that came out of the initial proposal was that people were uncomfortable with . . . the street being renamed. And I said, it's not about renaming the street . . . We're adding that name to this area. That's one. Number two . . . another concern that came out was well, when you say diversity, what diversity are you celebrating? . . . And I think the concerns mainly came out from the non-Asian groups. They said . . . does Golden Mile have to do with Hong Kong's Golden Mile? . . . So there was, again, some concerns about that, that I'm . . . primarily serving the Chinese American community by renaming this area.[84]

In contrast to the relative ease with which the city of Alhambra was able to wield a decontextualized diversity campaign, Huang's proposal to ground a vision of present and future diversity in an ethnic-Chinese dominated space was subjected to intense scrutiny and skepticism. Councilwoman Juli Costanzo, a longtime resident of north San Gabriel,

Figure 17. San Gabriel's proposed "Golden Mile" is a bustling shopping area that generates a large amount of revenue for the city of San Gabriel. Photographs by the author, 2012.

and a member of the Mission District Partnership (to be discussed in more detail later), wondered publicly whether "limited staff time and resources would be better spent on other commercial areas": "Valley is such a phenomenon to begin with. We're very well known for Chinese restaurants, but I would like more variety throughout the city and not just focused on one area."[85] Mexican American councilman David Gutierrez was also reluctant to support the initiative, although unlike Costanzo, he did not oppose it outright. Indeed, Gutierrez acknowledged that "we need an identity that will not only preserve the history of the city, but one that remains open to the new members of the community." However, regarding Valley Boulevard, he stated that "non-Asian residents," whom Gutierrez characterized as the "forgotten 50 percent of the population," complained about the lack of "Western world" restaurants like national chains Tony Roma's or the Claim Jumper. For many such residents, Gutierrez believed, shopping in an Asian supermarket was outside of their comfort zone, adding that he himself felt "more at home" buying groceries at a nearby Vons or a Mexican market: "I like my beans, my tortillas, my carne asada."[86]

It is notable that at least on the public record, Costanzo and Gutierrez focused their comments on food (restaurants and supermarkets), giving the impression that any opposition to municipal support of initiatives on Valley Boulevard such as the Golden Mile were based on a desire for more "variety" and balance in "ethnic" options;[87] it was a matter of culture and diversity, not race, and consumer options rather than civic representation. Further, although Gutierrez's evocation of the "forgotten 50 percent" might contain some ambiguity regarding who was forgotten, and who was doing the forgetting, his categorization of this segment of the population as "non-Asian" and encompassing both "Western world" restaurants and "my beans, my tortillas, my carne asada," aligned Mexican (American) culture together with "mainstream" Americanness and created a grouping from which Asian supermarkets were explicitly excluded.

In March 2009, I met again with a visibly beleaguered Huang. Huang seemed more dedicated to bringing the Golden Mile proposal to fruition than ever, but even though two years had passed, he was still fighting to get the proposal off the ground. After failing to get any definitive support from his fellow council members and the chamber of commerce in 2007, Huang began to approach Valley Boulevard–based businesses and ethnic organizations, trying to "get all the organizational support . . . the property owners' support, and the business support." He worked with Chi Mui's widow, Betty Mui, to raise money "to help buy the banners," "completely outside of city money."[88] In working primarily through private channels, Huang followed an already existing pattern of development among ethnic Chinese immigrants. The massive growth of restaurants, stores, and services on Valley Boulevard since the 1980s has been largely funded by private capital stemming from businesses and banks helmed by ethnic Chinese—an infrastructure that, it is important to note, stemmed initially from structural racism against Asians and other nonwhites.[89] Therefore, after the lukewarm reception of the Golden Mile proposal by city officials, Huang's choice to pursue funding through private, ethnic community–based channels confirmed the continuing need of ethnic Chinese immigrants to draw financial support from sources other than governmental (i.e., municipal) institutions. In 2009, the text of Huang's Golden Mile proposal included a sentence that stated, "The corridor is an economic phenomenon without any financial assistance from the government."[90] Indeed, few business owners on Valley Boulevard were members of the San Gabriel chamber of commerce—a situation Huang believed was due, at least in part, to the chamber not making sufficient efforts to recruit there. Since there was no unified Valley Boulevard merchants' organization either (such as Alhambra's DABA), Huang had to literally go door to door to drum up support for the proposal.

Huang was now also considerably more blunt about other city officials' and residents' reluctance to support the Golden Mile proposal. He stated that there was, in his opinion, definitely "persecution, discrimination" against Asian immigrants, especially from wealthy white residents in the north, signified by attitudes toward businesses and issues on Valley, such as the perception that there must be illegal activities going on and that "Asians are dirty." Further, since the "propensity to vote" was up north, Huang believed that many city council members believed that they should serve the people who voted them in: the north and not the south. Huang, still the sole Asian American on the council, felt that race and ethnicity was an element in city issues "all the time." In the city council campaign that had just ended, "We've heard people say, 'Valley Boulevard doesn't serve the residents of San Gabriel.' And that's *crazy*. Because 60 percent of the population is Asian American. And you're saying Valley Boulevard doesn't serve the residents? I mean, it obviously serves *some*body. It serves predominantly Asians, because there's so many Asian businesses here. But . . . you know, it's just very unfortunate that people speak of things like that."[91]

The concerns, posed by non-Asian groups to Huang, illustrate how Asian American politicians with immigrant backgrounds such as Huang had to contend with what Ruth Wilson Gilmore has called the "performance effect," in which an audience member or interlocutor attributes motivations and interests based on an identity (e.g., racial) ascribed to the speaker by the audience member or interlocutor himself.[92] Huang felt that, as the only Asian American member of San Gabriel City Council, "it was easy for them [city officials and members of the public who opposed the Golden Mile] to think that I'm doing this with a . . . selfish intention, for my ethnic community, you know, my Chinese heritage prompted me to do this." Therefore, when asking, "When you say diversity, what diversity are you celebrating?" and "Does Golden Mile have to do with Hong Kong's Golden Mile?" questioners seemed unable to separate Huang's appearance and position as the sole Asian American body on the council from his presumed motivations. As Huang put it succinctly, "some people thought when I say 'Golden Mile,' that it was meant to serve the Chinese." When he was told this, Huang said, "I [was] shocked because to *me*, it's essentially [the] opposite. . . . It's not to serve the Chinese, it's to serve the whole community. . . . I want Golden Mile, when it comes to fruition, to serve the entire community, to celebrate . . . not only the current vitality, prosperity, but also the diversity that we want it to achieve."[93] On the other hand, Huang believed that when non-Asians argued for the Golden Mile, including two economic consultants and a white city councilman, Kevin Sawkins, audiences were much more willing to listen. Referring to Sawkins, Huang said, it "absolutely" made a difference: "People have a tendency to think this is an Asian concept. So when he comes in and he speaks on . . . the Asian community's behalf, it's superb."[94]

In fact, "Golden Mile" is a popular name for numerous locales around the world in addition to Hong Kong's Golden Mile, from a stretch of banks and financial institutions in San Juan, Puerto Rico; to beachfront promenades in South Africa and England; to swaths of expensive real estate in Moscow; and even a stretch of Wilshire Boulevard in Los Angeles.[95] However, former mayor Chi Mui's upbringing in Hong Kong, Albert Huang's Taiwanese background, and the plethora of restaurants and shops on Valley Boulevard primarily targeting ethnic Chinese immigrants, made only the Hong Kong reference salient to the chamber of commerce.

Mission District Revitalization and New Claims to the Spanish Fantasy Past

The city's approach to the Mission District during the same time period was quite different from its treatment of Valley Boulevard. In marked contrast to the absence of any official city support for the Golden Mile proposal, the city was continuously and conspicuously involved in promoting and "revitalizing" the Mission District, which is central to its identity as "the city with a mission." In 1996, the city formed the Mission District Partnership, an organization of "businesses, residents, government, schools, organizations and various entities with an ongoing interest in the success of the San Gabriel Mission District."[96] The partnership's stated mission goal was "to cooperatively develop, promote and market the District as a destination for tourism, culture, entertainment, dining and shopping." Juli Costanzo—the city council member and longtime resident of North San Gabriel who consistently opposed the Golden Mile proposal—was an affiliate, and the city provided significant staffing and organizational support. As Huang put it, "the [Mission District Partnership] meetings are completely organized by the city. Versus the Valley Boulevard stakeholders meeting, this is something that, it's kind of like, thrown at us—'hey, you go and organize it.' It's a completely different idea."[97]

In the early 1990s, the city spent about $2.6 million in state and local funds in the push to develop the Mission District. Revitalization attempts continued through the 2000s. In 2009, one plan encompassed several new mixed-use developments and remodels. The first project to be built under this plan, Mission Villa, was a mixed-use development "designed in the Spanish Colonial Revival architectural style to complement the historic character of the district." Mission Village, another mixed-use project, proposed by the owners of upscale Chinese restaurant Mission 261 (brothers Harvey, Lewis, and York Ng) in a site adjacent to the restaurant, would include a "Spanish Colonial style boutique hotel."[98] The willingness of ethnic-Chinese immigrant business owners to participate in promoting a

Spanish or broadly Mediterranean theme—particularly in order to gain "mainstream" acceptance, also found expression on Valley Boulevard in retail developments such as those built by Sunny Chen, a Taiwanese businessman, who opened a $60-million-dollar Hilton Hotel across from San Gabriel Square in late 2004. Chen chose a "contemporary Tuscan décor" in order "to make non-Asian visitors feel more at home." A buffet featured both "Western" and "Asian" food, and the hotel's meeting rooms were named after California missions.[99]

The validating function of vaguely Spanish and Mediterranean references in the Mission District as well as on Valley Boulevard stood in stark contrast to city council members' pointed speculations about Golden Mile's possible linkage to Hong Kong. The contrasting civic investments and attitudes toward these two areas during this time period illustrated how an elite, white-dominated north continued to keep a tight grip on who could make claims to San Gabriel's identity and history and what the nature of those claims could be. City officials prioritized nurturing the Spanish fantasy past via Mission District revitalization and Mediterranean architectural styles, while maintaining a "let it be" attitude toward Valley Boulevard and coding it as a perpetually foreign, autonomous Asian space. In doing so, they reproduced in space the long-standing racial trope of Asians as unassimilable bodies that might be tolerated but could not be incorporated within official civic identities.

The following year, however, several new developments complicated the story. In March 2010, Albert Huang rotated into his term as mayor. By the fall, with the support of fellow council members Kevin Sawkins and the newly elected Mario De La Torre, Huang was able to win his push to designate Valley Boulevard the Golden Mile. The city allotted some funds and small projects to carry out the branding.[100] In September, city officials even proposed to change the city motto and logo of San Gabriel, from the long-cherished "city with a mission" to the more open-ended "history in the making," in order to be inclusive of more elements of the city. In particular, they hoped that the revised motto would draw more businesses to the Golden Mile District. They also proposed to add "way-finding" signs to various points of interest in the city, including the Mission District, Golden Mile, and La Laguna Park. Council member De La Torre, who led the proposal and was supported by Huang, believed that in addition to being more inclusive and reflecting the "reality" of present-day San Gabriel, "a new fresh look" for the city would help to bring in more revenue. "Our income and tax revenue has dropped and we need to make up that difference."[101] It seemed that there was room for change within the city council after all.

However, the proposal immediately met with virulent opposition from local residents—particularly Mexican Americans, whites, and representatives of the San Gabriel Band of Mission Indians (Gabrielinos). The Gabrielinos' attachment to the mission might seem unexpected. As in the California mission system as a whole, thousands of indigenous people were forced to labor in the San Gabriel Mission and suffered poor conditions and often brutal treatment. An estimated six thousand indigenous people died there. The San Gabriel Mission was also the site of a failed Gabrielino revolt.[102] But to the Gabrielino leadership it represented an important symbol of their history and presence in the region. "It's important because our history is at the mission. Our people built that mission," spiritual leader Ernesto Perez Salaz told the *Pasadena Star-News.* "We have a lot of history here in San Gabriel. We don't want to change anything."[103] "History has already been made," vice chairwoman Nadine Salas told the city council at a contentious meeting attended by some three hundred residents who opposed the proposed change.[104] Salas directly connected what she perceived as a move to eradicate native history with the Golden Mile: "To me it just seems like we have this one important piece of history. . . . Why change something that's been in our history for so long? Especially now with the creation of the Golden Mile." Since most businesses in the Golden Mile were owned by Asian Americans, she believed that the logo change was intended to "cater to" Asians.[105] Other residents also associated Asians unfavorably with the proposal: "The tagline creates a big issue of segregation and separation in the city," said Charles Salazar. "The new demographic doesn't want anything to do with us. It's assimilate or leave."[106]

Though the rationale for defending the mission-centered motto varied, one thing that stayed consistent with city officials' earlier objections to the Golden Mile was residents' unwillingness to see Asian Americans as a legitimate part of San Gabriel's civic identity and official history. They were still seen as "new" (an oppositional "them" versus "us") and relegated to a special interest group, rather than being recognized as over 60 percent of the population.[107] After hearing the concerns, the city council—including De La Torre and Huang—voted to keep the old motto. Some council members expressed strong opinions on both sides of the issue: David Gutierrez stated that the evening the council proposed to change the logo was "the worst evening I've had on the council," while De La Torre felt that bringing up race in the issue was "ridiculous." But Mayor Huang, still the only Asian American on the council, was relatively quiet on the issue, stating only that he understood the expressed concerns about assimilation.[108] In the end the original logo and motto remained unchanged.

Would residents have expressed their opposition to the proposed change in the same way if an Asian American had not recently become the mayor of the city? Could Valley Boulevard and its occupants ever be seen as a legitimate part of San Gabriel's civic identity and citizenry, rather than as oppositional, threatening, and generally nonnormative? Unfortunately, the experiment of Albert Huang's mayorship, like his predecessor Chi Mui's before him, was short lived. On October 15, 2010, only a few weeks after the city council voted to keep the old city motto, Huang was involved in a public altercation with a woman who was allegedly his girlfriend and arrested. Four days later, citing concerns for his family, he resigned his public office, holding back tears when Betty Mui, Chi Mui's widow, stated that she respected his choice.[109] Although Huang was later cleared of all charges, it seemed that his political career in San Gabriel had come to a halt. The following spring, for the two city council seats up for election, residents chose incumbent Juli Costanzo and John Harrington, a white resident of North San Gabriel, over two Asian American candidates.[110] For now, and once again, the city was restored to a white, Mexican American, and north San Gabriel–dominated leadership. Although the Golden Mile had been approved, more pressing city budget issues over the next years meant that the project was put on the back burner indefinitely. As of mid-2012, not a single sign or banner had gone up.[111]

Just a few blocks north of Valley Boulevard, however, during the same span of years Albert Huang spent struggling to make that space and its denizens a recognized part of San Gabriel, another fight over space was brewing, in which grassroots activists would seize an opportunity to put forth a rather different narrative of San Gabriel's identity and history—one that prioritized inclusion over exclusion, in which immigrant histories were central rather than peripheral.

Friends of La Laguna: Development of
Pan-Ethnic Immigrant Identity

*These are not individual sculptures but a historical and cultural
landscape.*

—Eloy Zarate, Friends of La Laguna[112]

In the mid-1960s, the city of San Gabriel commissioned seventy-year-old
cement sculptor Benjamin Dominguez, a Mexican immigrant, to create
more than a dozen whimsical sculptures and play structures of sea crea-
tures for a section of Vincent Lugo Park that was named "La Laguna de
San Gabriel." The park became known colloquially as "Monster Park" or
"Dinosaur Park." Dominguez's most well-known work in his native Mexico had been lion and tiger enclosures for the Mexico City Zoo. Since
emigrating to the United States in 1956 at the age of sixty-two, Dominguez
lived in Texas and Nevada and created zoo and playground structures
in the El Paso and Las Vegas areas before moving to La Puente, a predominantly Mexican American suburb in the eastern part of the SGV. In
Southern California, he designed imaginative and beloved parks, including Garden Grove's Atlantis in Orange County and play structures at Legg
Lake in Whittier Narrows in nearby Rosemead. La Laguna de San Gabriel
was his final commission and is the largest remaining example of Dominguez's work.

In the nearly fifty years since the park's opening, more than two generations of San Gabriel residents grew up playing among the brightly
colored cement sea lions, starfish, whale, dolphins, octopus, and sea-
serpent lighthouse slide. Many San Gabriel residents had lifelong and
multigenerational ties to the park. For instance, one woman recounted
how her father took her to play in the park as a young child. She took
her babysitting charges there as a teenager and was proposed to by her
future husband in the park. As a mother, her own three children grew up
playing at the park.[113] However, in November 2006, the San Gabriel City
Council approved a renovation plan for Vincent Lugo Park that called
for the removal of Dominguez's sculptures, since they did not comply with present-day safety standards. In their place, a soccer field and
baseball field extension were proposed.[114] The decision met rapidly with
opposition, led by longtime San Gabriel resident Eloy Zarate and his
wife Senya Lubisich, both history professors at local colleges. The Zarate

Figure 18. Opening day of La Laguna de San Gabriel in Vincent Lugo Park. The park would later be affectionately called "Monster Park." May 16, 1965. Courtesy of Benjamin Dominguez's family.

and Dominguez families had met by chance on Father's Day four years earlier, when Zarate and Lubisich brought their children to the park, and Fernando Dominguez and his wife were there photographing the structures, having just come from paying their respects at the cemetery where Benjamin Dominguez was buried.[115] After hearing of the renovation plan in late 2006, Zarate and Lubisich, with the support of the Dominguezes, began to rally residents, sending volunteers to make pitches door to door in the neighborhoods abutting the park. Speaking at an emotional rally at the park in December, Marta Dominguez, the youngest of thirteen Dominguez siblings, said that she believed that her brother's encounter with Zarate and Lubisich "was not a mere coincidence, I think, because God's hand is in this." Standing with Marta Dominguez and several of her family members, Zarate spoke: "This is no longer about my memories, this is about Benjamin Dominguez. . . . I am not going to let Benjamin Dominguez be forgotten. We're not going to let that happen."[116] Their appeals proved effective: At the end of the rally, nearly forty volunteers signed up to canvass the surrounding neighborhoods.

Zarate, who played in the park as a child and now brought his own children there, argued that the sculptures were "historical, cultural works," "artistically relevant," and that, as the works of a Mexican immigrant, they spoke to San Gabriel's immigrant past and present. "It is made by a Chicano artist in the '60s, mixing and combining his culture and the new American suburban way of looking at things. It's become a much larger issue for us than, 'Oh my kids play there.'"[117] Zarate and Dominguez's children foregrounded the sculptor's immigrant experience, arguing that Dominguez's personal story of "immigration and adopting a new home-land" reflected San Gabriel's diverse population.[118] Dominguez "wanted to express gratitude to his new homeland through the playgrounds," Fernando Dominguez, who had helped his father to build some of the structures, told the *Pasadena Star-News*.[119] In arguing that saving the park wasn't just about nostalgia but about a key aspect of the city's identity, Zarate and other Monster Park supporters articulated a specific vision of San Gabriel's past, present, and future that linked a pan-ethnic, pan-racial immigrant experience to suburban identities and priorities.

The park was located south of San Gabriel's literal and proverbial train tracks, about a mile south of the Mission District and less than two blocks north of Valley Boulevard. Zarate, himself a longtime resident of north San Gabriel, felt that knocking on doors helped him gain a better understanding of the "schism" in San Gabriel between north and south. He realized that many northern San Gabrielites' visions of south San Gabriel—specifically, its Asian residents—were wrong. In north San Gabriel, he said, there was a common belief that the city's problems stemmed from the city council "selling out to Asian businesses." Talking to Asian immigrant residents of the neighborhoods around Vincent Lugo Park, Zarate found that, "These people aren't benefiting from all those businesses. . . . They're working like anybody else to try to make it, to pay their rent. They're living in apartments . . . they're poor." These residents felt that "[c]ity council is selling out to rich people. They don't care about us." Zarate told the story of a Vietnamese man who took Zarate into his backyard, whose view was now completely dominated by the newly constructed Hilton Hotel: "He said, 'Look what they did. Look what they did to my backyard.' I'm like, 'Yeah, that sucks. You got people looking into your backyard!' He says, 'Look what the city did . . . all they care about is money.'"[120] The unhappiness Zarate heard from Asian immigrant residents about development on Valley Boulevard as well as sentiments regarding the park—that, as one Chinese man put it, "not all change is good"—complicates common local discourses that polarize a whiter, wealthier north San Gabriel of single-family homes and a densely populated, Asian south whose residents do not care for ostensibly white, suburban, quality-of-life concerns.

Zarate also based his feeling that such residents would support his cause on his observations: when he went to the park in the morning, "it's all Chinese people. Chinese people doing their tai chi, doing their martial arts." From such scenes, Zarate derived a sense of collective well-being that included himself, the son of a Mexican American father and an Argentinean immigrant mother, as well as them: "[T]hen I go there, and I love it.... It's like, they're *right*.... They enjoy the park and they enjoy the dinosaurs, and all these things that are there, and I knew that they did. And I knew that if I went and communicated to them what I was doing, what we were doing, that they would agree . . . that this *meant* something."

Friends of La Laguna (FoLL), led by Zarate and Lubisich, built an inclusive campaign that united people by class, shared immigrant histories, and longevity in area by positing coalitions based on voluntary affiliations and multiple identifications. In their emphasis on Benjamin Dominguez's Mexican immigrant background (which Zarate also characterized as "Chicano" more than once), FoLL's campaign to save Monster Park also pushed back against the erasure of the histories and *presence* of Mexican immigrants and Mexican American history in the region and in Southern California, more generally. With its grassroots campaign based on multiple, nonidentitarian affiliations, Zarate says that FoLL brought to the surface voices "in their broken English communicating [that] the park should stay, we love the park, we love the dinosaurs, that's a beautiful place."

In January 2007, FoLL entered into a Memorandum of Understanding with the city of San Gabriel to preserve and protect the structures.[121] According to Rebecca Perez, director of parks and recreation for San Gabriel, "We really didn't have much historical information about the playground, and because of that, we didn't realize how important this playground was."[122] In order to raise the funds necessary to bring the structures up to current safety codes, FoLL became a nonprofit organization. Lubisich became president, Zarate became chief financial officer, and their friends and fellow north San Gabriel residents Eric Kirchhoff and John Harrington (who would later be elected to fill Albert Huang's vacated city council seat, in March 2011) filled the remaining positions of vice president and secretary. Zarate described this core group as being indicative of the multiethnic families that made up a politically progressive segment of north San Gabriel: in addition to Zarate and Lubisich (who is white), Harrington is a "white guy raised in Seattle married to a Salvadorean," and Kirchhoff the son of German immigrants, raised in San Gabriel, and married to a Chinese woman. "Senya and I noticed, I go, do you notice the families? We have mixed kids. We have one white person married to a person of color. . . . That's north San Gabriel. And that's the United States. And we're all pretty liberal . . . we have liberal politics. But this has nothing to do with politics. Right? So we all have kind of these larger world views, and we understand even though we have different views and ideas, the park brought us together . . . [that] this is important for our community in San Gabriel." In the summer of 2007, FoLL received their first major grants of $50,000 and $70,000 from California Cultural and Historical Endowments and the Annenberg Foundation, respectively, to begin assessments for a historic structures report and preservation plan.[123] However, their first step to protect the park was to submit a nomination to the State Register of Historic Places to name La Laguna a historical landmark, making it eligible for official protection as a "historic and cultural resource." This was important, the organization believed, because it would "formally articulate the value that the park holds for our community." In 2009 the historical landmark status was granted, and La Laguna was also designated as a local landmark for the city of San Gabriel.[124]

In the broadening of FoLL's outreach in order to raise money and educate community members and organizations about the park's history (such as local Kiwanis and Rotary Clubs as well as preservation organizations), it became clear that some supporters had a slightly different narrative of the reasons for saving La Laguna—especially, perhaps, when speaking to a predominantly white, north San Gabriel–based board. Some voiced to Zarate the opinion that, "'you're saving San Gabriel. . . . They would have taken it all.'" The "they" in the statement Zarate interpreted to mean unequivocally, "those Asians": "So on one hand you're hearing this awful, racist stuff, but now you have to be diplomatic . . . to respond tactfully, without alienating the potential donor." However, the anxiety and hostility of such residents also clearly represented an opportunity for FoLL. The park activists tapped into a desire for history and identity in longtime residents. "Overwhelmingly, people have been very receptive to the idea that the park means something to the city because there are so few things that *are* San Gabriel. I mean, it's no longer the city that it was. Things are going. And that's why they kind of react to the Asian community: 'Look what they've done over there.' Well, what have they done?" Zarate argued that, in fact, white elites' shaky "idea of an [municipal] identity" was not put to the test "until all these Asians started coming in": "We have north San Gabriel, we have barrio San Gabriel, we have village San Gabriel . . . and now people are going, 'San Gabriel!' Who *is* that? I mean, I think this whole region is like that." Zarate also pointed out the fallacy of forming a collective identity against an essentially fictive "Asian" group: "With even the Asians that come in, are they Asian? You know . . . can they fit any of these ideas that we have of these groups?"[125] Zarate and his collaborators sensed that at this moment of rapid demographic transition, the city's history and identity was up for grabs, much as it was in the late nineteenth century, when newly arrived Anglo Americans enshrined the Spanish fantasy past as part of a national narrative of racial succession. The FoLL activists were always careful to affirm that the park was worth saving because it represented history. To people against saving the park who argued that it was not worth saving because to them it was "not history" because it was "just art," or because it had been built within their own lifetimes, Zarate replied, "Alright, well maybe it's not your history. But it's *mine.* I grew up there. I take my kids there."[126]

In fact, FoLL, who often represented their leadership to the press as "three families," made narratives of local family histories, children, and futurity central to its campaign.[127] Benjamin Dominguez's children and grandchildren spoke frequently of Dominguez's love for children. As one of his sons put it, "He just wanted to do something for this country that he loved and leave something for the enjoyment of the community, the kids."[128] "He was very passionate about kids and found children to be very special people," his youngest daughter told the *Pasadena Star-News.*[129] One of Dominguez's daughter-in-laws recounted how at the park's opening festivities, "I had three children then and I was carrying the smallest one in my arms."[130] Typical responses by supporters to the news of its possible demise included the following:

It would be a cultural tragedy to destroy this delightful park. It has been treasured by me, my children and, now, my grandchildren.

Dinosaur Park is a great park that my family and I have enjoyed since I was born some thirty-one years ago. Now, I take my godson and my cousin's children there to play. . . . The park is great and different, and should be saved for future children to enjoy.

I grew up in San Gabriel. . . . We spent much of our time in the then-brand-new park. I watched the park grow into a beautiful place. I took my children there to play. . . . I want to take my grandchildren there, as well.

My Aunt took me to Vincent Lugo Park when I was a little girl. . . . Now, as a mother of two, it has become a family treasure of sorts. . . . Monster Park doesn't just belong to the city of San Gabriel, it belongs to generations of children.[131]

Within the context of multiple available narratives, Zarate centered Benjamin Dominguez's immigrant, Chicano history as the story that "has driven everything." By affirming that personal family histories *are* San Gabriel's history, FoLL and their supporters seized the opportunity to redirect the narrative on a modest piece of the landscape in a way that could have lasting significance: they claimed a place for the immigrant, Chicana/o history of San Gabriel. Indeed, they affirmed that immigrants and Chicanas/os *have a place* in the history of San Gabriel and the region as a whole. In their successful grassroots campaign to save La Laguna de San Gabriel from demolition, they were able to direct narratives of San Gabriel's history from the ground up and to employ the contested nature of the city's identity and history in a moment of transition as an opportunity rather than a constraint. As Zarate put it, "Something is happening. And if you can tweak what happens, you can change the relationships. . . . Maybe the park is one of those tweaks, right? I mean, the park is something that everyone can come together [around] . . . that's important. So you've got to find something like that that draws people together."[132]

Five years later, in 2012, FoLL had completed some of the renovations needed to bring the sculptures up to code and had gone through $400,000 of funding but still needed another $500,000 to finish.[133] The park had now become officially accepted and beloved as a San Gabriel landmark. Although many of the organizers' original claims had been tempered by their success and the widespread embrace of the park, Zarate still saw the moment of organizing as an important instance in which north San Gabriel residents were able to make alliances with south San Gabriel residents to articulate one shared civic identity: that "this is about San Gabriel." In the future, besides finishing the renovation of the park, they also wanted to establish chapters of Friends of Laguna in the local high schools, so youth—such as their own children, many of whom had grown up with the struggle to save the park—could get involved and feel like they too had a stake in shaping and claiming San Gabriel.

Conclusion

In three distinct struggles over civic landscapes, West SGV civic officials and residents fought to put forth particular representations of history and identity. In Alhambra, the deployment of pluralist multiculturalism in the diversity and Mosaic on Main campaigns papered over a divisive process of redevelopment, in which implicitly white, "mainstream" businesses won space at the expense of a large number of predominantly Asian, immigrant-owned small businesses. On Valley Boulevard in San Gabriel, a predominantly white elite clung to promoting a Spanish fantasy heritage in the city's historic Mission District, while refusing a Taiwanese American council member's proposal to celebrate a predominantly Asian business district as an official part of the city's identity. Finally, at Monster Park in San Gabriel, multiethnic white and Latina/o grassroots activists led an inclusive campaign to save the park, affirming a space for immigrant and Chicana/o histories in the West SGV.

Throughout these three episodes, it was clear that state practices, in the form of local government, had the power to reproduce as well as create new racial meanings through the conflation of racial and spatial discourses. In the West SGV, despite rapidly transforming demographic and economic contexts, an old-guard white elite still held sway in its municipal governments, with significant contexts for the region's civic landscapes. If they were to be successful, aspiring Asian American and Latina/o politicians had to contend with this old guard one way or another, whether through incorporating themselves into the existing power structure or simply "not making waves." In contrast, in the grassroots campaign to save San Gabriel's Monster Park, activists managed to redirect established residents' anxiety over shifting demographics into more inclusive grounds for community affiliation, in which personal histories, articulated through relationships to the park, *were* San Gabriel's history. They found a way to, as Lisa Lowe puts it, "think through the ways in which culture can be rearticulated not in terms of identity, equivalence, or pluralism but out of contradiction, as a site for alternative histories and memories that provide the grounds to imagine subject, community, and practice in new ways."[134]

Taken together, Alhambra's diversity initiative, San Gabriel's Golden Mile proposal, and the campaign to save Monster Park illuminate how conceptions of history and diversity, as expressed in public space, can perpetuate or challenge inequalities based on notions of race. By looking closely at these dynamics, we can also see how regionally specific conceptions of race, space, and history work in tandem with state-structured processes to maintain—or potentially reorganize—power relations, which are then sedimented and recodified in the landscape. If we can better understand the power of ideological underpinnings of state practices to shape familiar, everyday landscapes, people who have been excluded or threatened with erasure from those same landscapes may be better prepared to mobilize for change at key moments when, in Zarate's words, "something is happening": "if you can tweak what happens, you can change the relationships."[135]

· CHAPTER 5 ·

SGV Dreamgirl

Interracial Intimacies and the Production of Place

I N THE LATE 2000s, the local street-wear brand called "SGV" produced
a T-shirt, which they called "SGV dreamgirl," featuring a black-and-
white image of an attractive, dark-haired and dark-eyed woman, overlaid
with the repeating three-letter brand logo (Figure 19). The website catalog
description of the shirt read, "meet your dreamgirl; she's half Asian, half
Latina." The T-shirt, along with several others designed by Paul Chan and
produced and distributed by Chan and a "motley crew" of skateboarding
buddies turned business partners who had grown up in the area, evoked
an explicitly multiracial, Asian American and Latina/o place identity.[1]
Other T-shirts produced around the same time included one featuring the
well-known red Sriracha hot sauce bottle (a staple in casual Asian restaurants and home pantries everywhere) with the letters "SGV" instead of
the Sriracha logo, another that sported the logo of a popular hair cream
favored by cholos, and yet another that riffed on the painted ivy walls created by local government agencies as an attempt to deter graffiti.

In the melding of their cultural, racial, and geographic imaginations,
the SGV brand's ethos and creations clearly evoked a shared *racial-spatial
imaginary* highly specific to the area. More specifically, the image of an
SGV dreamgirl who is half Asian and half Latina prompts the following questions: What is the relationship between place and interethnic
or interracial intimacy? In the West San Gabriel Valley (SGV), how is a
collective, place-based multiracial or multiethnic identity experienced
and expressed? What are the key components of such an identity, how
is it produced and sustained, and toward what ends? In chapter 2, we saw
that Asian Americans and Latinas/os who grew up in the SGV, especially those who came of age in the 1980s and 1990s, were likely to develop
close interethnic and interracial friendships in their neighborhoods

Figure 19. *In 2008, the SGV brand released a T-shirt design called "SGV dreamgirl," featuring the image of a woman who was half Asian and half Latina. Courtesy of Paul Chan.*

and schools, which often developed into a lasting sense of multiracial consciousness and collective nonwhite identity. The three subsequent chapters illustrated that while this multiracial consciousness and collective identity formed a pronounced regional structure of feeling in the SGV, with the potential to form a basis for antiracist politics, ideology supporting the reproduction of dominant national racial hierarchies nonetheless remained powerful among individuals and local institutions. In this chapter, we will look further at the question of multiracial identity and racial-spatial consciousness not only through the experiences of multiethnic and multiracial individuals but also through the lens of interethnic and interracial intimacy. The coexistence of more fluid affective and interpersonal identifications with the more hardened racial and social hierarchies expressed in civic institutions and spaces—and sometimes within or experienced by the same individuals—show the importance of affective, interpersonal, and cultural realms to the formation and expression of regional structures of feeling. These are the realms where we can consistently find a distinctive place-based racial consciousness, which, though not fully realized in institutions and more broadly based power structures, is nevertheless consistently present.

Considering the meanings and effects of interethnic and interracial intimacy in relationship to place is important for two primary reasons. First, interracial intimacy and ethnic identity are closely related. In the case of marriage—the institutional binding together of family lines and fortunes—scholars have argued that they are in some ways mutually constitutive. Following Max Weber's definition of ethnicity as "real or fictive kinship, a sense of common provenance and history," Paul Spickard argues: "People making marriage choices, and other people reacting to those marriage choices, do so largely around the notion of who is within their group. Perceptions of class and culture, and knowledge of social connections, all play parts in these decisions. But ultimately, after an individual's feelings for another individual, marriage choices seem mainly to embody judgments as to whether a particular person is one of us or not."[2] Place is similarly important to ethnoracial identity because, as we have seen, place-based understandings about racial and ethnic identity also have the potential to blur the boundaries and meanings of ostensibly discrete racial and ethnic categories. Seen in these ways, interethnic and interracial intimacies emerging from highly place-specific contexts have the potential to transform available terms of ethnoracial affiliation—how we decide "whether a particular person is one of us or not"—as well as challenge dominant racial hierarchies.

Building on the introspective and wide-ranging responses of my interviewees, I include in my conceptualization of intimacy not only dating, relationships, and marriage (which among my interviewees were predominantly heterosexual relationships), but also a more extensive notion of kin that does not depend on biology or a nuclear family–based trajectory of procreation but is nonetheless characterized by mutual caretaking, lasting emotional bonds, and personal and collective well-being. This approach— considering intimacy and ethnoracial identity as deeply connected to place and potentially transformative of social relations—complicates the two-fold focus of much of the existing scholarship on relationships between whites and nonwhites and heteronormative notions of family and procreation.[3] As the experiences of a range of West SGV residents will illuminate, on a day-to-day level, people live a broader experience of inter-ethnic and interracial intimacy than dating and marriage, encompassing familial and close friendship ties as well as romantic and sexual intimacy.[4] Conversely, the patterns of affiliation that bring together interethnic and interracial couples are strongly shaped by a broad range of factors, including class, culture, and location.

This diversity of intimacies and meanings is the dynamic terrain out of which cross-racial identification and affiliation emerge. Diverse forms of interracial intimacy born of proximity and familiarity can be uncomfortable and contradictory, but—in one way or another—they are often integral to challenging people's abilities to assert fixed and stable racial and ethnic identities and transform the range of identifications and affiliations available to them. This underscores the important point that multiethnic and multiracial *affiliations,* if not identities, are experienced by a much broader range of people than only those who identify as "mixed race." As George Lipsitz has pointed out, "As an embodied identity, 'mixed race' is an accident of history. As an epistemology and a situated knowledge, as a standpoint from which to create strategic anti-essentialism and branching out, it is a powerful weapon of the struggle available to everyone."[5] Through their diverse everyday enactments of interracial intimacy as *an epistemology born of place,* the experiences of West SGV residents teach us yet another way in which racial identities are fluid, "multi-ethnic and polycultural from the get-go."[6]

"Most of Us Had a *Tío* or *Tía*": Mexican Asians and Chino Latinos

Most commonly, cross-racial intimacy took the form of close friendships and nonbiologically based kinship ties. These included everyday intimacies such as moving freely in and out of one another's houses, eating food made by one another's parents and relatives, and participating in friends'

family events. Such activities could lead to developing familial relationships with friends' relatives and identifying oneself with one's friends and
their culture to a great extent. For many, these nonromantic and nonbiologically based forms of intimacy also engendered an understanding of
race as performative, an openness to other people and other cultures, and
a highly developed and self-reflexive understanding of one's own racial and
ethnic identity. For Japanese American Adam Saito,[7] growing up around
"a certain kind of Mexican American culture" in a lower-middle-income
neighborhood in Alhambra meant that "you learn some Spanish too, and
so that communication sort of lets you be part of any particular groups
regardless of your ethnicity . . . It didn't really matter what you looked
like. . . . My uncle would tell people he was Mexican because that's what all
the people were around in the neighborhood." In Adam's neighborhood,
this racial blending went both ways: although any Asian person was "auto-
matically" a "chino," "even if you're Mexican and if you have more Asian
features or closer to indigenous. . . . you were also chino."[8]

Milo Alvarez observed this cross-cultural blending as well, when he
spoke of "Asian American folks that kind of grew up there [Monterey
Park and Alhambra] for a long time" that had become "a little bit more . . .
Mexican"; later-generation Mexican Americans and Asian Americans, he
felt, were "more like each other" than necessarily their own ethnic groups.[9]
This was true for more recently arrived generations too: Albert Huang, the
former mayor of San Gabriel, was a first-generation Taiwanese immigrant
and was known to some people as "the Asian Mexican." When I asked him
about this nickname, he responded: "Oh, well, the fact is . . . [I'm] Latino.
I'm as Asian as I'm Latino." He attributed this to the fact that he and one
of his best friends growing up in the West SGV, a Mexican American, were
"like brothers," and his design partner in his architectural office, a Chilean
immigrant, was also a "brother."[10]

For interviewees Maya Garcia[11] and Anita Martinez, the high degree
of closeness they experienced with Asian American female friends engendered a strong sense of identification and experience-by-proxy.[12] As
discussed in chapter 1, through Anita Martinez's close friendship with
Tina, a Vietnamese American, Anita experimented with "passing" and
learned about the nuances and performativity of race and culture, as well
as the concerns that this youthful fluidity sometimes triggered in adults (as
when Tina's mother admonished her daughter to "stop acting Mexican").
This practice went beyond the level of play, though, in that Anita felt a

deep *familial* identification with Tina and her family. As a later-generation Mexican American, she described her experience spending time with Tina's immigrant Vietnamese family in the following way:

> I never really had a really strong Mexican cultural background because so much of my family grew up here. So it was kind of nice to be part of . . . this really intact, close-knit family and culture . . . and see how that worked. . . . It was nice to see things that were traditional . . . to learn all these new things and to go out—oh, what am I eating? And I never had duck before. . . . Stuff like that. And I liked going to her house and just seeing her family and how they lived, and I got along with all her brothers and sisters. . . . It was just me and my brother in my family, so it was nice to be around all these siblings and stuff.[13]

By intimately partaking in the daily food, culture, traditions, and structure of Tina's family as a quasi family member, Anita was able to explore a different way of being in the world that contrasted significantly with her own home life and cultural background. In some instances, the level of closeness she experienced with Tina blurred the boundaries between herself and her friend. At one point, the two became estranged "over a guy." Anita had developed a serious crush on a Mexican American friend. After Anita changed high schools, though, the friend and Tina started to spend more time together and got romantically involved. Although Anita felt deeply betrayed, she eventually accepted Tina's apology and explanation: "After I got over it, she's like, 'I'm sorry, I'm sorry. First it was about you, but then it grew into something else.' And I'm like, 'Mm, I can understand. . . . You and I are so much alike, it'd be natural we would like the same guy.' So then I got over it." The way Anita was able to come to terms with the betrayal was to tap into her sense of herself and Tina as nearly the same person, to the extent that "it'd be natural we would like the same guy."

Tina, on the other hand, cultivated Anita's sense of familial intimacy with Vietnamese and Asian cultures by encouraging her to "pass" as Vietnamese (and more specifically, as Tina's cousin [see chapter 1]) and predicting that Anita would marry an Asian. As Anita described it, "She [Tina] would always tell me, 'I know you're going to marry a nip [derogatory term for a Japanese person].' That's what she would say—she would use that kind of language.' [Meaning?] Like, I'm gonna marry an Asian guy. She would always tell me, 'I know you're gonna end up with an Asian guy. I know it, I know it, I know it.'" Anita admitted that in elementary school, she had "big crushes on all the Japanese American guys—they were so cute." In high school and college, she casually dated some Asian American men. Ultimately, however, when she was twenty, Anita met her long-term boyfriend, a first-generation Mexican American, and had been with him ever since (at the time of our interview, she was thirty-seven). He had, she said, "helped me be more Mexican, like teaching [me] Spanish and stuff like that." Her boyfriend helped her to fulfill her long-standing desire for a deeper connection to her own culture and traditions—a desire she had previously explored through the daily intimacies of a close cross-racial friendship.

Even now, however, she still felt resonance with the place where she had come from and its ability to create affinities across race. When working recently for a local clothing company, one of her coworkers was a Chinese American woman who, it turned out, had grown up in the same neighborhood. Their mothers lived close to one another, and Anita knew the woman's sister. "We would both answer the phone, and people kept thinking we were the same person. And I realized that we probably have the same accent, or we talk the same way. . . . And I figured, you know, it's because we grew up in the same neighborhood. . . . She's Chinese American, I'm Mexican American, but we both have a similar way of speaking. I thought that was kind of interesting. That even after all these years, you know?"[14] For Anita, the cross-racial intimacies fostered by the neighborhood in which she had grown up still resided in her voice, body, and mannerisms and were also evident in the way she described her connection to her Chinese American coworker through neighborhood and familial relationships.

Like Anita, Maya Garcia came from an English-speaking, Mexican American household. Growing up in Alhambra, Maya also identified strongly with her Asian American friends. As a sophomore in high school, she visited Japan with a close friend and her friend's family. Her friend was a Nisei (Japanese term for second-generation, child of immigrants), and Maya began to think about immigration "from that experience more than from my own family's experience, because it was extremely important to her family that she understood that she was second generation." Later, when she thought about immigrant identity,

she thought about it "from that one friend's perspective." These formative identifications led Maya later on, as a college student, to become an
ethnic studies major. She remembered a junior high history teacher, a
Chinese American, who had "made sure that all of his students had an
understanding of the Asian American experience. So when I saw those
[ethnic studies] classes I was drawn to them—I know a little about this.
These were my friends, this was my experience."[15] Her phrasing here
is subtle but important: just as her closeness to her Nisei friend had
fostered her interest in immigrant identity, the "Asian American experience" resonated with her on a deeply personal level—not as someone
else's experience but as *her own* experience.

Her nostalgic and affective ties to growing up in the SGV, which
later became quite influential to her choices in college and beyond (e.g.,
majoring in ethnic studies and working in the education nonprofit sec-
tor in a major city, where she felt comfortable "anywhere," talking to
people of diverse backgrounds), were clearly a blend of Asian American
and Mexican American cultures. This became especially apparent when
she talked about food, which she experienced as one of the highlights
of growing up where and how she did. Her favorite foods from growing
up included "Korean curry rice, Japanese food—red beans with pancake
around it for dessert, Mexican food at people's houses, *pozole*, *menudo*,
a Korean friend's mom made *maki* rolls with hot dogs and cucumber."
In this sense, interethnic, interracial, and even postcolonial intimacy—
embodied by a Mexican American girl eating *maki* rolls with hot dog
and cucumber made by a Korean mother—occurred at the scale of an
individual being cared for in friends' homes and being fed by friends'
mothers.[16]

For Chinese-Vietnamese American Jenny Tran[17] and her friends,
eating food in each other's houses was also an important site at which
interethnic and interracial intimacy occurred, which she explicitly connected to mixed and multiracial families: "So many of us came from
mixed backgrounds . . . And like, yeah, we would still go to someone's
house and we'd be eating carne asada, or we would be eating noodles
or whatever it is, but I don't think it was ever really talked about in such
a conscientious way, except sometimes I would be like, 'hey I feel like
having noodles.' And so we would go over to someone's house because
they had noodles."[18] Importantly, for Jenny, a pervasive sense of multiethnic and multiracial familial identification, particularly across Asian

American and Latina/o cultures, did not stop with her biological family. When she stated that "most of us . . . had an abuela [Spanish for 'grand-mother'], we had a tía or a tío [Spanish for 'aunt' or 'uncle']," she meant it on multiple levels—literal, fictive, and figurative. In the following anecdote, she referred to the figurative aspect:

> My [Mexican American] friend [name omitted] and I always joke about the fact that he had a barbecue . . . and I was over there, and one of the *tíos*. . . he comes in, he doesn't bring anything, he's sitting in the corner drinking whiskey. And I'm just like. . . . *Every* family has that uncle, and some of us have three—you know what I mean? And we were just laughing at that, because a couple months ago, he had come to *my* family barbecue, and my uncle . . . was doing the same thing: comes in, doesn't bring anything, except that he just starts drinking whiskey and beer and he's just sitting in the corner talking shit. . . . *And so I think that these kind of friend-ships, that we see these kinds of similarities in each other's families, and because we make it that we are part of each other's families . . . this kind of proximity just makes so much sense.* [emphasis added][19]

By "proximity," she meant "the proximity of our cultures, the proximity of our living spaces, the proximity of the way we interact." The special inti-macy enabled by these multiple proximities fostered extended notions of kinship among Jenny and her friends. In some of these relationships, this feeling of kinship was explicit. Jenny had literal Mexican kin—a biologi-cal uncle who had married a Mexican woman and now lived outside of Mexico City—and she also had fictive kin:

> One of my closest friends, [name omitted], he's Mexican and Hawaiian. . . . his *abuela* is like, my *abuela*. I've known her since I was a kid, and everybody in his family I've known forever. And they helped raise me. And I call them *tío* and *tía*, [his] grandma I always call grandma. His mom and dad, I call mom and dad. . . . I still get phone calls from my friends' grandparents or their aunts and uncles, that are like, "'ey, where you been? How come you don't come around no more? You don't like us no more?" . . . that boundary of what is family and what's not family is very blurry, at least for me and my circle of relationships.[20]

Of course, these racial and cultural cross identifications and inter-actions did not always occur without friction. Most often, this friction stemmed from perceptions that Asian Americans enjoyed a higher socio-economic status—or felt that they did—than Latinas/os. One needs only to recall Salvadorean and Mexican American Oscar Ixco's pleasure and pain at being mistaken for Asian (and middle class) while growing up in a housing project on the border of East Los Angeles and Monterey Park (see chapter 1) or the sharp admonition to Anita Martinez's friend Tina by her Vietnamese mother to "stop acting Mexican." Forty-year-old Mexican American Walter Ruiz,[21] who grew up in Echo Park and moved to Alhambra as a young married man, struggled with a vivid early experi-ence of being discriminated against by Asian waitstaff in a local Chinese restaurant. This contradicted his stereotype of Asians as "really good businesspeople . . . people who would do anything to make a buck," and contributed to his impression of SGV Chinese as being "exclusive," "arro-gant" and "self-centered."[22] Years later, however, after becoming actively involved with his children's Boy Scout troop (see chapter 3), he found that most of his friends were Asian Americans. His wife, having known his ear-lier sentiments, would prod him: "'[H]ey, all of your friends are Chinese, or Japanese, how do you feel about that?,'" to which Ruiz would reply, "'alright, alright, I know, I was growing up, I didn't know any better, give me a break.'" The intimacy of friendships that grew out of his involvement in a local civic organization forced him to reevaluate his negative racial stereotypes—or at least confounded any easy generalizations.

As with Anita Martinez's experiences, within Ruiz's own household, the fluid and performative aspects of cross-racial identification also became clear. Ruiz's three children, born and raised in Alhambra, ran the gamut of the West SGV's readily available racial identities: while their daughter was "a typical American kid," his older son was immersed in Chinese culture. As Ruiz described it:

His friends call him an honorary Chinese boy. All his friends are Chinese. . . . His girlfriends have been Chinese. And when you see him, the only thing that interests him are Chinese things . . . he's definitely influenced by . . . the area where he goes to school, and uh, Chinese culture. I mean, he won't even say "shoot" . . . when-ever he's frustrated or surprised he says, "Aiyaa!" [Chinese slang interjection]. . . . I mean, that's his way of speaking, you know?

Which I find really funny. 'Cause he's this tall, lanky Mexican kid, and yet everything that comes out of his mouth is very kind of— "wow, did *he* say that?"

Finally, his younger son, who was ten, was "Captain Mexico"—an avid soccer player who loved to wear his Mexican national team uniform and was "so proud of being Mexican." The Ruiz children exemplified a regionally specific understanding that race and ethnic identity were not necessarily fixed identities but could be performative choices. For Walter Ruiz, the cross-racial identifications born of place challenged his previously held racial stereotypes and were also intimately embodied in his own children.

As these diverse life experiences teach us, nonromantic forms of interracial intimacy born of proximity and familiarity could be uncomfortable and contradictory, but—in one way or another—they were often integral to challenging people's abilities to assert fixed and stable racial and ethnic identities and transformed the range of identifications and affiliations available to them.

Interethnic and Interracial Romance: Dating the Mexican Boy across the Street

Nonromantic forms of intimacy did sometimes cross the line into romantic relationships, ranging from casual dating to long-term partnerships and marriage. Interethnic and interracial dating was relatively common in the experiences of both Asian Americans and Latinas/os in the West SGV.[23] Most commonly, interethnic and interracial romantic interactions grew out of sharing neighborhood spaces or school-based social circles. Thirty-one-year-old Lia Chen[24] remembered dating the Mexican American boy who lived across the street, whom she had known "since the day I moved in," when she was in eighth grade.[25] In high school, Milo Alvarez and Maya Garcia, now both in their late thirties, had racially mixed groups of friends who freely dated one another across ethnic and racial lines. For Maya, this pattern continued into her adult life: her college boyfriend was Chinese and white, and for much of the rest of her twenties, she was in a long-term relationship with a Taiwanese American (who had also grown up in the SGV, in nearby South Pasadena). True to the demographics of the region, the majority of interracial relationships were between Asian Americans and Mexican Americans. Thirty-one-year-old Japanese American

Mark Nakamura[26] recalled having Asian and Chicano friends and dating "half Koreans, and half Chicanas." However, due to the prevailing racial-social divide Mark experienced, which was heightened by his own and his friends' involvement in gangs, the crossing of such lines did not go unremarked: of his Chicana girlfriend, "people would say she was 'Asian-washed,' because she hung out with just Asians." Chicanos would look at Mark like, "what the hell are you doing with her?," while some "Asian girls would be like, 'ew, he's dating a Mexican girl.'"[27]

Twenty-two-year-old Vietnamese American Nancy Do began to date "mostly Mexican guys" after switching from public school in Monterey Park into a predominantly Mexican American, all-girls Catholic high school, with similarly populated brother schools. Now she felt she had less in common with Asian American men than Mexican American men.[28] Nancy was careful to specify that her choice of friends had as much to do with culture as with race: she felt distanced from certain Asian American subcultures, while her "mostly Mexican friends" shared her musical tastes, social interests, and "views in life." However, she described her romantic preferences in clearly racial and cultural terms. Referring to a brief phase in which she dated white men, she described them as "the Other for me. . . . Just in the same way Asian women are exotified [sic], I exotified them." She articulated her preferences in counterdistinction to values and char-acteristics she associated with whiteness: "That's why I date Mexican boys because I mean, you have a lot in common. You have certain values that are the same. Whereas I feel like in the white community, they don't have the same values. Like one value would be family. Mexican people have a very strong sense of family, and so do some Asian people. And I feel like white people don't. They're very . . . dispersed and disconnected." Nancy also associated these values with a particular geography and specifically with coming from the SGV: one of the things she did not like about the white men she dated—whom she associated with the wealthier and less racially diverse Westside of Los Angeles—was their lack of understanding of where she came from, literally. If she had been from the Westside, she believed, "then maybe it would have worked with some of the white guys. But I'm not. I'm from here, which is like a different subculture, and [it's] something from out of their realm of reality and they couldn't accept that, or they didn't understand it . . . so I started dating Mexican boys again."

She linked a gradual growth in mutual understanding between Asians and Latinas/os in the area to necessity-by-proximity: "I like the fact that

Mexican people or Latino people and Asian people are . . . in such close quarters, and that we are learning to understand each other more." As an example, she referred to her parents' initial opposition to her Mexican boyfriends:

> When I first dated a Mexican boy my mom didn't like it. . . . My dad, he would never say much, but he had his feelings, and they would come out when he was drunk. Like uh, he has stereotypes. When I had a Mexican boyfriend before, he was like, "why would you want to date them"—he made up his own term, "they're boozers," meaning drunks, "they're gonna beat you"—and I just responded with well, you're Asian, and you drink, and you used to hit mom. So, there's no difference. And that pissed him off. But . . . they got used to the Mexican boys.

Through what Nancy characterized as "a lot of disobedience" on her part, including directly challenging her father's racial stereotypes, her cross-racial romantic relationships eventually forced her parents to change their expectations and accept their daughter's choices.

Lia Chen, the Taiwanese American who dated her Mexican American neighbor, also described a qualified acceptance by her mother that likely would not have occurred without the familiarity that had developed in being neighbors. In Lia's words, her mother was "so Chinese in her racialization of people," with "clear lines of who I can and cannot marry"— which Lia understood to include "really just deep, racist stuff that they have about Latinos." Her mother told her explicitly that she did not want Lia dating or marrying anyone Latino. Lia questioned her mother about this: "What about [the] [family name omitted]'s son . . . ? And she's like, 'Oh, they're OK, because they're kind of white anyways.' . . . So my mom's idea of Mexicans are like, the [family names omitted] across the street from me . . . [who] don't speak Spanish and like, are basically very Americanized, you know? And so she's like, very comfortable if I dated someone like that. But if it was somebody who was like, a recent immigrant or spoke Spanish? Then she wouldn't be comfortable with it."[29]

Although the boy Lia dated "looked completely um, Mexican—he was like, dark-skinned . . . because his family was like—you know, they had very American, like white, dinners like meatloaf . . . my mom was like, 'oh, it's OK.' So it's just strange."

For Nancy Do, Mexican Americans' distinctiveness from whites made them acceptable for dating in her eyes. In contrast, Lia Chen's mother believed that Mexican Americans' ambiguous whiteness—equated with conceptions of "Americanness" as being assimilated to white, middle-class culture and opposed to recent immigrants—made them acceptable. In both instances, however, the familiarity made possible by shared space and proximity, as well as their daughters openly challenging the parents' racist beliefs through their dating choices, made this growing acceptance possible.

Like Nancy Do, Chinese-Vietnamese American Jenny Tran, now in her early thirties, felt that her racially and ethnically diverse social group coalesced most importantly out of shared musical tastes and a countercultural orientation. They were the "gutter punks": most were punk rockers, some were metal heads, but "I think what really kept us together was just because we hated everybody else."[30] As for many Asian Americans and Latinas/os who grew up in working- to lower-middle-class households in the SGV, class was also an important part of her group's social identity. Part and parcel of their immersion in antiestablishment music subcultures, as reflected by their own everyday experiences, was a burgeoning understanding that race and class were inseparable: "The punk, the hip-hop that we were listening to, was very conscious of race and what it meant to be in a colored body . . . [That] was very much part of our identity and very much part of how we understood the world." For Jenny, the diversity and countercultural orientation of her friendship group extended into her dating life. She shared her first kiss with an African American boy whom she met through b-boy and b-girl circles. She dated Mexican Americans; Asian Americans, including a female South Asian classmate with whom she went to prom; and fell hard for a friend who was "Japanese and Mexican, and Native American, and some other things too." They were all "punk rockers and people on the fringes." These early patterns developed into clear priorities in her adult life. Until her current partner, she had never dated anyone "Anglo," and tended to choose partners with similar backgrounds (working class, coming from single-parent homes) and political views, "who understand the way that for me, American society is constructed . . . through a racialized body." Jenny understood her romantic preferences as explicitly political. She believed that these patterns had been heavily informed by where and with whom she had grown up and also by her mother's encouragement to date someone who shared "the same experiences." When her mother encouraged her to find someone "like her," Jenny understood this not in a conventional identitarian way (e.g., find someone with the same racial/ethnic background) but in a way consonant with Jenny's own notion of extended and nonbiological kinship: someone who was from the same area, who had had similar experiences, and who had a mixed race background. Jenny admitted, however, that her mother struggled with her daughter's current choice of a white partner: "I think that was like the only instance where my mom was like, 'are you sure?' And she didn't disapprove of it in a way that was like, 'I don't like him' . . . It was always in terms of, are you sure he's gonna understand you? Are you sure that he's the right choice for you? Are you sure that he is someone that is going to be able to stick by you? . . . But I know a large part of it was because he's Anglo." Similar to Nancy Do's experience but differing from Lia Chen's (in which whiteness was seen as desirable and equivalent to "Americanness"), for both Jenny Tran and her mother, whiteness was an Other that contrasted unfavorably with more familiar nonwhite groups. This stood out in contrast to several other Asian American women I interviewed as well as national intermarriage patterns and a generally acknowledged "racialized hierarchy of desire" among Asian Americans in which whites ranked with, and sometimes even above, other Asians as the most desirable partners (with the caveat that in some circumstances other Asian groups, even within the same ethnicity, ranked at the very bottom).[31] Most of the Asians I interviewed were familiar with this hierarchy, whether or not they adhered to it in their own personal lives.

For twenty-nine-year old Mexican American Ben Avila,[32] the intersection of race and class was also a salient category of experience. Raised by an immigrant single mother who worked as a housekeeper, the Avilas lived in rental apartments mostly in Alhambra but used a family friend's address to allow Ben and his sister to attend the desirable public schools in neighboring, wealthier South Pasadena.[33] While Ben was aware that this was a relatively common practice,[34] he felt that "kids of color" like himself—particularly Latinas/os and African Americans—were "profiled" by the high school, such as being followed by the principal or another administrator after school or receiving a surprise visit at their residential address. Especially if any students who fit these demographics were "getting into trouble, they'd be trying to figure out a way to maybe get rid of you." As a result, throughout junior high and high school, he felt that he and other working-class Latina/o students never completely fit in. This awareness extended to his dating life. While he did not have a problem with dating across racial and ethnic lines, he felt that "the harder connections were . . . across socioeconomic classes. . . . There were these very wealthy kids that we would never date, and they would never date us."[35]

Despite describing South Pasadena as a "white neighborhood" and "your typical suburbia,"[36] Ben also noted that "there were Latinos who passed for white" and Asians "who had a similar identity to some of the upper-middle-class wealthy whites."[37] His mostly Latino male friendship group dated a group of girls whom he characterized as "mostly white" but also "more complex than that." In fact, many of the girls he dated identified as having mixed ethnic and racial backgrounds. Through dating young women within this diverse social circle, "white identity for me started kind of disintegrating. Like girls that I would date, initially I would bet, oh, they're white. Then like, oh, wait, they're white and this. Or they're white but . . . they see themselves as Scottish American or Irish American. Something weird where they start tapping into their family history." Eventually, one of the women from this high school social circle, who is Dutch Indonesian, became Ben's long-term girlfriend. Four years after my initial interview with Ben, they had two young children and lived in South Pasadena—although Ben, with his ambivalent relationship to the class dynamics of South Pasadena, might have preferred to continue living in Alhambra. Alhambra, he felt, was "kind of this empty space" that afforded him a relative anonymity and freedom: "you don't feel like you get stuck anywhere." With its comparatively heterogeneous class composition and modest everyday landscapes, it was an escape from the predominating upper-middle-class and wealthy culture and carefully cultivated built environment of South Pasadena.

Close attention to the accounts offered by West SGV Asian Americans and Latinas/os who dated and formed long-term relationships interracially reveals that perceptions of shared values—such as valuing family, a countercultural orientation, or a similar class background—were important factors. While for some people, these were also important considerations for friendship, serious romantic relationships were often more consciously and introspectively evaluated and provided opportunities (welcomed or not) to work out complex identities tied to race and class among parents and children. Place served as an active factor in working out these relationships and identities, whether due to intimacies born of proximity or through identification or disidentification with one's surroundings.

SGV Dreamgirl? Multiracial and Multiethnic Families and Individuals

Out of these various forms of intimacy—whether part of longer or more recent histories—multiracial families and the melding of diverse cultural traditions became the norm for many SGV residents. For individuals with multiracial backgrounds, however, growing up in the SGV was sometimes less ideal than it might have seemed, despite—or even because of—its Asian American and Latina/o majority.

"I Had the Asian Look, but I Knew Spanish": Discomfort, Flexibility, and Passing

Thirty-year-old Elena Tanizaki-Chen's[38] Japanese American father and Mexican American mother grew up in Boyle Heights and Lincoln Heights and met through shared social circles within East Los Angeles's "large . . . Hispanic and Asian community."[39] After a stint in San Luis Obispo, where Elena was born, the couple divorced and moved the family back to Los Angeles, where they settled in Alhambra, Monterey Park, and Monte-bello (which neighbors Monterey Park to the south). Both of her parents remarried—her mother to a Mexican American man (who she later also divorced) and her father to a Japanese American woman. Elena spent the rest of her childhood living first with her mother and then with her father when she went to high school. In Elena's words:

> I talk about being a majority, yet only half of me at one time was
> a majority. So I never felt comfortable as a biracial person that
> looked 100 percent only one of those races. I think it was really
> just a societal thing, the way that I was constantly having to dispel
> people's perceptions of me. . . . People just assumed that I was
> 100 percent Asian. . . . Maybe if I was more immersed in either of
> my ethnicities, in the way of the native language or culturally or
> something, that I would not feel sort of half and half. I can't really
> explain it. But I always knew that I was sort of walking the line. I
> never felt a deep, deep identification with either of the cultures.[40]

She felt discriminated against by Latinas/os who thought she was "full Asian"; Japanese Americans who did not consider her to be "Japanese enough"; "non-Hispanic, non-Asian folks" who believed her to be "100 percent Asian"; and Asians who did not know she was also Latina. In the last instance, she might be "amongst a group of Asians, and someone in the group is stereotyping and making inappropriate comments about Hispanics."

In contrast to frequent interactions such as these, which she characterized as "really uncomfortable," if "not in such a hurtful way that you usually think [of as] discrimination," Elena found comfort in a long-term relationship with a boyfriend who had the same mixed, racial and ethnic background as she did: "It was definitely convenient. We just had a better understanding for each other because of it. A better understanding of his family. I probably felt comfortable a little quicker." Thinking of the future with this boyfriend, she found comfort in the fact that she would have "very similar experiences" as her children. After that relationship ended she eventually got together with the man who became her husband, a second-generation "100 percent Chinese" American whom she had first met in high school years earlier. Initially she felt "very cautious when I thought I would have kids with this guy who is not of Japanese and Mexican descent." She felt she had to learn a lot more in order to date her husband than she had to date her biracial ex. However, four years after our initial interview, after giving birth to their first child, Elena now felt "a lot more comfortable with the idea that my kids are more mixed than I am." They lived in a diverse neighborhood in West Los Angeles, where Elena felt that there was "a lot more variety" than in the SGV, which both she and her husband agreed was important for their child.

Elena experienced growing up biracial in the West SGV as far from a dream but instead something that was at once comfortable and constantly uncomfortable, even "stifling" (in her words). In her view, the predominantly Asian American and Latina/o mix was diverse, "but it could have been more diverse." To be what Elena "looked like" (Asian) was so common that her actual ethnicities were rarely recognized, leaving her with a constant feeling of being misrecognized. She noted:

> I probably would have been more comfortable living in Peru, or
> a lot of other places in the world, where it is more common that
> you would speak a language other than what you look like. I've

traveled through Central and South America, and they never really question my identity. When I was in Peru, I know that there were people that thought I was local. . . . Part of when I described the San Gabriel Valley being stifling, it's kind of a mentality—people don't really think globally. I think probably most of America is probably like that.

For Elena, then, as a biracial person, the West SGV did not function as a cosmopolitan and diverse space, but rather still represented a limited American mode of thinking about race, in which racialized expectations about one's character and behavior based on what one looked like were impossible to escape.

SGV brand cofounder Eladio Wu, who is ethnically Chinese and grew up in Costa Rica and Mexico until age eleven, also struggled to figure out where and how he fit in the SGV. When I asked whether he felt he fit in growing up, he answered:

Sometimes I did and sometimes I didn't—because I had the Asian look, but I knew Spanish. I had the Latino culture, and I didn't know English at the time, so it was kind of odd for me. Like, say, when I was outside I feel good, but when I go back inside I'm a different person, just because I couldn't relate to nobody.

Outside, do you mean, out of school?

Yeah. Out at school, out at social life. But then when you go home it's a different story. Everybody's different. So it's like you could relate, but I couldn't relate at the same time.[41]

Eladio made friends with Latinos, "a couple Asians," and some African Americans as well. But his mixed friendship group and multiple alliances, at a time at which tensions between young Asian Americans and Latinas/os were high, sometimes caused consternation. At school he might be approached by "random students" who would be "in your face" and ask him, "'are you with the Asians or with the Latinos?' And I just [said], 'I'm with nobody.'" At San Gabriel High School, his sister encouraged him to join the Mexican American Student Association, a club to which she had belonged. However, when Eladio went, "I walked in, and I was the only Asian there.

Everybody else was Latino, so everybody looked at me like, are you lost? What's going on? What do you need? Are you delivering anything? So after that . . . I didn't go no more."

In contrast to Elena and Eladio, Chinese and Mexican American Russell Lee-Sung felt quite at ease in the predominantly Asian American and Latina/o mix in which he grew up in Monterey Park. Lee-Sung's parents, a Chinese woman from Shanghai and a Mexican and Chinese American man from El Paso, Texas, met in Los Angeles, and Lee-Sung was born in Monterey Park in the mid-1960s. The family initially lived in Chinatown. Then, after his parents divorced, his mother took him and his sister to Monterey Park. Lee-Sung's father had been raised by his Mexican mother and "did not know his Chinese father at all":

> So pretty much his upbringing was a very Mexican upbringing. . . .
> When he came to Los Angeles, when he was about . . . maybe
> twelve, thirteen years old, he was not accepted either way. Because
> the Chinese people didn't accept him because he wasn't full
> Chinese, the Mexican people didn't accept him because he wasn't
> really Mexican. And so he did experience a lot of racism growing
> up in the L.A. area. But eventually he did tend to gravitate more
> to the Asian side because he started working in Chinatown and . . .
> ended up having a lot of contacts there. So even though he speaks
> fluent Spanish, he probably spends more time in Chinatown
> because of that. . . . He has a lot of friends that are Hispanic also. So
> it's both. And white.

Lee-Sung's father raised him and his sister to speak English only and assimilate to mainstream American culture as much as possible, "because when he grew up, in L.A., in order to really succeed, you had to speak English. You had to be more American, more mainstream."

Perhaps this directive influenced Lee-Sung to leave the area when it came time to go to college. He decided that the racial mix in the area felt *too* comfortable and decided to go to Pepperdine, a predominantly white private university in the exclusive beach community of Malibu, in part to socialize himself among whites. In his words, "I wanted to get away from the community that I was very comfortable in, which was Asian and Hispanic, and go and experience different people, and different culture, and that kind of thing. And it did exactly that [laughing]."[42]

As a result—of feeling "different" and in the minority for the first time in his life—Lee-Sung felt that after coming back to the area, he was able to engage with whites effectively and with ease in his position as a school administrator, in a way he would not have been able to otherwise (see chapter 2 and the conclusion).

As Elena Tanizaki-Chen, Eladio Wu, and Russell Lee-Sung's experiences illustrate, multiracial Asians and Latinas/os came to live in the SGV through crisscrossing local, intranational, and international pathways. Rather than embodying any kind of generalizable multiracial experience, they might feel uncomfortable and misunderstood or, like Lee-Sung, cultivate a chameleon-like flexibility and facility to thrive in any environment. In fact, in some ways, the heterogeneity of their histories and experiences, more than their Asian and Latina/o ancestries, was the aspect of their identities that was most representative of the West SGV. Indeed, a focus on Asian and Latina/o intersections in some ways obscures the highly heterogeneous experiences of individuals within these racial categories and even within ethnic categories.

Tanizaki-Chen, Wu, and Lee-Sung did have at least one experience in common, though. For all three, usually the Asian part of their heritage was assumed and often imposed on them to the exclusion of the Latina/o aspects. In contrast, for those with mixed white and Latina/o backgrounds (admittedly a redundant phrasing for many because of the legacy of European colonialism in Latin America), identifying wholly as Latina/o was comfortable, even as they were sometimes identified as white by others and might even use this to their own advantage. As mentioned earlier (chapter 2), Dora Padilla, a Mexican American whose Mexican father had German heritage, used her light-skinned appearance and German maiden name (turned middle name) to her advantage when running for the school board in Alhambra. Though she used her ability to "pass" for white strategically, this never conflicted with her strong identification as Mexican American. And even though twenty-year-old Jesse Boden[43] acknowledged that his Swedish last name "may speak differently" for him, he had grown up primarily with his Mexican American mother's side of the family and never identified as white. In his own words, "I don't really identify with my dad's . . . culture, you know, with that background. . . . I would say definitely growing up where I did and with the family I did, that it's definitely shaped my perspectives." While in general he was quite comfortable with a Latino and specifically

Mexican and Mexican American identity ("If someone asks me, I am Mexican because my family is from Mexico"), he did feel that his mixed-race identity was important when it came to social justice issues. Since he experienced it at an intimate level in his own family, being mixed race gave him a heightened understanding of the differences between living life as a white person with majority-racial status in contrast to a minority: "because of . . . my status as a minority *and* . . . someone [in the] majority . . . I see that division most clearly. I'm more aware of it when I'm concerned with, like, social justice issues and . . . politics and things like that."[44]

"We're a Little Different": The Heterogeneity of Asianness

For Asians with complex ethnoracial backgrounds, the pan-ethnic term *Asian American* proved useful.[45] Eighteen-year-old Annie Liu,[46] whose father is Chinese and mother is Korean-Chinese, usually tells people simply that she is "Asian American."[47] Similarly, Jenny Tran, whose ancestry is "mostly Chinese . . . Vietnamese and . . . partially Anglo" and identifies most strongly as "a woman of color," will generally "just say I'm Asian American, because they don't want a long matrix of how you identify yourself." Though she identified as multiethnic, she clarified that to her this meant not only "the ethnic or racial composition of my background" but also how she grew up.[48]

Twenty-one-year-old David Wong,[49] the son of a Japanese American mother and a Chinese American father, might explain that he is "half Chinese and half Japanese" or answer as he did in the following anecdote:

> Last week I was in North Carolina . . . And I was on the bus and someone said, "Are you from the Philippines?" And I said, "No, I'm from California." So . . . I don't feel like I identify so much as being Japanese or Chinese or mix[ed]—I feel more American really, than anything else. I mean, ethnically not, but you know, just culturally, I feel pretty much American.
>
> *Mm-hm. And how did that person respond [when you said] "I'm from California"?*
>
> Then they wanted to know where I was *really* from.

Did you kind of purposefully not come out with that right away?

Yeah. Yeah, I do that, you know. Because, well, they thought I was a foreigner.[50]

To David, saying he was from California provided relief from what felt to him like incomplete and ill-fitting "labels" (of which he declared himself to be "not a fan"). At the same time, he understood what was "really" being asked and took the opportunity to refuse to satisfy the questioner's presumptions, which equated his looks with foreignness.

For forty-eight-year-old Susie Ling, who is ethnically Chinese and grew up in the Philippines before immigrating to the United States as a young adult, her self-identification varied by context.[51] In "Chinese contexts," she identified herself as "Filipino Chinese, just to get away from expected norms, or where my language [referring to Mandarin Chinese] collapse[s]," while politically, she identified herself as "Asian American, no question." Married to a third-generation Japanese American, with whom she had children, a pan-Asian identity was very important to her "because of my political agenda as well as my cultural situation." She also described herself as "obviously very pro . . . multiculturalism, for personal agenda reasons. You know, it makes my children and me much more accepted by the community."[52]

For Jenny Tran, David Wong, and Susie Ling, the local heterogeneity of Asians—and specifically the predominance of upper-middle-class, immigrant ethnic Chinese—was also a factor in their identity formation. Jenny Tran remembered being conscious of skin-color hierarchies among Asians, being "very conscious of the fact that I was always one of the darker-skinned Asian Americans," and being "taller and bigger than everybody, so everybody always thought that I was Hawaiian or Samoan. And a lot of times a lot of their families wouldn't let me play with them because . . . they weren't sure . . . what my background was." In particular, she remembered being mercilessly teased by another girl, who was Chinese and "very fair-skinned":

> To this day, I still think she was one of the meanest girls I have
> ever met in my whole life. . . . And she said to me, something
> along the lines of, "Ew, why are you always out in the sun? It's just
> going to make you *darker*" . . . [My friend] Veronica and I, we were

both dark-skinned . . . she's the one who's mixed, Mexican and
Filipina. . . . Veronica and I would be running around, you know,
playing with the monkey bars, and hanging out with the boys. . . .
She [the mean girl] *always* sat in the shade. . . . And I was just like,
oh, is that what does it? It's the sun? So if I stay out of the sun, then
I won't be dark? And I told my mom that, and my mom was just
like, "no, honey, you were just born that way". . . . And it was just
like, OK, well maybe that's why *she's* staying out of the sun, because
she doesn't want to be *my* color. . . . And I remember what she was
wearing too, because during that time, everybody was rocking out
on LA Gears [tennis shoes]. . . . I could never afford LA Gears. And
I always remember that she had LA Gears and . . . and I was like,
man I wish I had those LA Gears [laughing].[53]

In this way, the mean girl as well as other Asian American students social-
ized Jenny to realize her difference from an Asian female norm that was
seen as desirable and valued light skin, wealth, small stature, and "ladylike"
behaviors. Instead, she found acceptance and identified with her ethno-
racially mixed friendship group, which included friends like Mexican and
Filipina Veronica, who like Jenny was "dark-skinned" and physically active.

David Wong felt that in areas in which Asians were more concentrated,
such as on Valley Boulevard, he and his family did not really fit in, "even
though we're Asian." Apart from his mother being Japanese American, his
father was a later-generation Chinese American:

I mean, my dad just barely speaks Chinese. . . . [H]e comes from
a more American Chinese [background]. So that really isn't us,
even though we might look Asian—going to 99 Ranch [a large
pan-Asian supermarket] really isn't us. I mean, we go there for
certain things, but really, we just go to Ralphs and Costco, or
whatever. Going to eat dim sum every weekend—a lot of people
do that—that's not us. . . . Whereas I know a lot of my friends,
perhaps whose parents immigrated here from China or Hong Kong
or whatever, they really like that, because they're very comfortable
and at home. But for us, we wouldn't be very comfortable.[54]

He gave another example, of when his parents enrolled him in group piano
lessons when he was five years old:

And everybody in the class was Chinese. . . . And so my dad and my mom would alternate taking me. Now, one day we have to get the pieces for the recital ready, and the teacher says, "[N]ow you gotta fill out this form with the name of the song." Well . . . the names of the songs were not in English. . . . Every other parent was doing it for the kid. Well, my dad cannot write Chinese. I mean, he can write his name, but not, you know, just start writing something down. So you know, you feel that you really don't fit in. You realize that you're not part of this [pause] enclave . . . because we're a little different.

From these experiences, David realized that while people might assume a racial and cultural sameness between him and his peers, he felt a clear distinction in his daily life: he was Asian "but not in the same way as these other people."

In Susie Ling's need to identify herself as Filipino Chinese to other ethnic Chinese and Jenny Tran and David Wong's sense of difference from other Asians, it's clear that certain characteristics were associated more strongly with a stereotypical "Asianness" (e.g., "going to 99 Ranch," "going to eat dim sum every weekend," or more class-inflected characteristics such as valuing light skin and dressing in brand name clothing). However, the heterogeneity of Asians in the SGV, even among ethnic Chinese, made each of them aware of the specificity of their own histories and identities within the mix and able to search for broader and less essentialized forms of identification: Susie Ling as Filipino Chinese and Asian American, Jenny Tran as a woman of color, and David Wong as a Californian.

Conclusion

In the late twentieth and early twenty-first centuries, the multiracial and multiethnic diversity of the SGV was undeniable. While these highly multiracial and multiethnic individuals and families were certainly shaped and informed by the social, historical, and political conditions that made the West SGV the place it is today, they were actually neither representative nor exceptional. In scratching the surface of the multiracial dream of the SGV, what one finds is an irreducible heterogeneity that cuts across gender, generational, racial, class, and ethnic lines. What people did have in common, though, was an awareness of this heterogeneity—which led to multifaceted possibilities for affiliation and identification as well as intimate interactions and connections that blurred ostensibly fixed boundaries. The multiple proximities both experienced and imagined by SGV residents ("the proximity of our cultures, the proximity of our living spaces, the proximity of the way we interact," in Jenny Tran's words) added up to a particular kind of situated knowledge, in which place served as both the binder and producer of transformative understandings of race, ethnicity, and identity.

A story from a San Gabriel resident, a Latino man in his forties whom I'll call J.,[55] illustrates this point well: At a recent meeting concerning a civic issue, the attendees—predominantly "old-guard," white, north San Gabriel residents—spoke disparagingly about Asians, evoking racist stereotypes in the process. Afterward, an elderly white woman, whom I'll call Mrs. M.—herself one of the old guard, who had stayed silent during the meeting—came up to J. Clearly pained, she asked, "Why do they have to talk that way? You know, my daughter-in-law . . ." J. knew that Mrs. M.'s son had married a Chinese woman, and so she now had half-Chinese granddaughters. Although to all outside appearances, Mrs. M. herself had not changed, she had been transformed by her daughter-in-law and granddaughters. The words her colleagues used might have seemed innocuous to her before, referring to a comfortable "them," but through familial intimacy, "they" had been transformed into a jarringly resonant "us." Perhaps this is what it really means to have an "SGV state of mind"—to see the dream of the place as a set of multiracial identifications, affiliations, and politics that have the potential to disorder dominant racial and social hierarchies and are potentially available to all of us.

How Localized Knowledges Travel

IN THE DECADES after World War II, channeled by systemic patterns of housing discrimination that steered them away from more exclusively white areas but valorized them relative to would-be African American homeowners, Asian Americans and Latinas/os became neighbors in the West San Gabriel Valley (SGV). In these communities, they forged friendships, especially as youths, and practiced a moral geography of differentiated space. Compared to whites, who fled the area en masse, an expectation and acceptance of difference rather than sameness kept Asian Americans and Latinas'/os' numbers relatively stable during a rapid influx of ethnic Chinese immigrants to the region that began in the late 1970s and has continued into the present day. Throughout, both Asian Americans and Mexican Americans took advantage of the availability of diverse housing options in the West SGV's lower-middle-income to middle-income residential landscape, in the process complicating the symbolic dimensions of American homeownership and giving rise to new paradigms of race and privilege. Through everyday practices of friendship, romance, love, and family, West SGV residents formed intimate cross-racial relationships that gave rise to strong multiracial affiliations and identifications and were often highly influential to their own identity formation. For many, the "multiple proximities" (e.g., of location and culture) experienced by Asian Americans and Latinas/os imbued the West SGV itself with a multiracial place identity.

At the same time, in the mid- to late 2000s, in school and other civic institutions, Asian Americans and Latinas/os formed an overwhelming majority but at key moments struggled to make sense of their daily worlds vis-à-vis powerful national discourses and ideologies about race including the model minority myth and color blindness. Individuals' ways of making sense of the social order were tied intimately to the particular regional context in which they lived. The nuances of their reactions and interpretations of the social order around them revealed dissonances and contradictions between regionally specific knowledges and dominant racial hierarchies. Civic institutions inculcated particular societal orders and mores, yet these were imperfectly internalized—never quite settling as commonsense, taken-for-granted truths. On several main public thoroughfares, racialized struggles regarding civic landscapes took place, revealing sedimented historical geographies of race as well as continuing uneven power relations.

Throughout this book I have shown how everyday landscapes and people's experiences within them can be simultaneously saturated with dominant racial ideologies and their attendant material outcomes and rich with alternative narratives of pasts, presents, and futures. These conflicts and emergent identities, shaped both within and against hegemonic ideologies and constituted by a host of often mundane interactions at neighborhood, municipal, and regional levels, make up the "accumulated history of a place."[1] Their contradictions and possibilities illustrate the importance of considering neighborhoods and regions as units of analysis in order to understand processes of racial formation. Cumulatively, they add up to a not fully articulated, yet definitely formed, *regional racial consciousness*, similar to Raymond Williams's idea of a "structure of feeling."

Although I have described at length several strong and persistent themes that I believe define the history and recent past of the West SGV, even in the five years that have elapsed since I began my research, the rapid pace of change in this area has continued. Although the 1980s through 2000s saw, for the most part, a relative parity between Asian Americans and Latinas/os in terms of relative numbers and socioeconomic status, the Asian—and especially ethnic Chinese—population has continued to grow, and the Latina/o population has begun to decrease. Although the SGV's Asian population remains ethnically heterogeneous and its ethnic Chinese population is actually highly heterogeneous as well (in terms of generational status, country of origin, and class), its *racial* heterogeneity may have begun to decline, with Asians becoming a clear majority presence in an increasing number of spaces. However, as we have seen throughout the book, this process is uneven and complex and often does not reflect deeply entrenched power hierarchies. Nor does it represent an inevitable trend, with easily predictable outcomes. Also, importantly, the relative socioeconomic parity of Asian Americans and Latinas/os in the area has remained consistent—especially when compared to whites' much higher economic status—creating a similarity in class strata that has

been integral to Asian Americans and Latinas'/os' abilities to share neighborhoods and build cross-racial affinities.

British cultural theorist Paul Gilroy has put forth a notion of conviviality, which he describes as the "processes of cohabitation and interaction
that have made multiculture an ordinary feature of social life in . . . urban
areas and . . . postcolonial cities." Distinct from multiculturalism and
color-blind racism, conviviality does not claim "the absence of racism or
the triumph of tolerance" but rather puts into practice a "radical openness
that . . . makes a nonsense of closed, fixed . . . identity and turns attention
toward the always unpredictable mechanisms of identification."[2] Looking
at racial formation through a regional lens allows us to locate this kind of
radical openness in everyday practices, feelings, and actions and to ruminate on its specific features, outcomes, and limitations. One of the most
important effects of regional racial formation is that the consciousness
that emerges from it, while rooted in place, is not limited to place. It can
constitute a lasting world view. This thought leads to a final and crucial set
of observations about regional racial formation—that it travels.

On a basic level, the ways people experience shifts and transformations in their understanding of racial orders and power hierarchies as they
move between different locations and contexts—a cognitive version of
what geographer Neil Smith has called "jumping scales"[3]—speaks to the
importance of grounded, everyday experiences in the formation of ideas
and attitudes about race. They also illuminate a range of possibilities and
limitations in further articulating a critical theory of regional racial formation. Within the context of the West SGV, salient examples of such
possibilities and limitations include Mexican Americans' experiences of
intraregional boundaries; the limits of Asian American racialized privilege; and finally, the development of multiethnic, multiracial knowledges
and affiliations that are both regionally specific and mobile.

Jumping Scales in *El Barrio Chino*

While many Mexican Americans proudly claimed the SGV as a fluidly
multiracial place, some, especially a few who had grown up poor and in
neighborhoods that experienced a rapid rate of change, struggled with
the new racial dynamics. The complexity of the area and their own family histories and personal geographies, however, gave them the tools to
engage in multiscalar analyses that did not simply construct Asians as

racial scapegoats. To take one example, Juan Ramirez[4] was able to link a transnational, historical interpretation to his experiences growing up and living in the area. After moving from Monterey Park to Alhambra in the 2000s, Ramirez remembered how one of his young son's friends, upon visiting the Ramirez family's newly purchased house, proclaimed that they had moved to "*el barrio de los chinos* [Chinatown or Chinese district; literally 'Chinese neighborhood']."[5] Ramirez's young son and the boy's friend were just beginning a process that Ramirez had gone through himself, having had Chinese neighbors his whole life and trying to make sense of what seemed to be their increasing dominance compared to Mexican Americans in the Monterey Park neighborhood where he lived as an adolescent. From very early on, Ramirez had made transnational associations, connecting "*la tiendita del chinito*" (a small grocery or store owned by a Chinese person[6]), where he grew up in Monterey Park, and "*la tiendita del chinito*," close to where he spent summers with relatives in a border city in Mexico: "I had grown up knowing that . . . Mexicans and Chinese people had interacted for a long time historically. I knew that just as part of the family history. For instance, my grandmother remembered the attacks on Chinese people in Mexico . . . when they were kicked out of California, a lot of them went to Mexico. There were lynchings and mob riots. My grandmother told us, when I was a little kid, that Chinese people would hide in her house, [because] of mobs of people attacking Chinese families. . . . There's a lot of memory about this."[7]

The understanding embedded in Ramirez's family history that "Mexicans and Chinese people had interacted for a long time historically" made him constantly aware of transnational and historical forces connecting the fates of Mexicans and Chinese, complicating his perceptions of and reactions to local developments. When sections of his childhood neighborhood were categorized as blighted in the late 1980s and began to be demolished, a move many in the predominantly Latina/o neighborhood blamed on "rich Chinese people," Ramirez's own strong emotions were tempered by the awareness that other forces, such as white elites who had long wielded power in the region, were also involved. The Ramirezes' family memories, tied to larger collective community memories and cumulative experiences up to the present, showed how day-to-day experiences that exposed the intricate, small-scale boundaries of the local world could also lay the groundwork for cognitively "jumping scales"—drawing connections and making meaning between geographic scales and across larger areas.

Forty-year-old Walter Ruiz's[8] account of an experience in a Chinese restaurant on Valley Boulevard after moving from Echo Park to Alhambra in the early 1990s (also described in chapter 5), offers another example of intra- and multiscalar analyses of classed and racialized dynamics. Ruiz and his wife—who was then pregnant—were going out to eat and decided to try a new restaurant. When the couple walked in, they noticed that only one table was occupied with diners, who appeared to be an Asian family, including a "Caucasian boyfriend or husband." After several minutes passed and they were blatantly ignored by two separate workers, "I realized what was happening. We were basically being ignored. They were waiting for us to leave."[9] Although his wife implored him to just walk away, Ruiz was so enraged that he picked up a chair and threw it across the restaurant before walking out. The incident "left an indelible mark on my psyche": "I remember walking away from that experience and feeling [long pause] I don't know how to [pause] feeling different. . . . Like I wasn't treated like a human being. I was less than a human being to them, because they were willing to let me just stand there with my [pregnant] wife. . . . I was so contemptible to them that I wasn't even worth sitting down and you know, [being] offered a glass of water or a menu or something like that." His incredulity that this experience was the "first time I'd really been discriminated against," and the sting of feeling like he was considered "less than a human being" led to a number of reflections about place-based experiences of interracial and interethnic interactions. As previously mentioned, the experience also disrupted stereotypes he had previously held of Asians as "really good businesspeople . . . people who would do anything to make a buck," marking class- and race-inflected boundaries within Alhambra in a way that Ruiz had not previously felt and forcing him to make connections regarding class divisions within Asian as well as Latina/o communities:

I don't look at the Chinese in Chinatown the same as I look at the Chinese in Monterey Park. I think of Monterey Park, they're much more exclusive . . . they have more walls around them. And I think they're more arrogant . . . self-centered. . . . But you get the same thing from Hispanics in Montebello. I have friends who are from Montebello, when they look at people from let's say, East L.A., they have the same mentality: "[W]e've pulled ourselves out of the muck, and we don't want to be like that anymore, so we're gonna build walls, and we're different from you."

He also speculated about how one racial minority could treat another in this fashion. Being treated by Asians as lower in the racial hierarchy disturbed his expectations of how the racial hierarchy worked. He "genuinely believe[d] that any Asian person walking into a Mexican ... restaurant—in Echo Park or anywhere like that, I don't think they [would] ever be turned away." Thinking that the Asian restaurant workers must themselves have experienced overt racial discrimination in the past "from other cultures, maybe Anglos, or maybe even Hispanics," and that it was a "learned trait" or "defense" helped Ruiz somewhat to make sense of it. However, he also made the comparison that for him, "it was like being a Black person in the South": "I'm not saying I have four hundred years of oppression behind me, but it was difficult to swallow. It still is. It's still a very vivid memory that I don't think I'll ever get over."

Ruiz's struggle to make sense of the experience led him to analyze it at multiple scales. Instead of attributing the actions of the Chinese restaurant's Asian workers to individual racism, he thought about the complexity of class differences within ethnic and immigrant groups and made intraregional and national connections. (Still, his comparison to being treated like a Black person in the South shows how racism is often reduced to and naturalized as a Black and white problem.) Simultaneously, the experience marked lasting boundaries within the local area, changing his "outlook on ... where I could go." Now, for fear of losing his temper again if a similar incident occurred, he did not feel he could go to "*any* restaurant": there were ones he might avoid or only go to with a Chinese-speaking friend. Although none of this ultimately helped Ruiz to "get over it," his thought process in trying to sort through the experience, which remained vivid in his mind, showed the potential for "jumping scales" in the analysis of interracial and interethnic interactions and how the incident's meanings were not fixed, even years later.

The Limits of Racialized Privilege

While Mexican Americans, as sometime minorities in the West SGV, had plenty of opportunities to ruminate on racial hierarchies at multiple scales, for Asian Americans, the transformation of localized knowledges into racial consciousness often occurred upon leaving the West SGV. As discussed in chapter 2, in some local contexts—particularly institutional ones—many Asian Americans experienced a racialized form of privilege.

However, when Asian Americans left the area—especially middle-income Asian Americans who left for the first time to attend college—they were often disoriented by the presence of much larger numbers of white people. Their previous sense of relative privilege evaporated. While Mexican Americans wrestled with a perceived Asian–Latina/o divide within the West SGV, Asian Americans more often focused on white–Asian divides and discussed the effects of jumping scales via traveling or moving outside of the area. For example, eighteen-year-old Annie Liu,[10] who grew up in Alhambra under close supervision of her Taiwanese father and Korean-Chinese mother, had this to say about her experience at a UCLA orientation only twenty-five miles west, on the Westside of Los Angeles: "When I went to UCLA, I felt that I was really a minority . . . because when you're in Alhambra, you don't feel like a minority. It's sort of like when you see a Caucasian, the Chinese term [is] . . . 'foreigner' [*laowai*], right? . . . but when you go to a college campus, you're the minority again, so it's like, you're the foreigner. So it was kind of a wake-up call . . . a surprise for me to see, like, wow, there are so few Asians compared to where I come from."[11] In the fall of that year, however, Asians actually constituted the relative majority of UCLA's undergraduate enrollment (38 percent). Where UCLA differed the most from the West SGV was not actually the number of Asians but a higher percentage of whites (34 percent) and a lower proportion of Latinas/os (15 percent).[12] It seems possible, then, that although she did not understand it as such, Annie may have been reacting to the latter differences more than to the scarcity of Asians—a hypothesis that is well supported by her fellow West SGV residents' reflections that follow. In either case, Liu's experience expressed the degree to which the particular mix of the West SGV was normalized for residents, especially those who had grown up there.

For Grace Ahn (Korean American, Alhambra), Russell Lee-Sung (Chinese Mexican American, Monterey Park), and Lisa Beppu (Japanese American, South San Gabriel/Rosemead), going to college was also a significant moment in which they realized that the place they had grown up in was not like other places. For many Asian Americans, college represents a key setting in which pan-Asian or Asian American identities are developed for the first time.[13] For West SGV Asian Americans, however, going to college often had a much different meaning: Instead of constituting their first opportunity to encounter concentrations of Asian American youth, it was often the first time they had encountered large numbers of white people. As discussed in chapter 5, Russell Lee-Sung left Monterey Park in the mid-1980s to attend Pepperdine, a private, "almost entirely white," Christian university in Malibu, "because I wanted to get away from the community that I was very comfortable in, which was Asian and Hispanic, and go and experience different people, and different culture, and that kind of thing. And it did exactly that [laughing]." Lee-Sung recalled his first days there: "I did not know a single person at Pepperdine. . . . So that right there was pretty scary. And then the other part is you walk onto campus and *everybody's* white, you know. So *that* was strange. I mean, I could just feel it. Because when you're in Monterey Park, everyone is dark-haired, dark-eyed, you know. You go to Pepperdine, everyone has, you know, light hair and light eyes. And so, walking through there . . . I felt, like, everyone looking at me because I looked very different."[14] Lisa Beppu's experience at Chapman College in the early 1980s (a small private college approximately thirty-five miles south, in inland Orange County) was similar to Lee-Sung's: "[I]t was a *very* uh, awakening experience for me, because until that time there are things that I had never experienced. Like, the thing that always sticks with me, is that I had never felt short before. You know? Like, for a Japanese girl, I'm pretty tall, you know? I'm like, about 5'4" and a half, and all of a sudden, I felt short! 'Cause there was all these six-foot guys, and a sea of blue eyes and blond hair."[15] Grace Ahn, traveling a hundred miles north from Alhambra to attend coastal UC Santa Barbara in the mid-1990s, "felt like an alien there":

Did it feel really white to you?

Yes. [emphatically] I felt really small on campus.

Physically?

[pause] Maybe. Physically. Emotionally, I think. . . . I felt like an alien there.[16]

The vivid, visceral nature of Lee-Sung, Beppu, and Ahn's memories of these initial displacements from the West SGV shows how race is always an embodied experience in place: "You walk onto campus and everybody's white. . . . *I could just feel it." "The thing that always sticks with me,* is that I had never felt short before." "A sea of blue eyes and blond hair." "*I felt really small. . . . I felt like an alien* there [my emphases]." Similarly, twenty-one-year-old David Wong,[17] who is Chinese and Japanese American and grew up in Alhambra before attending UC Berkeley for college, described the difference for him between walking "into a room full of Asians versus walking into a room of all white people": "I would feel much more comfortable—I mean, just to be honest—with the Asian. . . . Maybe it's a stature thing . . . you know, like height difference." Wong traced this feeling back to an experience in high school, when he attended Boys State, a selective, week-long camp in Sacramento for teenaged boys with demonstrated leadership skills. Wong felt "intimidated" by the white boys, who constituted the majority of the participants. He felt that they were "older," "taller," and "more sophisticated" than him. The other boys treated him badly, "but I just took it, because for some reason, I felt like they were all my superiors rather than peers." Wong felt his own unease had very much to do with growing up in a predominantly Asian American, majority-nonwhite environment. If he had grown up in a predominantly white area, he probably could have "gone there and just been one of the bunch." As it was, the experience still stung years later: "I still feel—I think about it, and I feel [pause] different."[18]

For Lee-Sung and especially Beppu, their sense of unease or not belonging was sometimes substantiated by the way they were treated. Lee-Sung remembered an incident in which a university staff member assumed he was a foreign student:

> I remember . . . coming up to a table, standing in line . . . and
> the person asked me for my green card! . . . [brief pause] I was
> like, I can't believe you just assumed I'm a foreign student, you
> know? [laughing] And it's like, "No, I was born here in the United
> States"—in a very firm voice, looking [at him] right in the eyes.
> 'Cause that's not right—you can't just *assume* that I'm a foreigner
> like that. I was kind of upset. And that had never happened to me
> before. But that was kind of how they looked at anybody who
> wasn't white.

Lisa Beppu related several incidents, while attending college in Orange County or traveling in other areas, when she would get "that *look*," which said, "What are you doing? You don't belong here." She recalled going to apply for jobs in the summer and getting the feeling that "they're not even going to consider me" and one incident in which "some kid" rode past her on a bike yelling, "You Jap!" Beppu's brother told her that he didn't like to visit her there, following an experience at a restaurant in which he sat at the counter and was never served.

Clearly, then, there were limits to a West SGV–developed sense of what I have called Asian American racialized privilege. Moving as little as twenty-five miles away, people could feel physically and emotionally alienated. From Lee-Sung and Beppu's accounts, it is apparent that, in some moments, they struggled simply to be treated like human beings (echoing Walter Ruiz's experience in the Chinese restaurant on Valley Boulevard). Racist assumptions and attitudes (that Lee-Sung was not American or that Beppu could not even be considered as a prospective employee) could make a material difference in their opportunities at a basic level. The trappings of Asian American racialized privilege, predicated on racial expectations that reinforced white dominance such as the model minority myth, failed when transported to contexts in which whites were clearly dominant. Confronted with unpleasant contradictions upon leaving, many Asian Americans now saw their experiences growing up in the West SGV in a much different light.

Jinny Hong[19] (ethno–Chinese Vietnamese, thirty-one), who grew up in Monterey Park and now lived in San Gabriel with her Mexican American boyfriend, was strongly aware of the opportunities she felt she had as a result of the area's particular ethnoracial mix. Specifically, in high school, she was class president all four years and traveled the country in youth leadership circles. Later, she was elected Miss Junior Chinatown and "worked the Miss Chinatown circuit" for a few years. When I asked Jinny how growing up in the West SGV had influenced how she thought about race and ethnicity, she responded in part with an anecdote stemming from her travels as a youth leader:

> As a child I wasn't exposed to many white people or Black people, but . . . when I did have to go to the South for leadership and such, the first person to call me a "nip" was a white person, and the first person to come to and defend me was a Black person. . . . I won't forget those things. . . . So I'm just very open to trying to understand people, and part of it is just growing up here. . . . I'm not too sure if I would have been given all the opportunities, you know, something as simple as being class president, something as simple as somebody

take you under their arm and being exposed to all these things at a very young age. Something like Miss Junior Chinatown—is there a Miss Chinatown in Missouri? So just all those experiences.[20]

For Jinny, the racial consciousness she developed "just growing up here" meant that she was able to link her simultaneous experiences of the opportunities and limitations of racialized privilege with a consciousness of a larger-scale racial hierarchy informed by white privilege and a connection between anti-Asian and anti-Black racism.

"As a Community, People Have a Personality"

As Jinny Hong's sentiments indicate, while the limits of racialized privilege were just as real as the sense of subordination some Mexican Americans felt about living in a "barrio chino," these coexisted with a pattern of regional racial thinking in the West SGV that *did* travel. This was the idea that "as a community . . . people have a personality," as Lisa Beppu put it. The "personality" of the West SGV—as discussed extensively in chapters 1 and 5—frequently included among its characteristics a sense of affiliation tied to place and linked to a majoritarian nonwhite identity and the development of particular kinds of knowledges. As discussed, this way of thinking was sometimes generational and associated with having grown up in the West SGV. Often, however, it did not develop in a more conscious way until people moved away from the area or traveled and then evaluated how they felt and what they found in comparison with what they had known growing up. For example, Beppu described how her perception of subtle daily interactions in and outside of the West SGV changed after she moved to Orange County for college:

> At college . . . and then just even out and about that town, there's always one thing that stands out in my head. As a woman, right, if you go in and out of the door, they would just close the door right in front of your face, OK, with not a backwards glance. Whereas here [in the West SGV], in this community, a woman comes towards the door, a man will hold it open for you, even wait for you, if they see that you have bags in your hand. And you don't always experience that in Orange.[21]

Later in our interview, when I asked Beppu how she would describe what she called the "personality" of the West SGV, she elaborated:

> You know, like, what I was telling you about before about how men will hold the door open for you? So I think because most of us in this community have an immigrant background, people tend to still have a little bit of the old-school manners, you know, just common courtesy about certain things. . . . And I like that there's a mix of cultures, you know? Because my kids, they're all mixed up. That's the world. . . . You need to be able to know how to live with, work with, be friends with different cultures, backgrounds, communities. That's the future, you know? And it does still feel to me like family.

Like Eloy Zarate and the Friends of La Laguna in their struggle to save Monster Park, Beppu, who is a third-generation Japanese American, located shared "immigrant" mores as a source of commonality for West SGV residents, although she then widened the description to "you know, just common courtesy about certain things." Ultimately, like many other West SGV residents, she tied the sense of the community feeling like "family" to knowing "how to live with, work with, be friends with different cultures, backgrounds, communities"—a localized and community-based expression of cosmopolitanism.

Jinny Hong described the West SGV as "a community where people are supportive of you." After her family arrived in Monterey Park in the early 1980s as refugees from Vietnam (via a refugee camp in Hong Kong and a brief stint in North Carolina), her father passed away suddenly. Her mother, who did not speak English and was functionally illiterate, was left to be the sole provider for their family of eight. To get by (as mentioned in chapter 1), her mother grew vegetables in the backyard of their rented triplex to sell to local Asian markets and sewed piecework for a factory, as well as receiving government assistance. Jinny felt that there were few communities in which her mother would have been able to find these types of opportunities: "[W]here else would she have had that opportunity to go sell vegetables at a supermarket, right? Or where else would she have the leverage to say, sew from home and watch kids at the same time?" Even now, whenever she passed by the markets that had bought vegetables from her mother, Jinny would think, "'[T]hose people gave my mom the opportunity,' you know?" Jinny, like Lisa Beppu, also felt that this sense of support and understanding crossed racial and ethnic boundaries. As an example, she related an anecdote about her mother purchasing a propane tank from a worker who was a Mexican immigrant:

> Her English is very broken, and she'll go speak to the man who's going to hook her up with like a propane tank, you know, because she needs a propane tank, and they understand each other, because I think that you know, he speaks broken English, she speaks broken English, he's Mexican . . . she's Chinese, right. They can barely understand each other, but I do think that there's also this understanding of, "You know what? We're both here and this is what we want and this is how we're going to get it, and this is how we're going to help each other." And there's a lot of that. There's a lot of that on many, many scales. I do business here now in the San Gabriel Valley, and a lot of the businesses that I come across, there's that kind of camaraderie. . . . there is that support.[22]

David Wong and Anita Martinez also experienced a sense of camaraderie that exceeded singular racial or ethnic identities and traveled with them to other locations and contexts. Wong related an experience when he was visiting relatives in North Carolina and was stranded on a Greyhound bus:

> We got completely stuck. And they took a lot of people off and transferred them to another bus, so there were only maybe about a dozen of us left on the bus. And there were a Hispanic . . . mother and son. And then there was a white guy who was about my age, and then there were three German girls . . . and then there was a Black couple. Pretty diverse group. But just thinking about it, in retrospect, I was talking to the Mexican couple, in Spanish even, and I'm terrible at Spanish. But I felt more at ease than . . . when I was talking to the white guy . . . That's just the way I am, and maybe you know, I have a problem. [laughs] But yeah, I guess if you think about it, I felt very comfortable with them. I laughed, I joked, it was very enjoyable.

Anita Martinez described a similar sense of comfort when as an adult, she moved to Lincoln Heights, a hilly, working-class Asian and Latina/o neighborhood just north of Los Angeles's Chinatown:

It was almost kind of like being in the San Gabriel Valley. . . .
Where I live now, we live in a four-plex. . . . The bottom floor,
it's . . . me and my boyfriend, the other family [is] Mexican, and
upstairs, Chinese. And it feels natural to me . . . it's not weird or
anything. Although they [the Chinese neighbors] can't really
communicate that well, we still get by with gestures and hand
signals. And if I really need to tell 'em something, I'll go to, what
is that, Babblefish [a translation website], I'll type it out and
print it in Chinese [laughing] so I could give it to them. And it
works![23]

Martinez and Wong expressed a high level of comfort and even pleasure
with the labor of communicating across linguistic and cultural divides,
even with very limited tools, indicating a sense of ease and familiarity that was clearly defined by factors outside of shared language and
culture.

Like Martinez and Wong, Mexican American Gina Alvarez, growing up in Alhambra, articulated a sense of being part of a multiracial,
nonwhite majority. Alvarez, as mentioned in chapter 1, moved slightly
out of the area to Temple City as an adult and decided when choosing
schools for her two daughters that she wanted them to grow up with a
similar sense of comfort in being part of the "majority." For Alvarez, this
meant choosing schools with fewer whites and more children of color.[24]
For these children of the West SGV, then, the sense of "feeling like the
majority" was not necessarily defined by which racial or ethnic group
had the largest numbers. Instead, it often translated into a traveling sense
of comfort in multiracial, multiethnic, *nonwhite* settings, and sometimes
even purposefully seeking out such settings. They also learned particular
skills and developed a comfort with communicating across racial, cultural, and linguistic divides, leading to a sense of connection that was
both familiar and deeply exhilarating. Milo Alvarez (Gina's older brother) explained:

Having been to some places—I've been to the Midwest . . . the
East Coast . . . New Mexico . . . I've never seen anything like this
community here. . . . I feel very connected to it as a place that was
home. Now what does that home represent? It represents these
sort of changes that took place in my lifetime, that I witnessed

with my own eyes. . . . I have this good feeling about that. . . . It was like, these groups that sort of worked together in this weird, sort of crazy way, trying to figure each other out, you know?[25]

Conclusion

A large part of my challenge in this work has been to make sense and meaning of relationships that are complicated, while not compromising their complexity. However, as a famous thinker with better words than mine has pointed out, the task here has not been to "introduc[e] from scratch a scientific form of thought into everyone's individual life" but "renovating and making 'critical' an already existing activity."[26] Accordingly, Milo Alvarez's insight that "these groups that sort of worked together in this weird, sort of crazy, way" was tied to "trying to figure each other out" is an important one. It points to how studying regional processes of racial formation can unearth knowledges and practices that constitute already existing alternatives to dominant notions of interracial relations among nonwhites in the United States. Instead of supporting a pendulum-like model, in which "race relations" swing perpetually between the two poles of conflict and cooperation, a multiracial regional analysis illuminates a spectrum of experiences that are constantly shifting and often contradictory. A regional field of analysis allows a fine-grained analysis of the production of both hegemonic ideologies and counterhegemonic ways of thinking in everyday landscapes and institutions of civil society. It also opens up a "third space"[27] that shows us how people find commonality and connection in ways that escape and disorder dominant hierarchies of power, without ignoring or denying them. In fact, more often than not, this indeterminate space of connection and commonality is explicitly informed by a clear-eyed consciousness of the destructiveness and injustice of racial and social hierarchies.

By defining the "region" in relation to racial formation as a set of social relations and processes common to a place or set of places, a regional approach provides a comparable lens through which to consider suburban as well as central urban and rural racial hierarchies, as well as those processes that link and define different "types" of space. In further research, a comparison of dynamics across multiple regions would certainly enrich and extend these arguments. While I have examined in detail some aspects of neighborhoods, schools, and civic spaces, considering other elements, such as labor and workplace dynamics, should also be important to further developing a regional racial frame of analysis. Ultimately, however, my hope is that one could use these principles to think through just about any area, toward a deeper understanding of how racial dynamics and norms, as well as the creation and practice of alternative world views, are inextricably tied to place and scale.

Cognitive Maps of Race, Place, and Region

WHAT DEFINES the West SGV as a place? How do regional racial hierarchies shape its contours, its internal and external boundaries? How does this vary for individuals whose bodies are differentially racialized, gendered, and classed? To begin to get an idea of the answers to these questions, cognitive mapping proved to be illuminating. I asked forty of the people I interviewed to draw maps of their regular pathways within the West SGV and how they imagined it cohered as a region. A sampling of the resulting maps and some brief discussion of their implications follows.

Thirty-five-year-old Salvadorean and Mexican American Oscar Ixco mapped his world growing up in the Maravilla public housing projects, literally at the border of East Los Angeles and Monterey Park. Three

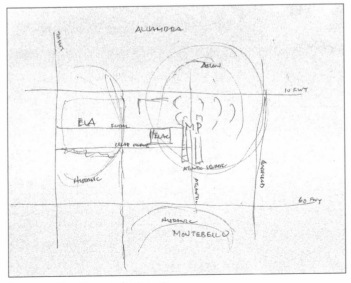

Figure 20. Cognitive map by Oscar Ixco.

freeways defined the structuring lines. East L.A. and Monterey Park adjoined at the center at East Los Angeles College, and the cities of Alhambra and Montebello flanked the north and the south, respectively. Ixco also marked Asian and Hispanic spheres: the Asian in Monterey Park and Alhambra, and Hispanic in Montebello and East L.A. Ixco went to elementary school and junior high in Monterey Park but lived just across its borderline: indeed, in a land grab by Monterey Park in the 1951, the city had taken land right up to, but not including, the Maravilla projects.[1] Ixco lived this municipal bifurcation, happy to be occasionally mistaken for Asian at school—since in his mind, those were the middle-class kids who lived in single-family homes in Monterey Park— and ashamed at the end of the day to go back to the projects (which, although predominantly Mexican American, housed people of a variety of racial and ethnic backgrounds).

People's maps also showed a regional cohesiveness to adjoining municipalities and challenged traditional conceptions of urban versus suburban functions.

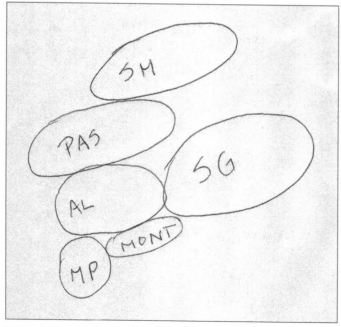

Figure 21. *Cognitive map by Karen Toguchi.*

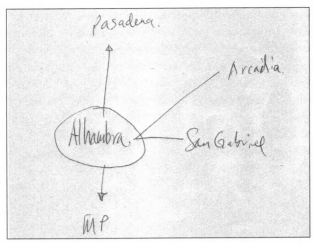

Figure 22. *Cognitive map by Stephen Sham.*

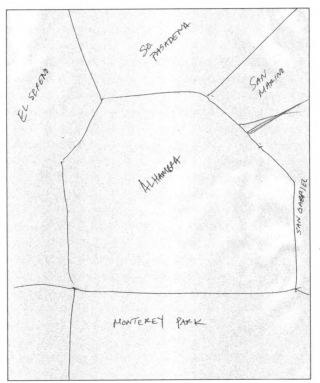

Figure 23. *Cognitive map by Ben Avila.*

These maps above—drawn by Karen Toguchi, a sixty-three-year-old, third-generation Japanese American woman living in Monterey Park; Stephen Sham, a forty-two-year-old, first-generation Chinese American from Hong Kong living in Alhambra; and Ben Avila,[2] a twenty-nine-year-old, first-generation Mexican American—show how people's regular paths in the West SGV are likely to consist of five or six adjoining municipalities and often do not take them west of Monterey Park, Alhambra, and Pasadena (with the exceptions, for some Mexican Americans, of El Sereno and occasionally East L.A., which are directly west of Alhambra and Monterey Park). The following maps, drawn by Elena Tanizaki-Chen,[3] a twenty-nine-year old Japanese and Mexican American woman who grew up in Monterey Park and Montebello, and Romy Uyehara, a thirty-three-year-old Japanese American woman raised in the Monterey Park hills, show a similar sensibility—and again, that freeways and major roads are important dividing lines.

Some maps also showed an even broader regional fetch, dictated by family ties and work and school obligations (but still not conforming

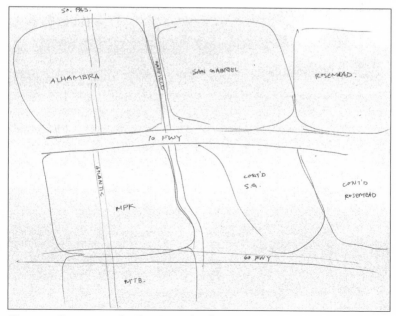

Figure 24. *Cognitive map by Elena Tanizaki-Chen.*

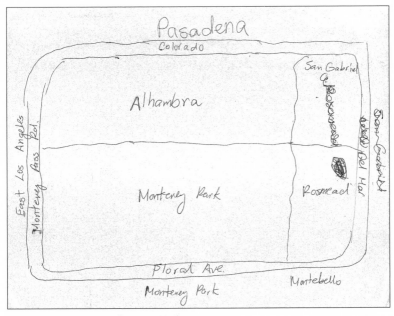

Figure 25. *Cognitive map by Romy Uyehara.*

to traditional conceptions of city-suburb interconnections). Thirty-one-year-old Korean American Grace Ahn, who grew up in Alhambra, now lives and works further east in the SGV but still retains ties to Monterey Park and Alhambra, in a southwest-to-northeast arc of municipalities that, with the exception of Monrovia, all have majority-Asian American populations (and conspicuously exclude the whiter and wealthier northwestern SGV cities of Pasadena, South Pasadena, and San Marino; Figure 26). Similarly, twenty-six-year-old Mexican immigrant Gloria Enriquez's[4] map of her regular pathways (directionally flipped) moves east from where she lived in Rosemead to El Monte, a predominantly Mexican immigrant and Mexican American municipality where she worked at a locksmith business owned by an aunt and uncle, and significantly further (about twenty miles) to Pomona, where she attended community college.

In contrast, maps drawn by people who had only just completed high school or left the area shortly after high school are considerably smaller-scaled than either of the types already mentioned. Ethno–Chinese Vietnamese American Paul Pham's[5] map features a subsection of

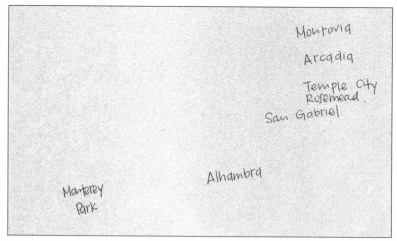

Figure 26. *Cognitive map by Grace Ahn.*

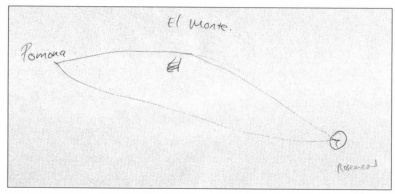

Figure 27. *Cognitive map by Gloria Enriquez.*

Alhambra and Monterey Park not more than four miles square, bounded at the north and south by Main Street and Garvey Boulevard. Similarly, Korean American Riva Kim's map is bounded primarily by Main Street in the north and the 60 Freeway at the south (an additional two miles south of Garvey Blvd; Figure 29)—although Pham and Park both indicate trips outside of the immediate area for restaurants, groceries, and shopping.

While not surprising, considering the constraints and dependencies of adolescents' worlds, these are nonetheless indicative of the relatively small geographic scales at which people develop first—and

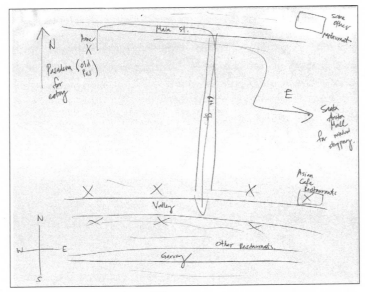

Figure 28. Cognitive map by Paul Pham.

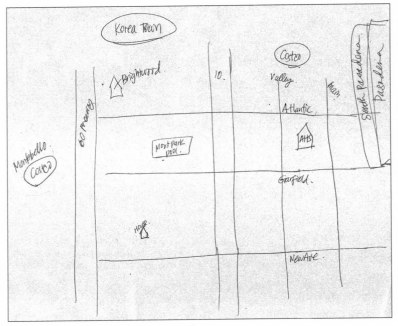

Figure 29. Cognitive map by Riva Kim.

formative—understandings of the relationships between race and place. They also suggest the grounded material effects of racial divisions at multiple scales: at the metropolitan level, discriminatory housing policies that pushed nonwhites into the Greater Eastside of Los Angeles, and at the neighborhood and municipal and intermunicipal levels, major thoroughfares that serve as contested dividing lines between different populations.

Notes

Introduction

1. All ages mentioned refer to the age of the person at the time of the interview, unless specified otherwise.

2. Interview with Laura Aguilar, March 10, 2007.

3. SGV brand website, http://www.sgvforlife.com.

4. Ibid.

5. Interview with Paul Chan and Eladio Wu, June 5, 2008.

6. U.S. Census 2010.

7. Zhou, Tseng, and Kim, "Rethinking Residential Assimilation," 53–83.

8. South San Gabriel is an unincorporated community between Rosemead and Monterey Park with a relatively small population, whose history is tied to that of the larger region in several important ways. (In 2010, South San Gabriel's population was 8,070, compared to Alhambra, 83,089; Monterey Park, 60,269; Rosemead, 53,764; and San Gabriel, 39,718 [U.S. Census 2010].)

9. Moctezuma and Davis, "Policing the Third Border." See also Fong, *The First Suburban Chinatown*.

10. As of 2010, Asian Americans made up 59.5 percent of the total populations of Alhambra, Monterey Park, Rosemead, and San Gabriel, and Chinese and Taiwanese made up 67.5 percent of the Asian Americans (calculated from 2010 U.S. Census).

11. This was cumulatively 30.9 percent (calculated from 2010 U.S. Census).

12. This was approximately 236,840 (calculated from 2010 U.S. Census).

13. Saito, *Race and Politics*, 158–80.

14. This was cumulatively 81.7 percent in Alhambra, Monterey Park, Rosemead, and San Gabriel, ranging from 77.5 percent in Alhambra to 85.2 percent in Rosemead (calculated from 2010 U.S. Census). On the longer histories of Mexican Americans in the region, see Ochoa, *Becoming Neighbors in a Mexican American Community*; and Garcia, *A World of Its Own*.

15. Fong, *The First Suburban Chinatown*.

16. Garcia, *A World of Its Own*; Ling, "Pre-War Japanese Americans in the San Gabriel Valley"; Ling, "The Early History of Chinese Americans in the San Gabriel Valley," 25–52. For instance, Alhambra resident David Tong's father, a Chinese American immigrant from Hawaii, sold fruit from a cart in South Pasadena and Alhambra in the 1930s and had previously worked as a ranch hand in

Diamond Bar, at the eastern edge of the SGV, approximately twenty miles east of Alhambra (Interview with David Tong, September 28, 2007).

17. Saito, *Race and Politics*; Fong, *The First Suburban Chinatown*; Ochoa, *Becoming Neighbors*; Toyota, *Envisioning America*.

18. Gilmore, *Golden Gulag*, 30–86.

19. Ong, Bonacich, and Cheng, eds., *The New Asian Immigration*; Saito, *Race and Politics*.

20. Tseng, "Suburban Ethnic Economy"; Zhou, "How Do Places Matter?," 531–53; Li et al., "Chinese-American Banking and Community Development," 777–96; Li, "Spatial Transformation of an Urban Ethnic Community," 74–94. Zhou has estimated that ethnic Chinese in Los Angeles have more bank branches per capita than any other group (although of course this does not guarantee use or access) (Zhou, "How Do Places Matter?"; see also Li et al., "Chinese-American Banking and Community Development").

21. Ong, Bonacich, and Cheng, *The New Asian Immigration*, 3–35; López-Garza and Diaz, eds., *Asian and Latino Immigrants in a Restructuring Economy*.

22. 32.2 percent of Latinas/os living in Monterey Park, San Gabriel, Alhambra, and Rosemead were foreign-born, and 12.9 percent were recent immigrants (since 2000), compared to 67.4 percent and 26.6 percent of Asians, respectively (calculated from U.S. Census, 2006–2010, American Community Survey). For Latinas/os, these proportions stayed nearly the same as in 2000 (32.9 percent and 12.6 percent, respectively); however, the percentage of foreign-born Asians decreased (from 73.2 percent in 2000). The percentage of recently immigrated foreign born also went down for Asians: in 2000, 37.3 percent of foreign-born Asians had immigrated in the previous ten years (since 1990; calculated from U.S. Census 2000, Summary File 4).

23. In 2010, median household income for Asians in the core area was $51,704, compared to $50,730 for Latinas/os. The countywide median household income was $55,476 (calculated from U.S. Census 2006–2010, American Community Survey).

24. In 2010, Asians' per capita income in the West SGV was $21,511, while Latinas/os' per capita income was $20,002. Non-Hispanic whites' per capita income was $40,843 (calculated from U.S. Census 2006–2010, American Community Survey).

25. In 2010, the median household income for Latinas/os in Los Angeles County was $44,989, compared with an average median household income of $50,730 for West SGV Latinas/os. West SGV Asians earned a median household income of $51,704, compared to $64,367 for Asians countywide (calculated from U.S. Census 2006–2010, American Community Survey).

26. In 2010, the median household income for Latinas/os in Los Angeles County was $45,076, compared with an average median household income of $54,507 for West SGV Latinas/os. In Alhambra, median household income among

Latinas/os was $52,372, compared to $49,972 among Asians. Non-Hispanic whites made the most, with $60,278 (calculated from U.S. Census 2006–2010, American Community Survey). In these cities, as of 2010, approximately one in five Latina/o workers were employed by the state (compared to around one in seven of Asian workers; calculated from U.S. Census 2006–2010, American Community Survey).

27. A total of 47.5 percent of West SGV Asians lived in owner-occupied housing, compared to 44.3 percent of Latinas/os. Also, 32.8 percent of Asians held management and professional jobs, compared to 27.9 percent of Latinas/os. Exactly 19.7 percent of both groups held service jobs. About 30 percent of both groups held sales and office-related occupations. Whites held management and professional jobs at much higher rates than either Asians or Latinas/os (49.7 percent) and service jobs at a much lower rate (10.3 percent; calculated from U.S. Census 2006–2010, American Community Survey).

28. This reflects available data (U.S. Bureau of the Census, 2007 Survey of Business Owners). In 2002, approximately two in three businesses in Monterey Park and San Gabriel (and nearly half in Rosemead) were owned by Asians, while only one in ten were owned by Latinas/os. Number of Latina/o-owned businesses in Rosemead not available; numbers for both groups were not available for Alhambra (U.S. Bureau of the Census, 2002 Survey of Business Owners).

29. Fong, *The First Suburban Chinatown*; Saito, *Race and Politics*; Pardo, *Mexican American Women Activists*; Horton, *The Politics of Diversity*; Calderón, "Mexican American Politics in a Multi-Ethnic Community"; Tseng, "Suburban Ethnic Economy."

30. Li, "Building Ethnoburbia," 1–28; Li, "Beyond Chinatown, beyond Enclave," 31–40; Li, "Spatial Transformation of an Urban Ethnic Community"; Li, *Ethnoburb*.

31. Zhou et al., "Rethinking Residential Assimilation"; Zhou, *Contemporary Chinese America*; Zhao, *The New Chinese America*; Toyota, *Envisioning America*.

32. Omi and Winant, *Racial Formation in the United States*, 55.

33. On the production of geographical scale and the social production of space more generally, see Lefebvre, *The Production of Space*; Smith, "Contours of a Spatialized Politics," 55–81; Marston, "The Social Construction of Scale," 219–42; Brenner, "The Urban Question as a Scale Question," 361–78; Brenner, "The Limits to Scale?," 591–614; Marston and Smith, "States, Scales and Households," 615–19; Swyngedouw, "6 Scaled Geographies," 129–53. On "place" and "region" within conceptualizations of scale, see Paasi, "Place and Region," 536–46. For a critique that advocates the abandonment of the conceptual use of scale altogether, see Marston, Jones III, and Woodward, "Human Geography without Scale," 416–32. For an overview of debates regarding scale within the field of geography, see Sheppard and McMaster, *Scale and Geographic Inquiry*.

34. In his discussion of racialized landscapes, Richard Schein uses the phrase

"moments of racial formation" in his own analysis of Omi and Winant: "The concept of race becomes a matter of 'both social structure and cultural representation,' and the ideological linkages between those *moments of racial formation* take place through racial projects" (emphasis added). Schein goes on to connect these concepts to "racialized landscapes": "Clearly, a racialized landscape is a racial project, one that is not only sociohistorical, but also sociospatial. As such, a racialized landscape serves to naturalize, make normal, or provide the means to challenge racial formations and racist practices" (Schein, "Normative Dimensions of Landscape," 203–4). See also Schein, *Landscape and Race in the United States*, and Cheng, "The Model Minority in the Model Home."

35. Pulido, "Rethinking Environmental Racism," 12–20. Pulido quotes Melvin Oliver and Thomas Shapiro.

36. Massey, *Space, Place, and Gender*, 156.

37. Ibid., 139.

38. Pulido, *Black, Brown, Yellow, and Left*, 26–27.

39. See Robinson, *Black Marxism*.

40. Gilmore, "Race and Globalization," 22. Therefore in Gilmore's oft-quoted definition of racism, as "the state-sponsored and/or extra-legal production and exploitation of group-differentiated vulnerabilities to premature death," the second part of the definition—that these processes occur "in distinct yet densely interconnected political geographies"—though often left out, should not be overlooked (Gilmore, *Golden Gulag*, 243).

41. Woods, *Development Arrested*.

42. McKittrick and Woods, *Black Geographies and the Politics of Place*, 4.

43. Pulido, *Black, Brown, Yellow, and Left*, 26–27, 29. Pulido's comparative study of Black, Latina/o, and Asian American Third World left activist groups in Los Angeles in the 1970s is anchored by an understanding of the regional economy of Southern California at the time, each racialized group's structural position within it, and how their corresponding socioeconomic positions in turn shaped their political priorities. See especially chapters 3 and 4. For example, for the Black Panthers, whose communities were suffering from massive unemployment, ghettoization, and police harassment, survival and self-defense were primary concerns, while the more middle-class-based Japanese American East Wind activists foregrounded issues of leadership and community service, and the Chicana/o organization CASA (El Centro de Accion Social y Autonomo) focused on issues of immigrant rights and labor organizing. Pulido also found that residential demographic patterns—informed by residential discrimination as well as by affirmative decisions by residents—played a large role in activists' development of political consciousness. As one Japanese American described such sociospatial relations: "If you lived in Boyle-Heights, you hung out with Chicanos and acted Chicano. If you grew up in South Central, you hung out with Blacks and acted Black" (56).

44. Among these Pulido (*Black, Brown, Yellow, and Left*) is the only one who explicitly theorizes the phrase "regional racial hierarchies" (26–27).

45. I capitalize "Black" to signify the distinctive identities and cultures that have arisen from the racial designation (just as "Asian" and "Latina/o" are capitalized). I do not, however, capitalize "white," since rather than being constituted by distinctive identities and cultures, this is a category that is typically formed by the exclusion of others.

46. Respectively, Loewen, *The Mississippi Chinese*; Almaguer, *Racial Fault Lines*; Foley, *The White Scourge*; Glenn, *Unequal Freedom*.

47. Leonard, *Making Ethnic Choices*; Molina, *Fit to Be Citizens?*.

48. Kurashige, "The Many Facets of Brown," 56–57.

49. Ibid., 57.

50. On coalition building in labor and political activism, see, for example, Pulido, *Black, Brown, Yellow, and Left*; and Kurashige, "The Many Facets of Brown." On the day-to-day formation of interracial friendships and alliances, see Garcia, *A World of Its Own*; Widener, "'Perhaps the Japanese Are to Be Thanked?,'" 135–81; Sánchez, "'What's Good for Boyle Heights Is Good for the Jews,'" 633–62; Kurashige, *The Shifting Grounds of Race*; Varzally, *Making a Non-White America*.

51. Garcia, *A World of Its Own*. Also see Tongson, *Relocations*. Tongson evokes a queer-of-color suburban imaginary in Southern California's Inland Empire.

52. Pardo, *Mexican American Women Activists*, 39–40. Pardo partakes in the same sense of wonder as many people I interviewed by following this comment with an exclamation mark: "In a racial/ethnic survey used by the local school district, the 'other' category refers to anyone who is *not* American Indian, Asian, black, or Hispanic. The 'total minority' category is the sum of the whites . . . ! Now, the one-time minorities are the majority and the 'others' are white" (39–40).

53. Interview with Nancy Do, March 21, 2007.

54. On how people-of-color identities have been mobilized in pursuit of specific political aims, see, for example, Pulido, "Development of a 'People of Color' Identity," 145–80; and Lipsitz, "'To Tell the Truth and Not Get Trapped.'"

55. For examples, see Tuan, *Forever Foreigners or Honorary Whites?*; Clark, *The California Cauldron*; Portes and Rumbaut, *Legacies*. Some notable exceptions include Wiese, *Places of Their Own*; Kurashige, "The Many Facets of Brown"; and Garcia, *A World of Its Own*.

56. Respectively, Yancey, *Who Is White?*; O'Brien, *The Racial Middle*; Kim, "Racial Triangulation," 105–38; De Genova, "Latino and Asian Racial Formations," 1–22; Bonilla-Silva, "We Are All Americans!," 3–17.

57. Molina, *Fit to Be Citizens*, 6. See also Almaguer, *Racial Fault Lines*, and Saxton, *The Indispensable Enemy*.

58. See Kim, "Racial Triangulation"; Almaguer, *Racial Fault Lines*; Gutiérrez, *Walls and Mirrors*.

59. On the "heterogeneity, hybridity, and multiplicity" of Asian Americans, see Lowe's now classic text *Immigrant Acts*. For a discussion of the heterogeneity of U.S. Latinas/os and the construction of a common category "Latino" through an examination of Mexicans and Puerto Ricans in Chicago, see De Genova and Ramos-Zayas, *Latino Crossings*.

60. On double colonization, see Gómez, *Manifest Destinies*.

61. Saxton, *The Indispensable Enemy*.

62. Although Californios were racially mixed, the fiction of "Spanish" descent was important to their elite class identity as well as to their acceptability to Anglo Americans as marriage partners. See Almaguer, *Racial Fault Lines*, and Pitt, *The Decline of the Californios*. For a full discussion of the importance of the Spanish fantasy past to California history and everyday landscapes, see chapter 4.

63. Ngai, *Impossible Subjects*.

64. See Garcia, *A World of Its Own*; Quintana, "National Borders, Neighborhood Boundaries"; Guevarra Jr., *Becoming Mexipino*; Leonard, *Making Ethnic Choices*; and Sánchez, "'What's Good for Boyle Heights.'"

65. Molina, *Fit to Be Citizens*, 9.

66. See Spivak on strategic essentialism, or the "strategic use of positivist essentialism in a scrupulously visible political interest." Spivak, "Subaltern Studies," 13.

67. On the idea of brushing history against the grain, see Benjamin, "Theses on the Philosophy of History," 253–64.

68. Harris, "Whiteness as Property," 1707–91.

69. Massey and Denton, *American Apartheid*; Sugrue, *The Origins of the Urban Crisis*; Kurashige, *The Shifting Grounds of Race*; Nicolaides, *My Blue Heaven*; Wiese, *Places of Their Own*; Shapiro, *The Hidden Cost of Being African American*; Lipsitz, *The Possessive Investment in Whiteness*; Lipsitz, "The Racialization of Space and the Spatialization of Race," 10–23; Lipsitz, *How Racism Takes Place*; Oliver and Shapiro, *Black Wealth/White Wealth*.

70. Tuan, *Forever Foreigners or Honorary Whites?*; Palumbo-Liu, *Asian/American*; Lee, *Unraveling the "Model Minority" Stereotype*; Orenstein, "Void for Vagueness," 367–408; Gómez, *Manifest Destinies*; Robinson and Robinson, "The Limits of Interracial Coalitions"; Basler, "White Dreams and Red Votes," 123–66.

71. McWilliams, *Southern California*; Deverell, *Whitewashed Adobe*; Kropp, *California Vieja*.

72. See Arnold, *Culture and Anarchy*; Althusser, "Ideology and Ideological State Apparatuses," 85–126; Gramsci, *Selections from the Prison Notebooks*.

73. Schein, "Normative Dimensions of Landscape"; see also Hall, "Gramsci's Relevance," 411–40.

74. Althusser, "Ideology and Ideological State Apparatuses"; Gramsci, *Selections from the Prison Notebooks*.

75. Pardo, *Mexican American Women Activists*, 39.

76. Massey, *Space, Place, and Gender*, 154.

77. Williams, *Marxism and Literature*, 132–34.

78. Hall, "Cultural Identity and Diaspora," 226.

79. Hayden, *The Power of Place*, 27–29; Lynch, *The Image of the City*.

80. Hayden, *The Power of Place*, 27.

81. Ibid., 27–29.

82. Sugrue, *The Origins of the Urban Crisis*. Sugrue describes how in mid-twentieth-century Detroit, the near total exclusion of African Americans from the building trades, which operated primarily on friendship and kin networks—a virtually insurmountable barrier to Black people because of Black–white residential and social segregation—led them to work as casual or subcontracted labor. They gathered at informal outdoor labor markets at intersections (one in particular was known as the "slave market"), making a ready supply of cheap labor. To the masses of suburban white commuters who drove past them every day, the labor markets crystallized an image of Black male shiftlessness that reinforced ideologies of race and became a cognitive racial geography of the city.

83. Massey, "Travelling Thoughts," 231.

84. On the concept of jumping scale, see Smith, "Contours of a Spatialized Politics."

85. Takaki, *Debating Diversity*; Muskal, "Census Bureau."

1. Not "For Caucasians Only"

1. Interview with Milo Alvarez, February 27, 2008.

2. See Garcia, *A World of Its Own*; Sánchez, "'What's Good for Boyle Heights Is Good for the Jews,'" 633–62; and Varzally, *Making a Non-White America*.

3. Lipsitz, "The Racialization of Space and the Spatialization of Race," 10–23; Lipsitz, *How Racism Takes Place*.

4. Robinson, *Black Marxism*. Robinson describes Blackness as an "ontological totality," or a way of thinking and being not informed solely by white domination, thus recuperating a whole history. As Fred Moten has emphasized, this ethos is characterized by what W. E. B. Du Bois articulated as an absence of the "wish . . . to exploit" (Moten made this point during a graduate seminar, "Readings in Race and Ethnicity," held at the University of Southern California in Los Angeles in Spring 2005). The original passage in Du Bois reads, "Above all, we must remember the black worker was the ultimate exploited; that he formed that mass of labor which had neither wish nor power to escape from the labor status, in order to directly exploit other laborers, or indirectly, by alliance, with capital, to share in their exploitation" (Du Bois, *Black Reconstruction in America*, 15). See also Clyde Woods's theorization of a "blues epistemology," a distinctly

African American way of knowing and being that grew out of regional racial and economic hierarchies in the Mississippi Delta (Woods, *Development Arrested*).

5. Harris, "Whiteness as Property," 1707–91; Pulido, "Rethinking Environmental Racism," 12–20; Lipsitz, *The Possessive Investment in Whiteness*; Lipsitz, "The Racialization of Space and the Spatialization of Race," 10–23; Lipsitz, *How Racism Takes Place*.

6. See Saito, *Race and Politics*, 158–80; and Fong, *The First Suburban Chinatown*.

7. Moctezuma and Davis, "Policing the Third Border."

8. On the earlier, 1920s developments in Monterey Park, see Fong, *The First Suburban Chinatown*.

9. Interview with Winston Gin, August 14, 2007.

10. Fong, *The First Suburban Chinatown*; Saito, *Race and Politics*.

11. Jackson, *Crabgrass Frontier*; Massey and Denton, *American Apartheid*; Freund, *Colored Property*; Lipsitz, "The Racialization of Space and the Spatialization of Race"; Lipsitz, *How Racism Takes Place*.

12. HoSang, *Racial Propositions*, 53–90.

13. Brooks, *Alien Neighbors, Foreign Friends*, 194–239; Cheng, "Out of Chinatown and Into the Suburbs," 1067–90; Pattillo-McCoy, *Black Picket Fences*.

14. HoSang, *Racial Propositions*, 79.

15. Kurashige, *The Shifting Grounds of Race*, 225–29.

16. Fong, *The First Suburban Chinatown*, 21–22.

17. Interview with Karen and Ed Toguchi, July 7, 2007.

18. Saito, *Race and Politics*, 23. In 1950, the U.S. Census reported a mere nineteen "nonwhites" living in Monterey Park, out of a total population of 20,395—although at that time, it should be noted, there was no separate category for Mexican Americans and they were usually counted as white. U.S. Census 1950, General Characteristics, Table 33, http://www2.census.gov/prod2/decennial/documents/37778768v2p5ch3.pdf. All other uses of "white" with regard to demographic data refer to "non-Hispanic" whites, unless otherwise specified.

19. Interview with Karen Toguchi, July 21, 2007.

20. Inouye, "Interview with Kazuo K. Inouye Conducted by Leslie Ito"; Kurashige, *The Shifting Grounds of Race*, 250–51.

21. Interview with Winston Gin, August 14, 2007.

22. Quoted in Fong, *The First Suburban Chinatown*, 24–25.

23. Wiese, *Places of Their Own*; Nicolaides, *My Blue Heaven*; Garcia, *A World of Its Own*; Sánchez, *Becoming Mexican American*, 188–206; Sides, *L.A. City Limits*, 95–130; Gonzalez, "'A Place in the Sun.'"

24. Interviews with Lisa Beppu, June 28, 2007, and Anita Martinez, June 20, 2008.

25. Interview with Mike Murashige, March 30, 2007.

26. Interview with David Tong, September 28, 2007. For a fictionalized account of the complexities of various forms of anti-Asian racism from the perspective of a young Japanese American woman in Los Angeles in the immediate years after World War II, see Hisaye Yamamoto's short story, "Wilshire Bus" (Yamamoto, *Seventeen Syllables and Other Stories*).

27. California Real Estate Association annual directory, quoted in HoSang, *Racial Propositions*, 56. In 1960, Glendale was 99.5 percent white. In 1970 it was, 98.4 percent white. Calculated from U.S. Census 1960, General Population Characteristics for California, Table 20, http://www2.census.gov/prod2/decennial/documents/12533879v1p6ch03.pdf; and U.S. Census 1970, Vol. 1, Part 6 (California), Sect. 2, Table 138, http://www2.census.gov/prod2/decennial/documents/1970a_ca2-01.pdf.

28. Inouye, "Interview with Kazuo Inouye."

29. Indeed, Inouye's record of purposeful "blockbusting" in the Crenshaw area of Los Angeles, in which he sold large numbers of homes to African Americans as well as Japanese Americans, indicate his multiracial ethos (Kurashige, *The Shifting Grounds of Race*, 250–51).

30. Fong, *The First Suburban Chinatown*, 23–24.

31. For the now classic overview of late twentieth-century processes of urban residential segregation, see Massey and Denton, *American Apartheid*. On African Americans in Los Angeles in the postwar period, see Sides, *L.A. City Limits*.

32. Harris, "Whiteness and Property."

33. Shapiro, *The Hidden Cost of Being African American*; Lipsitz, "The Racialization of Space and the Spatialization of Race," 19. See also Massey and Denton, *American Apartheid*; and Oliver and Shapiro, *Black Wealth/White Wealth*.

34. See Massey and Denton, *American Apartheid*; Sugrue, *The Origins of the Urban Crisis*; Kurashige, *The Shifting Grounds of Race*; Nicolaides, *My Blue Heaven*; Wiese, *Places of Their Own*.

35. Freund, *Colored Property*.

36. See Roediger, *Working toward Whiteness*, for a detailed exposition of how homeownership and the whitening of formerly racially "in between" European immigrants became intertwined after World War II. For other historical studies of the whitening of European immigrants, see Jacobson, *Whiteness of a Different Color*; Allen, *The Invention of the White Race*; and Roediger, *The Wages of Whiteness*; among others. On whiteness and "color-blind" self-interest, see HoSang, *Racial Propositions*.

37. Tuan, *Forever Foreigners or Honorary Whites?*; Palumbo-Liu, *Asian/American*; Lee, *Unraveling the "Model Minority" Stereotype*; Orenstein, "Void for Vagueness," 367–408; Gómez, *Manifest Destinies*; Robinson and Robinson, "The Limits of Interracial Coalitions," 93–119; Basler, "White Dreams and Red Votes," 123–66.

38. For examples of excellent studies of the spatial effects of white privilege and ghettoization, see Massey and Denton, *American Apartheid*, and Sugrue, *The Origins of the Urban Crisis*.

39. Kurashige, *The Shifting Grounds of Race*; Wiese, *Places of Their Own*; Garcia, *A World of Its Own*. Also see Sides, *L.A. City Limits*.

40. On intraethnic dynamics, see (among others) Lin, *Reconstructing Chinatown*; Chen, *Chinatown No More*. On economic flows, see (among others) Zhou, "How Do Places Matter?," 531–53; and Li et al., "Chinese-American Banking and Community Development," 777–96. On transnational connections see, for example, Ong, *Flexible Citizenship*. While geographer Wei Li, in her conceptualization of "ethnoburbs," points out that most so-called "suburban Chinatowns" are in fact multiethnic, multiracial communities, she does not discuss the long, multiracial "prehistories" of many such spaces. See Li, "Building Ethnoburbia," 1–28; Li, "Spatial Transformation of an Urban Ethnic Community," 74–94.

41. Lipsitz, "The Racialization of Space and the Spatialization of Race," 15.

42. Hong, in her analysis of African Americans' and Asian Americans' shared histories of racialized denial of property rights (through, for example, segregation and Japanese American internment), has argued that in liberal democracy's privileging of private property, "[i]f the purpose of the state is to maintain property relations, criminality becomes defined as the threat to private property." Therefore, in Hong's reading of Hisaye Yamamoto's memoir "A Fire in Fontana," African Americans shown "looting" on television during the Watts Riots justify white supremacist notions that black people do not deserve private property because they don't respect it (Hong, "'Something Forgotten Which Should Have Been Remembered,'" 291–311). See also Clement Lai on how the differential racialization of African Americans and Japanese Americans in San Francisco's Fillmore District strongly affected that area's redevelopment in the mid- to late twentieth century (Lai, "The Racial Triangulation of Space," 151–70).

43. Gómez, *Manifest Destinies*; Almaguer, *Racial Fault Lines*; Foley, *The White Scourge*; López, *White by Law*.

44. Inouye, "Interview with Kazuo Inouye," 194. For a discussion of this anecdote in the context of Inouye's "blockbusting" tactics as a realtor in Crenshaw, see Kurashige, *The Shifting Grounds of Race*, 250.

45. Robinson and Robinson, "The Limits of Interracial Coalitions," 100–101, 116n27. Marcus's argument was extended to two significant court cases during the mid- to late 1940s dealing with school segregation and interracial marriage, respectively: *Mendez v. Westminster* (1946), in which Marcus served as the plaintiff's attorney, and *Perez v. Sharp* (1948). In *Mendez v. Westminster*, a California U.S. District Court ruled that the segregation of Mexican American children into separate schools was unconstitutional. Although *Mendez v. Westminster* served as an important precedent to *Brown v. Board of Education* (1954), the case did

not argue directly against racial discrimination. Instead, Marcus won the case by asserting that Mexican American children were white and therefore could not be segregated on grounds of race (Jeanne Powers, "Mendez V. Westminster [1946] as a Window into Mid-Century Racial Ideologies" [paper presented at Annual Meeting of the American Sociological Association, New York, N.Y., August 11, 2007]). Similarly, the ambiguity of Mexican Americans' racial status under the law made for a gray area in their ability to intermarry across racial lines: In *Perez v. Sharp* [1948], the judge ruled a law forbidding nonwhites to marry whites "void for vagueness"— the bride, Mexican American Andrea Perez, could not be definitively categorized as white or *not* white (Orenstein, "Void for Vagueness").

46. Robinson and Robinson, "The Limits of Interracial Coalitions," 100–101; HoSang, *Racial Propositions*, 53–90.

47. Inouye, "Interview with Kazuo Inouye," 194.

48. Kurashige, *The Shifting Grounds of Race*, 250.

49. Interview with David and Soume Tong, September 28, 2007.

50. Interview with Dora Padilla, October 24, 2007.

51. Quoted in HoSang, *Racial Propositions*, 79.

52. See Tuan, *Forever Foreigners or Honorary Whites?*

53. Interview with Milo Alvarez, February 27, 2008.

54. Tuan, *Forever Foreigners or Honorary Whites?*

55. This is similar to Claire Jean Kim's theorization of a "field of racial positions," in which Asian Americans are "triangulated" relative to African Americans and whites—simultaneously valorized in comparison to African Americans and ostracized as outsiders or foreigners while African Americans are not (Kim, "Racial Triangulation," 105–38).

56. Ong, *Flexible Citizenship*.

57. Lipsitz, "The Racialization of Space and the Spatialization of Race."

58. Fong, *The First Suburban Chinatown*; Saito, *Race and Politics*; Calderón, "Mexican American Politics in a Multi-Ethnic Community"; Li et al., "Chinese-American Banking and Community Development"; Zhou, Tseng, and Kim, "Rethinking Residential Assimilation," 53–83.

59. Quoted in Saito, *Race and Politics*, 31. The man also recalled how the land behind his house used to be farmland worked by a Japanese American family—he and his wife would help farm sometimes in exchange for free fruit—and how upset his wife was when her Japanese American best friend had to leave for World War II internment camps. "My wife's best friend had to go and my wife drove her to the train, and they cried. We still have some pictures of her." Saito notes that in this account, the man foregrounds how "Latinos and Japanese Americans shared the experience of battling segregation, and because they were neighbors and friends they were also linked intimately and emotionally to the major events in each other's lives" (31).

60. Interview with Bill Gin, April 30, 2007.

61. Oliver and Wong, "Intergroup Prejudice in Multiethnic Settings," 567–82.

62. Charles, "The Dynamics of Racial Residential Segregation," 167–207.

63. Quoted in Fong, *The First Suburban Chinatown*, 64–65.

64. Compiled from U.S. Census Data 1980–2000.

65. Interview with Karen Toguchi, July 21, 2007.

66. Ibid.

67. Interview with Romy Uyehara, September 28, 2007.

68. Interview with Tony Gonzalez, November 29, 2007.

69. Ibid.

70. A pseudonym.

71. Interview with Juan Ramirez, October 4, 2007.

72. Interview with Anita Martinez, June 20, 2008.

73. Ibid.

74. Ibid.

75. Interview with Eloy Zarate, April 18, 2007.

76. Interview with Juan Ramirez, October 4, 2007.

77. A pseudonym.

78. A pseudonym.

79. Interview with Mike Murashige, March 30, 2007.

80. Interview with Anita Martinez, June 20, 2008.

81. Interview with Juan Ramirez, October 4, 2007.

82. See Freund, *Colored Property*.

83. Interview with Oscar Ixco, July 18, 2007.

84. Interview with Grace Ahn, January 16, 2008.

85. Ibid.

86. For related literature, see Rojas, "The Cultural Landscape of a Latino Community," 177–85, on Latina/o uses of homespaces in East Los Angeles; and Amam, "Cosmopolitan Suburbs," on the ways Asian immigrants in California's Bay Area have challenged prevailing spatial and architectural norms. On the dominant aesthetics of privilege in white suburbs, see Duncan and Duncan, *Landscapes of Privilege*, and Duncan and Duncan, "Aesthetics, Abjection, and White Privilege in Suburban New York."

87. A pseudonym.

88. Interview with Paul Pham, August 14, 2007.

89. Interview with Milo Alvarez, February 27, 2008.

90. A pseudonym.

91. Interview with Lisa Sun, April 20, 2005. Willow Lung Amam has written extensively about how the educational priorities of Asian immigrant parents have shaped the racial geography of neighborhoods in Fremont, in California's Bay Area (Lung Amam, "Cosmopolitan Suburbs").

92. Interview with Dora Padilla, October 24, 2007.

93. Interview with Nancy Do, March 21, 2007.

94. Wiese, *Places of Their Own*; Nicolaides, *My Blue Heaven*.

95. Interview with Juan Ramirez, October 4, 2007.

96. A pseudonym.

97. Interview with Jinny Hong, February 8, 2012.

98. Interview with Gina Alvarez, April 4, 2008.

99. Interview with Nancy Do, March 21, 2007.

100. Kurashige, "The Many Facets of Brown," 56–57.

101. See Amam, "Cosmopolitan Suburbs"; and Li, "Unneighbourly Houses or Unwelcome Chinese," 14–33.

102. Interview with David and Soume Tong, September 28, 2007.

103. Interview with Lisa Beppu, June 28, 2007.

2. "The Asian and Latino Thing in Schools"

1. Interview with Nancy Tran, March 9, 2007. All names in this chapter, except those of Robin Zhou, school and district administrators, and persons quoted in publicly available media, have been changed to protect the privacy of respondents.

2. Alhambra's residents currently number approximately eighty-four thousand. Its city motto is the "gateway to the San Gabriel Valley," and its residents are primarily lower-middle-income to middle-income Latinas/os and Asian Americans (52.9 percent Asian and 34.4 percent Hispanic or Latina/o, according to the 2010 U.S. Census).

3. Interview with Russell Lee-Sung, April 18, 2007.

4. Education Data Partnership, "Students by Ethnicity, Alhambra High School, 2004–2005," http://www.ed-data.k12.ca.us/App_Resx/EdDataClassic/fsTwoPanel.aspx?#!bottom=/_layouts/EdDataClassic/profile.asp?tab=1&level=07&ReportNumber=16&County=19&fyr=0405&District=75713&School=1930163#studentsbyethnicity. As of 2009, Latinas/os of Mexican origin constituted 76 percent of the Hispanic or Latina/o population in Alhambra. A third of Latinas/os in Alhambra were foreign born, compared with nearly 80 percent of Asians living in Alhambra (calculated from U.S. Census, 2005–2009 American Community Survey, http://factfinder2.census.gov).

5. Williams, *Marxism and Literature*, 132–34.

6. Althusser, "Ideology and Ideological State Apparatuses," 105.

7. Schein, "Normative Dimensions of Landscape," 217. Like everyday landscapes, common sense itself appears self-evident; as Stuart Hall reminds us, it "represents itself as the 'traditional wisdom or truth of the ages,' but in fact, it is deeply a product of history, 'part of the historical process'" (Hall cites Gramsci; Hall, "Gramsci's Relevance," 411–40).

8. See Willis, *Learning to Labour*; Hall, "Race, Articulation, and Societies," 305–41; Carby, "Schooling in Babylon," 183–211.

9. Althusser, "Ideology and Ideological State Apparatuses."

10. Education Data Partnership, "Students by Race/Ethnicity, Alhambra High School, 2010–2011."

11. Interview with Gabriela Fernandez, March 28, 2007.

12. Interview with Annie Liu, July 27, 2007.

13. Interview with Nancy Tran, March 9, 2007.

14. Interview with Paul Pham, August 14, 2007.

15. The establishment of norms, especially binaries, which eventually pass as "common sense" has been central to the operation of race as a political system of categories that, for most of modern world history, has defined "who should get what." Analyzing Black–white–Asian racial dynamics in the United States, Claire Jean Kim has theorized "a field of racial positions" that works as "a normative blueprint for who should get what" (Kim, "Racial Triangulation," 105–38). At a global scale, the legacies of an imperial-colonial order justified and dictated by categorizing people non-European peoples as "others" still continue to shape the life-and-death chances of much of the world today. See Said, *Orientalism*; Williams, *Capitalism and Slavery*; Fanon, *The Wretched of the Earth*; Blaut, *The Colonizer's Model of the World*; and Chakrabarty, *Provincializing Europe*; among others. In the United States, national ideologies of race—effectively hierarchical notions of citizenship and humanity—have been deeply shaped by a Black–white binary developed through the enslavement of forcibly displaced Africans, the production of whiteness, and the erasure and displacement of Native Americans. See Fields, "Slavery, Race and Ideology," 95–118; Jacobson, *Whiteness of a Different Color*; Allen, *The Invention of the White Race*; De Genova, "Latino and Asian Racial Formations, 1–22. These continue to define structural privilege, deprivation, and neglect in racial terms today. See Gilmore, "Fatal Couplings of Power and Difference," 15–24; Gilmore, "Race and Globalization"; Gilmore, *Golden Gulag*; Mills, *The Racial Contract*. Also see Fredrickson, *White Supremacy*, for an illuminating comparative study of white supremacy as a political system in South Africa and the United States. White supremacy is an overarching political ideology and system that supports the production and perpetuation of white privilege, which is the participation in, and exercise of, particular benefits and advantages accrued historically by whites, such as disproportionate ownership of property and other sources of capital. See Mills, *The Racial Contract*; Harris, "Whiteness as Property," 1707–91; Pulido, "Rethinking Environmental Racism," 12–20; Lipsitz, *The Possessive Investment in Whiteness*; Lipsitz, "The Racialization of Space and the Spatialization of Race," 10–23; and Lipsitz, *How Racism Takes Place*.

16. See Ladson-Billings, "From the Achievement Gap to the Education Debt," 3–12.

17. See HoSang, *Racial Propositions*, 91–129.

18. Becerra, "Trying to Bridge the Grade Divide."

19. Interview with Adam Saito, June 12, 2011.

20. See Willis, *Learning to Labour*.

21. Phone conversation with Scott Mangrum, June 18, 2008. At the time I spoke with Mangrum, his position had been eliminated due to funding problems, and he was being transferred to a different job at a high school at the end of the month.

22. In 2006–7, while the number of California State and University of California–eligible Latina/o students had increased from previous years, 60 percent of graduating Asian students as compared to only 24 percent of graduating Latinas/os completed California State / University of California entrance requirements. In 2004–5, just over half of Alhambra's senior class took the SAT (51.1 percent); 62.8 percent of the test takers were Asian, while only 27 percent were Hispanic or Latina/o. In 2006–7, 24 percent of Latina/o students at Alhambra High (as compared with 18.3 percent in the AUSD district as a whole) met state college and university entrance requirements. In 2008–9, both groups improved their numbers, although the gap between them remained nearly the same: 70.6 percent of graduating Asian students had completed California State and University of California requirements, while only 32.3 percent of Latino students completed the requirements. All data from California Department of Education, Educational Demographics Unit, http://dq.cde.ca.gov/dataquest.

23. As cited by Paik and Walhlberg, *Narrowing the Achievement Gap*, 4.

24. The language used in education scholars Paik and Wahlberg's edited anthology on the subject is representative: in the introduction, Paik and Wahlberg describe "the strengths and challenges of minority children," and ask, "How can we diminish the achievement gaps . . . ? Educators and allied professionals are interested in improving the efforts of these growing minority populations" (Paik and Walhlberg, *Narrowing the Achievement Gap*, 4).

25. Ladson-Billings, "From the Achievement Gap to the Education Debt," 4.

26. Further, it easily partakes in coded racist discourse veiling the same-old "underclass" rationale, whose opposite is the model minority (see Kim, *Bitter Fruit*), in which individual failure may be traced to a "cycle of pathology" in families and communities (Carby, "Schooling in Babylon").

27. Ladson-Billings, "From the Achievement Gap to the Education Debt."

28. See Foucault, *Power/Knowledge*; Foucault, *The Archaeology of Knowledge*; Foucault, *Discipline and Punish*; Foucault, *"Society Must Be Defended"*; Hall, "Re-Thinking the 'Base-and-Superstructure Metaphor,'" 43–72; Hall, "Race, Articulation, and Societies Structured in Dominance"; Hall, "Gramsci's Relevance"; Althusser, "Ideology and Ideological State Apparatuses"; Said, *Orientalism*.

29. Interview with Nancy Tran, March 9, 2007.

30. Interview with Annie Liu, July 27, 2007.

31. Interview with Gary Wong, February 19, 2008.

32. On Asian American students' espousal of cultural scripts, see Louie, *Compelled to Excel*.

33. Interview with Paul Pham, August 14, 2007.

34. Bourdieu, "Forms of Capital," 96–111; Stanton-Salazar, *Manufacturing Hope and Despair*, 265–70; Prado, "A Critical Social Capital Analysis"; Fong, *Complementary Education*; Zhou, *Contemporary Chinese America*. Prado, in his study of social networks and academic achievement at a similar, unidentified West SGV high school, concluded that while available statistical evidence showed "no large or significant class differences" between Asians and Latinas/os at the school, a greater amount of social capital on the part of the Asian American students (in terms of the factors named previously) played a significant role in their ability to do well academically. Vivian Louie has made similar observations in her study of 1.5- and second-generation Chinese American college students in New York City; while many of the Chinese immigrant parents she interviewed attributed their approach to education to Confucian values and educational norms in their sending countries, their children rarely understood these values with any ethnonational or historical specificity and instead cited generalized "Asian" values (Louie, *Compelled to Excel*).

35. Interview with Gabriela Fernandez, March 28, 2007.

36. Interview with Paul Pham, August 14, 2007.

37. For a critique of this tendency, see Nguyen, *Race and Resistance*.

38. Kim, "Racial Triangulation"; Pulido, *Black, Brown, Yellow, and Left*, 45; Chuh, *Imagine Otherwise*. Chuh uses a phrase originally from Gayatri Spivak.

39. Tuan, *Forever Foreigners or Honorary Whites?*. Tuan adapts Robert Blauner's discussion of white racial privilege (Blauner, *Racial Oppression in America*, 1972).

40. Ibid., 96. However, Tuan's theorization of racial privilege as experienced by Asian Americans ends here and is thus limited by her focus on neighborhood comfort and the discrete experiences of individuals, as well as her use of largely middle-class, later-generation Chinese and Japanese Americans to stand in for Asian Americans as a whole, rather than on the dialectic between these and larger structural and historical forces.

41. Ho, "(E)Racing the Model Minority," 192, 198.

42. Ibid., 184.

43. Ibid., 219; my emphasis.

44. Gilmore, "Race and Globalization," 261.

45. Interview with Paul Pham, August 14, 2007.

46. Interview with Annie Liu, July 27, 2007.

47. Louie, *Compelled to Excel*, 187–89.

48. In contrast, see Lee, *Unraveling the "Model Minority" Stereotype*, in which Lee details how Asian American students in a high school dominated by white

students were used as a buffer between white and Black students. Lee further delineates how distinct groups of Asian American students either complied with or resisted the model minority stereotype and how the stereotype operated in the production of particular race relations at the school among students, teachers, and administrators.

49. Interview with Lia Chen, October 24, 2007.

50. Valenzuela, *Subtractive Schooling*, 20. A rapidly growing body of research in education and sociology including Valenzuela's book has begun to address factors and causes of Latina/o disaffection with schooling in a variety of settings. See also Stanton-Salazar, *Manufacturing Hope and Despair.*

51. Steele, "Race and the Schooling of Black Americans," 68–78. In the early 1990s, in an effort to understand higher college dropout rates for Black students across the board regardless of socioeconomic status and level of achievement, Steele argued that what was at work was a mainstream culture that fostered "disidentification" with academics among Black students. From an early age, Black children suffered academic stigma and were expected to fail or need remedial attention. Subsequent studies showed that by junior high and certainly by high school, Black male students detached their measures of self-worth from academic achievement, while white students, for example, did not—that is, they ceased to *identify* with academics (Osborne, "Academics, Self-Esteem, and Race," 449–55). Steele also noted that Black college students performed better academically in the 1950s, when legal segregation was still in effect, than they did in more recent decades, with a host of support programs and organizations supposedly tailored to their needs available to them. In contrast, several programs at levels from elementary school to college that focused on challenging Black students, taking for granted their intelligence and potential (and not assuming that they needed extra support and remedial attention), were unqualified successes (Steele, "Race and the Schooling of Black Americans").

52. Interview with Gabriela Fernandez, March 28, 2007.

53. Interview with Matt Ramos, June 29, 2007.

54. Interview with Russell Lee-Sung, April 18, 2007.

55. Chong, "Morphing Outrage into Ideas."

56. Interview with Paul Pham, August 14, 2007.

57. Interview with Alan Fernandez, February 27, 2008.

58. This discourse tends to align Asians politically with whites, raising the often-implied notion that particular minority groups can only make it with lowered standards and that certain forms of affirmative action amount to "reverse discrimination." This argument was made famous by *Regents of the University of California v. Bakke*, 1978, in which Allen Bakke, a white man who had twice been rejected from University of California, Davis, medical school, claimed discrimination and won in the Supreme Court by a narrow margin. In 2006, Jian Li, a

Chinese American applicant who was rejected from Princeton, made such comparisons explicit when he filed a federal complaint alleging racial bias. Dana Y. Takagi has written about how the controversy over Asian admissions at elite universities such as UC Berkeley eventually resulted in anti–affirmative action discourses and practices, despite attempts by Asian American activists to distinguish themselves ideologically from such outcomes (Takagi, *The Retreat from Race*). See also Robles, *Asian Americans and the Shifting Politics of Race*, on the development and expression of neoconservative politics among Asian Americans in a struggle over racial quotas in high school admissions in San Francisco.

59. Of course there are always counterexamples. For instance, Alan recalled fondly a Mexican American vice principal who "took me under his wing, and saw that I was doing well," who invited Alan to college banquets and encouraged him to apply to many colleges. Alan also noted that among the teachers and administrators, this man "was the only one I felt like was proud to be Mexican." He contrasted him with the principal at the time, who was also Mexican American:

I remember bringing up one time something that had to do with being the only Mexican in class, and he [the principal] was just like . . . "don't dwell on things like that"—kind of like, "you're just exaggerating," or "this is not really important, just worry about going to school." And I just remember feeling really pissed off at him—like, "you're not really acknowledging what I'm telling you. It sucks!" . . . But Mr. ____ [the vice principal] . . . he seemed more proud of who he was. He was Mexican American. He wasn't anything else, he wasn't "Hispanic"— they used to use "Hispanic" a lot back then. . . . He would say he was Mexican American. Whereas [the principal] was just like a white person, you know?

The importance of being recognized ("he saw that I was doing well") and feeling affirmed in his ethnic identity ("Mr. ____ was Mexican American. He wasn't anything else.") was invaluable for Alan, who at the time of our interview was earning his PhD and writing a dissertation on Chicano history.

60. According to Principal Lee-Sung. Over the four years of Lee-Sung's tenure as principal, a large proportion of these veteran white teachers retired, and Lee-Sung strove to replace them with "culturally sensitive" teachers (whom, he was careful to specify, could be of any ethnicity).

61. Valenzuela, *Subtractive Schooling*, 30.

62. Interview with Matt Ramos, June 29, 2007.

63. Takagi, *The Retreat from Race*. In her study of controversies in the late 1980s over Asian American admissions to UC Berkeley and other elite institutions, Takagi draws attention to the importance of rhetoric and language in what she calls "shifting discourse," in which the central focus of debate changes as participants redefine and rearticulate others' definitions of the problem (9). In the case of Asian American admissions, through dialectical exchanges between Asian Americans, university officials, liberals, and neoconservatives, the terms of debate

morphed over time from discrimination to diversity to affirmative action, finally effecting a "subtle but decisive" shift in public and intellectual discourse about, and some universities' practices of, affirmative action. Also see Robles, *Asian Americans and the Shifting Politics of Race*, on Asian Americans' embrace of model minority stereotypes and neoconservative, color-blind discourse to oppose affirmative action at a San Francisco high school.

64. Chang, "Column Creates Uproar."

65. Interview with Russell Lee-Sung, April 18, 2007.

66. Chong, "Morphing Outrage into Ideas."

67. Interview with Russell Lee-Sung, April 18, 2007.

68. Ibid.

69. Alhambra High School, "Moors Say What?", *The Moor,* April 12, 2005.

70. Interview with Russell Lee-Sung, April 18, 2007.

71. Comment sheet from a meeting between Russell Lee-Sung and students, shared verbally by Lee-Sung during our interview, April 18, 2007.

72. Interview with Gabriela Fernandez, March 28, 2007.

73. Althusser, "Ideology and Ideological State Apparatuses," 105.

74. Muñoz, *Disidentifications*.

75. Ibid., 33.

76. Interview with Gabriela Fernandez, March 28, 2007.

77. Ibid.

78. Alhambra High School, "Moors Say What?"

79. Open enrollment was instituted progressively beginning in the fall of 2006. In the response to the fallout over Robin's column, students also formed a local high school chapter of MEChA (Movimiento Estudiantil Chican@ de Aztlán) and Latina/o parents founded an organization to support students (Chong, "Morphing Outrage into Ideas"). In addition, after Lee-Sung chose to leave for an opportunity at another high school, the district hired Maria Elena Sanchez, a Latina, as principal.

80. Interview with Paul Pham, August 14, 2007.

81. Interview with Annie Liu, July 27, 2007.

82. Interview with Matt Ramos, June 29, 2007.

3. "Just Like Any Other Boy"?

1. Interview with Joe Castillo, October 19, 2007. In order to protect the privacy of respondents, I have changed the troop number and all names in this chapter and omitted the specific municipality in which the troop is situated, with the exception of Boy Scouts of America officials not directly affiliated with the troop.

2. Interview with Marie Johnson, October 5, 2007.

3. Troop 252 documents, housed in the basement of the church in which they are chartered. Viewed July 31, 2008.

4. Interview with Bob Lee, April 30, 2007. Referring to the few white people present as "token whites" was a joke I heard often in the course of interviewing SGV residents, most often from Asian Americans. The pleasure they took in revising this phrase, which is typically applied to the minimal inclusion of nonwhites in various contexts, was obvious.

5. Interview with Marie Johnson, October 5, 2007.

6. Interview with Bob Lee, April 30, 2007.

7. Wong, *Democracy's Promise.*

8. Macleod, *Building Character in the American Boy*; Peterson, *The Boy Scouts*; MacDonald, *Sons of the Empire*; Mechling, *On My Honor*; Townley, *Legacy of Honor* (New York: Thomas Dunne Books, 2007).

9. MacDonald, *Sons of the Empire.*

10. Deloria, *Playing Indian*, 111; Huhndorf, *Going Native.* On the myth of the frontier and its utility in justifying racial violence, exploitation, and conquest in the history of the American West, see Horsman, *Race and Manifest Destiny*; Limerick, *The Legacy of Conquest*; and Slotkin, *Regeneration through Violence*; Slotkin, *The Fatal Environment*; and Slotkin, *Gunfighter Nation.*

11. Deloria, *Playing Indian.*

12. Ibid.

13. Quoted in ibid., 110.

14. BSA National Council website, http://www.scouting.org/Media/Fact Sheets/02–503a.aspx.

15. Weiss, *The American Myth of Success.*

16. In the 1990s and 2000s, the BSA became nationally controversial for repeatedly asserting its right to exclude gay members. In 2000, the BSA won a Supreme Court case in which the court ruled that affirmed that private organizations have the right to decide their membership, thereby upholding the organization's prohibition against gay members and leaders (Costello, "Some Backers Pull Boy Scouts' Funding").

17. Deloria, *Playing Indian*, 5. Similarly, British Army general Lord Baden-Powell's original vision of scouting in England incorporated colonial African and Indian themes and aimed to make boys into men able and willing to defend the British Empire (MacDonald, *Sons of the Empire*).

18. Mills, *The Racial Contract.*

19. Lowe, *Immigrant Acts*, 12.

20. Ibid., 26–7.

21. Townley, *Legacy of Honor*, 5.

22. Parallels can be made here with the U.S. Army's recruitment of immigrants, nonwhites, and semicolonial subjects.

23. Townley, *Legacy of Honor*, 38–9.

24. Peterson, *The Boy Scouts.*

25. African American Registry, "The Black Boy Scout."

26. One incident in particular encapsulates the fraught position in which a Japanese American scout could find himself at that time: In the Manzanar detention camp, at the close of 1942, conflict erupted between dissidents, accused War Relocation Authority (WRA) collaborators, and the WRA administration (Weglyn, *Years of Infamy*). When protesters headed for the flagpole to tear down the American flag, Japanese American scouts surrounded the base of the pole, arming themselves with "stones the size of baseballs" in order to defend it. Ultimately, after military police released tear gas and opened fire on the crowd, the protest ended with two fatalities and at least nine wounded—but due in large part to the efforts of the scouts, the flag stayed, camp director Ralph Merritt told the Associated Press (Peterson, *The Boy Scouts*).

27. Little Tokyo Historical Society, "Koyasan Betsuin Temple," http://discovernikkei.org/dj/nikkeialbum/files/filemanager/public/active/5/Koyasan%20Summary.doc.

28. On the racial state, see Omi and Winant, *Racial Formation in the United States*.

29. Ringle, "The Patriot."

30. Bunting, *So Far from the Sea*, 28.

31. Boy Scouts of America, "2006–2010 National Strategic Plan Boy Scouts of America," http://www.scouting.org/Media/AnnualReports/2006/05nsp.aspx.

32. BSA website, http://www.scoutreachbsa.org.

33. Campo-Flores and Kliff, "Campfire Questions," 66.

34. Boy Scouts of America, "2006–2010 National Strategic Plan," 6.

35. Ibid., 9.

36. BSA Fact Sheet, "Hispanic/Latino American Demographics in a Changing America," http://www.scouting.org/Media/FactSheets/02-972.aspx.

37. My emphases; Boy Scouts of America, "2006–2010 National Strategic Plan," 9.

38. Campo-Flores and Kliff, "Campfire Questions."

39. E-mail correspondence from Paul Reyes, Senior District Executive, Verdugo Hills Council, September 19, 2008.

40. Takagi, *The Retreat from Race*.

41. Interview with Jack Pan, July 21, 2008.

42. When I asked whether or not Boy Scouts enrollment in the area had increased after 9/11, Pan answered yes, but in the absence of significant qualitative data, it is difficult to make a case for a causal relationship.

43. Includes Boy Scout troops, Cub Scout packs, and co-ed Venture Crew teams.

44. Interview with Bob Matsumoto, August 1, 2008.

45. Interview with Jack Pan, July 21, 2008.

46. Macleod (*Building Character in the American Boy*) argues that much of the success of the BSA as an organization can be attributed to its early development of a central infrastructure made up of paid, professional bureaucrats.

47. Interview with Joe Castillo, October 19, 2007.

48. Interview with Bob Lee, April 30, 2007.

49. Interview with Gary Wong, February 19, 2008.

50. Interview with Joe Castillo, October 19, 2007.

51. Interview with Gary Wong, February 19, 2008.

52. Interview with David Wong, August 7, 2008.

53. Interview with Bob Lee, January 28, 2008.

54. Interview with Mary Hernandez, August 25, 2008.

55. Interview with Walter Ruiz, August 8, 2008.

56. Interview with Jesse Boden, November 12, 2007.

57. Interview with Joe Castillo, October 19, 2007.

58. Interview with Walter Ruiz, August 8, 2008.

59. Interview with Jesse Boden, November 12, 2007.

60. On the co-constitutive links between race, immigration, and citizenship, see Ngai, *Impossible Subjects*.

61. Interview with Bob Lee, January 28, 2008.

62. Interview with Joe Castillo, October 19, 2007.

63. Interview with Marie Johnson, October 5, 2007.

64. Interview with Shawn Smith, October 4, 2007.

65. I have omitted the name of the paper and direct citation of the article in order to preserve the privacy of those involved. Both Scoutmaster Lee and his wife Karen Lee, who has also been actively involved in Troop 252 for years, mentioned to me on separate occasions that the writer of the story was an Asian American woman. Bob Lee said, "Of all things, too, I think it was written up by an Asian girl." And Karen Lee said, "The person was an *Asian* person, Wendy. So I think she had her stereotypes of things, you know what I'm saying?" (interview with Bob Lee, April 30, 2007; interview with Karen Lee, January 28, 2007). Their statements implied a complex and somewhat contradictory set of charges, perhaps (1) that this added to the offense, since the Asian-surnamed reporter should not have portrayed Asian Americans in a bad light or should have written about race in a less incendiary way, and (2) that being Asian meant that the reporter carried unfair stereotypes of race relations.

66. Bonilla-Silva, *Racism without Racists*, 2.

67. Kim, *Bitter Fruit*, 17.

68. My listing of these elements combines the analyses of Bonilla-Silva (*Racism without Racists*) and Kim (*Bitter Fruit*). The last element has become particularly prevalent in the "postracial" Obama era, in which the election of a Black president is seen as definitive proof that race is no longer a problem in the United

States. For critiques of this perspective, see Bonilla-Silva, *Racism without Racists*; López, *White by Law*; and Wise, *Colorblind*; among others.

69. Kim, *Bitter Fruit*, 18. Once a progressive ideology espoused by civil-rights leaders, post-1960s color-blind discourse has become "a powerful tool for racial retrenchment" (Kim cites Neil Gotanda), and its language is often employed by conservatives in backlashes against affirmative action and other progressive reforms.

70. Kim, *Bitter Fruit*.

71. Interview with Bob Lee, April 30, 2007.

72. Interview with Gary Wong, February 19, 2008.

73. See Allen, *The Invention of the White Race*, and Gould, *The Mismeasure of Man*.

74. Interview with Karen Lee, January 28, 2008.

75. Interview with Bob and Karen Lee, January 28, 2008.

76. Interview with Mary Hernandez, August 25, 2008.

77. Interview with Gary Wong, February 19, 2008.

78. Williams, *Playing the Race Card*, 3–4.

79. An example from the 2008 U.S. presidential campaign illustrates this point as well. In late July 2008, after Barack Obama, who was then the Democratic candidate, said in a speech that the Republican campaign would try to elicit fear based on the fact that he "doesn't look like all those other presidents on the dollar bills," Republican John McCain's campaign accused Obama of "playing the race card . . . from the bottom of the deck" (Cooper and Powell, "McCain Camp Says Obama Is Playing 'Race Card'"). During roughly the same time period in which I was conducting interviews for this chapter, radio talk host Don Imus was fired for referring to the Rutgers University women's basketball team as "nappy-headed ho's" (April 2007), and three white Duke University students charged with raping a Black woman were prosecuted (2006–7). In both cases, the role of race, intent, and appropriate consequences were hotly debated. A representative opinion piece published in the *Washington Post* in response to the two incidents alleged "racial opportunism" and suggested that people should "drop the race card" (Hicks, "Drop the Race Card").

80. Chow, *The Protestant Ethnic*. On the reverse mirror-image relationship between the model minority and underclass myths, see Kim, *Bitter Fruit*.

81. Crenshaw, "Framing Affirmative Action." Crenshaw points out that, in fact, white women have been the primary beneficiaries of affirmative action programs.

82. Interview with Walter Ruiz, August 8, 2008.

83. Interview with Bob Lee, April 30, 2007.

84. Bonilla-Silva, *Racism without Racists*, 171.

85. Interview with Walter Ruiz, August 8, 2008.

86. Interview with Joe Castillo, October 19, 2007.

87. Interview with Jesse Boden, November 12, 2007.

88. Interview with Shawn Smith, October 4, 2007.

89. Interview with Bob and Karen Lee, January 28, 2008.

90. Baldwin, *The Fire Next Time*, 68.

91. Bonilla-Silva, *Racism without Racists*, 9.

4. Diversity on Main Street

1. Greenberg, *Branding New York*, 35.

2. Ibid., 10.

3. Widener, "'Perhaps the Japanese Are to Be Thanked?,'" 135–81.

4. McWilliams, *Southern California*.

5. Dávila, *Barrio Dreams*.

6. Kim, "Racial Triangulation," 105–38; Lai, "The Racial Triangulation of Space," 151–70. Lai writes about the "racial triangulation of space" in the redevelopment of San Francisco's Fillmore district, in which developers and city officials valorized "Japanese" (used interchangeably with *Japanese American*) space relative to "Black" space. In the case of the Fillmore, Lai argues, the racialization of "Asian" space as foreign and exotic enabled its relative valorization. In contrast, in the SGV, the ability of the Europeanized "Spanish"/ Mexican past to be claimed by whites was crucial to its continued legitimization in space.

7. Lowe, *Immigrant Acts*; Cocks, *Doing the Town*; Lai, "The Racial Triangulation of Space."

8. See Ong and Nonini, eds., *Ungrounded Empires*.

9. Anderson, "The Idea of Chinatown," 580–98; Anderson, *Vancouver's Chinatown*.

10. Anderson, "The Idea of Chinatown," 583–85.

11. Li, "Building Ethnoburbia," 1–28; Li, "Beyond Chinatown, beyond Enclave," 31–40; Li, "Spatial Transformation of an Urban Ethnic Community," 74–94; Li, *Ethnoburb*.

12. Anderson, "The Idea of Chinatown"; Anderson, *Vancouver's Chinatown*; Molina, *Fit to Be Citizens?*; Shah, *Contagious Divides*; Lin, *Reconstructing Chinatown*.

13. Li, "Beyond Chinatown, beyond Enclave"; Li and Park, "Asian Americans in Silicon Valley"; Amam, "Cosmopolitan Suburbs." For discussions of similar discourses in Canada, see Li, "Unneighbourly Houses or Unwelcome Chinese," 14–33; Mitchell, *Crossing the Neoliberal Line*.

14. Deverell, *Whitewashed Adobe*.

15. Jackson and Castillo, *Indians, Franciscans, and Spanish Colonization*; Smith, *Freedom's Frontier*; Kropp, *California Vieja*.

16. Camarillo, *Chicanos in a Changing Society*; Villa, *Barrio-Logos*.

17. Acuña, *Anything but Mexican*; Valle and Torres, *Latino Metropolis*; Villa, *Barrio-Logos*.

18. Saito, *Race and Politics*; Saito, "The Political Significance of Race."

19. Saito, *Race and Politics*; Toyota, *Envisioning America*. However, in 1985, only one year later—at the height of the nativist "slow-growth movement"—Chen, along with two Latino incumbents, was voted out of office, and whites regained control of the Monterey Park City Council for a time (Toyota, *Envisioning America*).

20. Chang, "Population Gains Slowly Taking Hold." Chi Mui, a first-generation immigrant from Hong Kong, was elected to the San Gabriel City Council in 2003 and became the city's first Asian American mayor in 2007. In 2004, third-generation Japanese American Gary Yamauchi was elected to Alhambra City Council and became the city's first Asian American mayor in 2007. Rosemead elected first-generation Vietnamese American John Tran to city council in March 2005; in 2007, Tran became the first Asian American mayor of Rosemead as well as the first Vietnamese American mayor of any city in the United States.

21. Calderón, "'Hispanic' and 'Latino,'" 37–44, 41.

22. See Sánchez, *Becoming Mexican American*.

23. Calderón, "'Hispanic' and 'Latino,'" 41.

24. Pardo, *Mexican American Women Activists*, 44. Both Pardo and Saito (*Race and Politics*) note that in Monterey Park, this sentiment was shared among later-generation Japanese American residents as well.

25. A search of data provided by city clerks of city council members with Spanish surnames yielded the following information: In Rosemead, Roberta Trujillo was a member of city council from 1974–1978, Joe Vasquez served from 1992 to 2005, William Alarcon from 2003–2005, John Nunez from 2005–2009, and Sandra Armenta was elected in March 2009. In San Gabriel, Richard Montes was elected to city council in 1972 and served until 1976, Edward T. Lara from 1976 to 1986, James Castaneda from 1988 to 2000, and David R. Gutierrez from 2001 to the present.

26. Latinos Daniel Arguello and Efren Moreno were elected in 1998 and 2000, respectively. In the several years that followed, the council became bitterly divided between Arguello and Moreno, on one side, and council members Paul Talbot and Mark Paulson, who were both white. Arguello and Moreno characterized Talbot and Paulson as a corrupt, probusiness, prodevelopment "old guard." In turn, the Talbot faction accused Arguello and his supporters of cronyism, practicing "East-LA style politics" (Chang, "Alhambra Mayor at Center of Storm") and "playing the race card." See Chang, "Alhambra Council a House Divided" and Chang, "Alhambra Race Has Been Ugly." On "playing the race card," see chapter 4.

Arguello called these accusations racist. Arguello and Moreno maintained that they had an obligation to bring up race. "Everyone thinks that Dan or myself are the bogeymen coming from the East Side," commented Moreno (Chang, "Bribery Scandal Deepens Council Split"). According to the manager of Arguello's unsuccessful campaign for state assembly, "Latinos and other ethnicities network, and it's called corruption. The old guard networks, and it's called networking" (quoted in Chang, "Alhambra Mayor at Center of Storm"). Paulson, who often took a more conciliatory stance than Paul Talbot and had on occasion tried to broker truces between Talbot and Arguello, was upset by Arguello's charges of racism: "Alhambra has been a racially diverse community for 40 years, and we've never had this kind of tension with regard to race. If Paul and I were anti-Latino, we would have moved out of town years ago. It seems like the race card is being played, and that upsets me" (quoted in Chang, "Alhambra Council a House Divided").

27. In a heated race in 2004, the Talbot and Paulson faction regained control over the council with the elections of Japanese American Gary Yamauchi—the first Asian American elected to Alhambra City Council—and Steven Placido (both endorsed by Paulson and Talbot). In 2006, Arguello ran for a third term and was defeated by Barbara Messina (an Italian American), who was endorsed by Paulson and Talbot. Although Paulson and Talbot both reached the end of their twelve-year term limits in 2006, they had endorsed four of the five successfully elected city council members (Yamauchi and Placido in 2004, and Messina and Chinese American Stephen Sham in 2006). The "old guard's" influence had been preserved. See Chang, "Alhambra Election Season to Be 'Bloodbath'"; Chang, "Turning out the Asian Vote"; Chang, "Talbot Faction Gains Majority on Council"; Ho, "Arguello's Road to Re-Election Rocky"; Ho, "Termed-out Councilmen Loom Large".

28. Quoted in Chang, "Population Gains Slowly Taking Hold." Chang quotes David Lang, head of the Indochinese American Political Action Committee, who has served as campaign consultant to Judy Chu and former Los Angeles city councilman Michael Woo.

29. Saito, *Race and Politics*, 63. In part, this was due to the absence of any Asian American political organizations (with the exception of local chapters of organizations such as the Japanese American Citizens League, which were not particularly active in local politics). According to Korean American councilman Alfred Song, who was the first Asian American elected to city council in Monterey Park in 1960, "In all of the years that I have campaigned for elective office, I have never had the help, financial or otherwise, of any organized Oriental group; whatever their origin may be—Korean, Japanese, Chinese, Filipino or any others . . . in twenty years, I think I could count the individual Asians who have come to my assistance on one hand and still have a couple of fingers left over" (quoted in Saito, *Race and Politics*, 64).

30. The challenges Asian American politicians in the West SGV faced in tapping into an ethnoracial voter base offers a partial explanation for why they had to clear the hurdle of the "old-boy" network. Many in the predominantly ethnic Chinese immigrant population did not have the legal status to vote; those that did were often preoccupied with the more immediate concerns many immigrants face in establishing themselves in a new country or faced language barriers and discrimination (Chang, "Population Gains Slowly Taking Hold").

31. According to Leland Saito, the elections of three Asian American politicians in the 1980s in Monterey Park, with substantial support and funding from Asian Americans, signaled a turning point: "the demise of the white old boy network and the emergence of Latino and Asian American political networks" (Saito, *Race and Politics*, 64).

32. Chang, "Alhambra Race Has Been Ugly."

33. Chang, "Cities Develop Marketing Plans to Lure Patrons."

34. E-mail correspondence with Gregory Thomas, May 24, 2010.

35. Widener, "'Perhaps the Japanese Are to Be Thanked?,'" 136.

36. Lowe, *Immigrant Acts*, 96.

37. Ibid., 96.

38. Ibid., 84–96.

39. See Waters, *Ethnic Options*.

40. Cocks, *Doing the Town*, 194. Also see Kropp, *California Vieja*, 207–60; Deverell, *Whitewashed Adobe*, 49–90; Valle and Torres, *Latino Metropolis*, 67–99.

41. Interview with Susie Ling, April 16, 2007.

42. The most conspicuous example of north-of-Huntington wealth is railroad tycoon Henry Huntington's vast estate in exclusive San Marino. In 1913 Huntington and a group of wealthy ranchers incorporated San Marino, which borders both eastern Alhambra and San Gabriel to the north, when neighboring cities threatened to annex their extensive land holdings. Ever since, San Marino has prided itself on being what the local newspaper calls "the finest, exclusively residential community in the West," with a host of supporting city ordinances from the seemingly trivial (such as a ban on placing trash cans in view of the street) to the more significant (such as a ban on apartment buildings, and a limit of one family per home). Since the 1980s, the historically old-money, white community has changed substantially with a large influx of affluent, ethnic Chinese immigrants. Currently, Asians are a slight plurality, making up nearly half of the residents. However, the community's commitment to preserving property values and exclusivity has otherwise changed very little (Pulido, Barraclough, and Cheng, *A People's Guide to Los Angeles*).

43. Ling, "The Early History of Chinese Americans in the San Gabriel Valley," 25–52; Garcia, *A World of Its Own*.

44. Horton, *The Politics of Diversity*; Fong, *The First Suburban Chinatown*; Saito, *Race and Politics*.

45. Saito, *Race and Politics*, 39–54.

46. Field notes taken by Leland Saito in 1989, quoted in Horton, *The Politics of Diversity*, 92.

47. Further, in the United States, the commonly accepted connotation of the term "Mediterranean" as exclusively European serves to create an ideological erasure of the geographical fact that the Mediterranean Sea is encircled by North Africa and the Middle East as well as Europe.

48. Interview with Susie Ling, April 16, 2007.

49. Horton, *The Politics of Diversity*, 79; Fong, *The First Suburban Chinatown*, 4.

50. Interview with local council member, June 14, 2007. I have omitted the council member's name due to the potentially sensitive nature of his remarks.

51. Shirey, "Show Me the Money."

52. Chavez, "Alhambra Banks on Charming Them."

53. Liu, "Downtown Alhambra Revival"; Vincent, "Big Condo Complex Planned for Alhambra"; Peschiutta, "City Playing Active Role."

54. Peschiutta, "City Playing Active Role."

55. Liu, "Downtown Alhambra Revival."

56. Chavez, "Alhambra Banks on Charming Them."

57. Peschiutta, "City Playing Active Role."

58. Liu, "Downtown Alhambra Revival."

59. Ibid.

60. Chavez, "Alhambra Banks on Charming Them."

61. Here I refer broadly to the rise of the entrepreneurial state, in which decentralization and increased mobility of capital forces municipal governments to compete for investment and wherein public spaces are reshaped as arenas of privatized consumption. See Harvey, *The Urban Experience*; Gregory, *Black Corona*; Weber, "Extracting Value from the City," 519–40; Brenner and Theodore, "Cities and the Geographies of 'Actually Existing Neoliberalism,'" 349–79; Dávila, *Barrio Dreams*.

62. Interview with Albert Huang, March 3, 2009.

63. Phone conversation with Sharon Gibbs, February 11, 2009.

64. Downtown Alhambra Business Association website, http://downtown alhambra.org.

65. Continuing the theme, Alhambra High School's mascot is the Moor. Writer Hisaye Yamamoto makes a brief comment on Alhambra's connection to its Iberian namesake in her memoir, "A Fire in Fontana," 156. In her analysis of the Yamamoto's memoir, Grace Kyungwon Hong quotes this brief passage and discusses it at length:

Once, when hospitalized for an unspecified illness, [Yamamoto] lies next to a woman whose brother confides to her that "he kn[ows] it's wrong, but he didn't want Blacks moving into his neighborhood in Alhambra—no Moors in Alhambra?—because of the drop in property values that would ensue." The ironic question "no Moors in Alhambra?" bursts through [Yamamoto's] summary of the man's statement, underscoring the hypocrisy of naming an all-white town after the famed palace in Granada, Spain, built by Arab conquerors whose name was for a long time synonymous with blackness. This seemingly flippant and sarcastic question also disinters the buried legacies of Spanish colonialism, as well as the acquisition of wealth and property, including what is now Los Angeles, through the American expansionism of the U.S.-Mexico War. Like the "Spanish-style" architecture and Spanish street names so common in California, the name of the incorporated municipality of Alhambra is a facile, sanitized signifier that recalls in a palatable way the history of Los Angeles—a history filled with violent conflicts over property. (Hong, "'Something Forgotten Which Should Have Been Remembered,'" 291–311)

66. Lowe, *Immigrant Acts*, 96.

67. Deverell, *Whitewashed Adobe*.

68. Interview with Mike Murashige, March 30, 2007.

69. Median household income was $56,657 compared to $38,085; per capita income was $24,786 compared to $14,229.

70. The homeownership rate was 64 percent, compared to only 39 percent in the south. Median value of single-family, owner-occupied homes was 41 percent higher in the northern zip code than in the southern ($282,400 compared to $199,900).

71. Approximately one in three residents in the northern zip code were white, while south of Las Tunas Drive, in the southern zip code, only one in ten were (U.S. Census 2000, Summary File 1, DP-1; Summary File 3, DP-2, DP-3, and DP-4).

72. Interview with Albert Huang, May 4, 2007.

73. Interview with Eloy Zarate, April 18, 2007.

74. Pierson, "Dragon Roars in San Gabriel."

75. Huang prevailed in a 4–0 vote over attorney Frank Chen and John Hou, former planning commissioner and president of San Gabriel-based Asian Pacific National Bank (Ho, "Huang Named to San Gabriel City Council").

76. Huang, "The Golden Mile of San Gabriel."

77. As quoted in Ho, "Huang Named to San Gabriel City Council."

78. Carpenter, "From Healing Hands to Haute Handbags."

79. See Zhou and Tseng, "Regrounding the 'Ungrounded Empires,'" 131–54.

80. Ho, "San Gabriel Has Plans."

81. Quoting Deputy City Manager Steve Preston; Ho, "San Gabriel Has Plans"; Ho, "City Wants to Travel Golden Mile." In 2005, San Gabriel Square brought in $378,000 in sales-tax revenue for the city, which receives 1 percent of all taxable sales (Ho, "San Gabriel Has Plans").

82. Huang, "The Golden Mile of San Gabriel."

83. As quoted in Ho, "City Wants to Travel Golden Mile."

84. Interview with Albert Huang, May 4, 2007.

85. Ho, "City Wants to Travel Golden Mile."

86. Chavez, "New Look Reflects an Old Pattern."

87. See Waters, *Ethnic Options*.

88. Interview with Albert Huang, March 10, 2009.

89. See Li, "Building Ethnoburbia"; Li, "Spatial Transformation of an Urban Ethnic Community"; and Tseng, "Suburban Ethnic Economy." Cathay Bank, the first Chinese American bank, was founded in Los Angeles's Chinatown in the early 1960s specifically to counteract mainstream lending discrimination and to help new immigrants navigate U.S. financial institutions. Cathay Bank proceeded to open the first Chinese American bank branch in Monterey Park in 1979, planting the first seed of what would subsequently become the largest concentration of ethnic community-oriented banks in the United States (Li et al., "Chinese-American Banking and Community Development," 777–96; Zhou, "How Do Places Matter?," 531–53).

90. Huang, "The Golden Mile of San Gabriel."

91. Interview with Albert Huang, March 10, 2009.

92. Gilmore, "Profiling Alienated Labor."

93. Interview with Albert Huang, May 4, 2007.

94. Interview with Albert Huang, March 10, 2009.

95. King, "Projects Move Forward on Westwood's Golden Mile."

96. San Gabriel Mission District Partnership, "2005 Business Plan," http://www.sangabrielcity.com/pointsofinterest/documents/Missiondistrictbusinessplan.pdf.

97. Interview with Albert Huang, March 10, 2009.

98. *San Gabriel Grapevine* 13, no. 1 (Winter 2009).

99. Chavez, "New Look Reflects an Old Pattern." Indeed, even across the Pacific, a Spanish-fantasy or faux-Mediterranean architectural style has become emblematic of the "good life" that can be achieved by Asian immigrants in Southern California—as apt an indication as any of the potent ideological cache of this fabricated regional history. See, among others, Rosenthal, "American Dream, Chinese Style."

100. Di, "San Gabriel Golden Mile Development Project Will Continue."

101. Interview with Mario de La Torre, June 11, 2012; Flores, "Council Keeps 'City with a Mission' as San Gabriel's Official Motto."

102. Hackel, "Indian Testimony," 643–69; Pulido et al., *A People's Guide to Los Angeles*.

103. Flores, "Council Keeps 'City with a Mission.'"

104. Flores, "Gabrielinos Balk at San Gabriel's Plan to Change City's Motto"; interview with Mario De La Torre, June 11, 2012.

105. Flores, "Council Keeps 'City with a Mission.'"

106. Flores, "Gabrielinos Balk at San Gabriel's Plan."

107. U.S. Census 2010.

108. Respectively, Flores, "Gabrielinos Balk at San Gabriel's Plan"; Flores, "Council Keeps 'City with a Mission'"; and Flores, "Gabrielinos Balk at San Gabriel's Plan."

109. Flores, "Emotional San Gabriel Mayor."

110. The defeated Asian American candidates were Chin Ho Liao, a retired engineer and president of the San Gabriel Rotary Club, and Philip Ho, an English professor at a local college. *San Gabriel Valley Tribune*, "San Gabriel Council Race Too Close to Call Early"; *San Gabriel Valley Tribune*, "Harrington, Costanzo Win Bids in San Gabriel."

111. In early 2012, in the context of a multiyear budget crisis, the state of California dissolved all city redevelopment agencies, including San Gabriel's. In mid-2012, city council members were also embroiled in bitter conflicts with San Gabriel police officers and firefighters over pension reform (Gold, "San Gabriel Makes Deal in Labor Negotiations").

112. Ho, "Group Rallies to Keep Playground Structures at Park."

113. Lubisich, "Save 'Monster Park.'"

114. Ho, "Lugo Park Playground Sculptures in Jeopardy."

115. KCET, "Life and Times."

116. National Public Radio, "Residents Unite to Save Concrete Animal Park."

117. Ho, "Lugo Park Playground Structures in Jeopardy."

118. Ho, "Group Rallies to Keep Playground Structures."

119. Ho, "Lugo Park Playground Structures in Jeopardy."

120. Interview with Eloy Zarate, April 18, 2007.

121. Friends of La Laguna website, http://www.friendsoflalaguna.org.

122. Rees, "Fairy-Tale Ending."

123. "Around Pasadena."

124. Friends of La Laguna website.

125. Interview with Eloy Zarate, April 18, 2007.

126. Ibid.

127. See Pardo, *Mexican American Women Activists*, on the moral power of motherhood in the environmental justice activism of the group Mothers of East L.A. Also see Gilmore, *Golden Gulag*, 181–240, on how the group Mothers Reclaiming Our Children wielded the "ideological power of motherhood" to challenge the legitimacy of the state's investment in prison expansion.

128. KCET, "Life and Times."

129. Ho, "Group Rallies to Keep Playground Structures."

130. KCET, "Life and Times."

131. Supporters included Margaret Chirivella, Arlene Chavez, Linda Takeuchi, and Kim Totten (KCET, "Life and Times"; KCET, "Monster Park Headed for Extinction?").

132. Interview with Eloy Zarate, April 18, 2007.
133. Ibid., May 3, 2012.
134. Lowe, *Immigrant Acts*, 96.
135. Interview with Eloy Zarate, April 18, 2007.

5. SGV Dreamgirl

1. Interview with Paul Chan and Eladio Wu, June 5, 2008.
2. Spickard, *Mixed Blood*, 12, 15.
3. Two well-known works in mixed-race studies that exemplify this two-fold focus are, respectively, Spickard, *Mixed Blood*; and Root, *Love's Revolution*.
4. In his legal and historical analysis of interethnic social and erotic interactions involving South Asian migrant men in the early twentieth-century American West, Nayan Shah includes in his theorization of "stranger intimacy" a host of relationships. These include fleeting sexual encounters with strangers, heterosexual marriages meant to strengthen claims on property and labor, and dense social networks both produced by and supportive of shifting racial-economic hierarchies. Shah argues that through practices that asserted "bodily autonomy and the ability to associate widely," South Asian migrant men "challenged the conspicuous barriers of race and class segregation and redefined civic participation beyond the narrow confines of legitimate and official politics" (Shah, *Stranger Intimacy*, 266). While the rubrics of strangerhood and transience are key to Shah's expanded concept of intimacy, I found that shared experiences of place and rootedness can also be instrumental in fostering unexpected and potentially transformative forms of intimacy.
5. Lipsitz, "Noises in the Blood," 19–44.
6. Kelley, "Polycultural Me."
7. A pseudonym.
8. Phone interview with Adam Saito, June 13, 2011.
9. Interview with Milo Alvarez, February 27, 2008.
10. Interview with Albert Huang, May 4, 2007.
11. A pseudonym.
12. On the depths and nuances of female friendship, see Faderman, *Surpassing the Love of Men*; and Marcus, *Between Women*. In particular, Marcus argues that female friendships, during the Victorian era in England, allowed women a flexible realm in which they could explore sentiments and behaviors that were not permitted with men and that these friendships regularly blurred lines between friendship, kinship, and romantic love, as these are understood in the contemporary period.
13. Interview with Anita Martinez, June 20, 2008.
14. Ibid. A similar observation to Anita's has been reported in a story that ran

in the *Los Angeles Times* in 2011. Reporter Hector Becerra described an East L.A. accent rooted in Chicano English but common among individuals of multiple races and ethnicities who grew up in particular neighborhoods. (Becerra, "East L.A. Speaks from Its Heart").

15. Phone interview with Maya Garcia, June 16, 2011.

16. See also chapter 1, when Eloy Zarate discusses his fond memories growing up in San Gabriel, with ethnically and racially diverse friends moving freely in and out of one another's houses. Allison Varzally has made similar observations regarding the importance of food and comfort in one another's houses, concerning youthful intimacies of people growing up in Boyle Heights in the early to mid-twentieth century. As Leo Frumkin, a Jew who grew up in Boyle Heights during that time, described it, "[y]ou'd sleep in each other's homes. You'd eat at each other's homes . . . you became internationalists" (quoted in Varzally, *Making a Non-White America*, 64).

17. A pseudonym.

18. Interview with Jenny Tran, June 10, 2011.

19. Ibid.

20. Ibid.

21. A pseudonym.

22. Interview with Walter Ruiz, August 8, 2008.

23. Out of the twenty-three people I interviewed who were in their thirties at the time of the interview, two-thirds discussed dating outside of their own race or ethnicity, either in their current relationships or in the past. The vast majority of women had dated interracially (ten out of twelve), while for men the ratio fell to just less than half (five of eleven). A higher proportion of Asian American women dated interracially than Latinas, while the reverse was true for men. Interracial or interethnic dating was also common among those in their twenties and forties. People in their fifties and older tended to have dated and married people from their same ethnic group, with a few exceptions. In her study of later-generation Chinese and Japanese Americans, Mia Tuan found that the vast majority of those she interviewed who were under forty dated interethnically or interracially, while for those over forty, this was much less common (Tuan, *Forever Foreigners or Honorary Whites?*).

24. A pseudonym.

25. Interview with Lia Chen, October 24, 2007.

26. A pseudonym.

27. Interview with Mark Nakamura, July 17, 2007.

28. Interview with Nancy Do, March 21, 2007.

29. Interview with Lia Chen, October 24, 2007.

30. Interview with Jenny Tran, June 10, 2011.

31. Bonilla-Silva and Embrick, "Black, Honorary White, White," 41. See also Tuan, *Forever Foreigners or Honorary Whites?*, and Spickard, *Mixed Blood*.

32. A pseudonym.

33. As of 2010, South Pasadena's per capita income was close to double that of Alhambra, its immediate neighbor to the south ($44,915 compared to $23,527), and the median property value of owner-occupied housing units was 60 percent higher ($823,199 compared to $493,100). See the 2008–2010 American Community Survey, http://factfinder2.census.gov.

34. Indeed, two other people I interviewed, both Asian American women, mentioned that their families had used circuitous means to gain entry into more prestigious school districts; one, like Ben Avila's family, used a family friend's address. In the other case, the family rented an apartment in South Pasadena for the sole purpose of being able to enroll their children in that school district.

35. All quotations from an interview with Ben Avila, August 17, 2007.

36. In 2010, South Pasadena was more than four times as white as Alhambra (43.6 percent non-Hispanic white compared to 10 percent). Of the remaining residents, 34.5 percent were Asian, 18.6 Hispanic or Latino, and 4.1 percent Black (2010 U.S. Census).

37. For more on this topic, see Bonilla-Silva and Embrick, "Black, Honorary White, White," and George A. Yancey on the positioning of Asian Americans and Latinas/os in the U.S. racial hierarchy (Yancey, *Who Is White?*; Yancey, "Racial Justice in a Black/Nonblack Society"). Bonilla-Silva and Embrick argue that the biracial U.S. hierarchy is developing into a triracial order involving whites, honorary whites, and "collective black"—and that distinct subsets of Asian Americans and Latinas/os fall into all three of these categories. Yancey argues that the United States' white/Black racial order is changing into a Black/non-Black order, in which Asian Americans and Latinas/os will gradually become assimilated into the dominant non-Black category, effectively becoming white.

38. A pseudonym.

39. Phone interview with Elena Tanizaki-Chen, June 23, 2011.

40. Ibid.

41. Interview with Eladio Wu, June 5, 2008.

42. Interview with Russell Lee-Sung, April 18, 2007.

43. A pseudonym.

44. Interview with Jesse Boden, November 12, 2007.

45. See Espiritu, *Asian American Panethnicity*.

46. A pseudonym.

47. Interview with Annie Liu, July 27, 2007.

48. Interview with Jenny Tran, June 10, 2011.

49. A pseudonym.

50. Interview with David Wong, August 7, 2008.

51. Nearly a quarter of ethnic Chinese in Los Angeles are immigrants from

somewhere other than Hong Kong, Taiwan, or China (Zhou, Tseng, and Kim, "Rethinking Residential Assimilation," 53–83, 59).

52. Interview with Susie Ling, April 16, 2007.

53. Interview with Jenny Tran, June 10, 2011.

54. Interview with David Wong, August 7, 2008.

55. Due to his involvement in the community, J. did not wish to be named in relation to this anecdote.

Conclusion

1. Massey, *Space, Place, and Gender*, 156.

2. Gilroy, *Postcolonial Melancholia*, xv.

3. Smith, "Contours of a Spatialized Politics," 55–81.

4. A pseudonym.

5. Interview with Juan Ramirez, February 18, 2008.

6. *Chinito* is a diminutive form of *chino*, or male Chinese; both are often used to refer to a person of any Asian ethnicity.

7. Interview with Juan Ramirez, October 4, 2007.

8. A pseudonym.

9. Interview with Walter Ruiz, August 8, 2008.

10. A pseudonym.

11. Interview with Annie Liu, July 27, 2007.

12. The same year (2007), Black students were 3 percent of the undergraduate student body. UCLA Office of Analysis and Information Management, http://www.aim.ucla.edu/enrollment/enrollment_demographics_fall.asp.

13. Espiritu, *Asian American Panethnicity*; Kibria, *Becoming Asian American*.

14. Interview with Russell Lee-Sung, May 18, 2007.

15. Interview with Lisa Beppu, June 28, 2007.

16. Interview with Grace Ahn, January 16, 2008.

17. A pseudonym.

18. Interview with David Wong, August 7, 2008.

19. A pseudonym.

20. Interview with Jinny Hong, February 8, 2012.

21. Interview with Lisa Beppu, June 28, 2007.

22. Interview with Jinny Hong, February 8, 2012.

23. Interview with Anita Martinez, June 20, 2008.

24. Interview with Gina Alvarez, April 10, 2008.

25. Interview with Milo Alvarez, February 27, 2008.

26. Gramsci, *Selections from the Prison Notebooks*, 330–31.

27. Bhabha, *The Location of Culture*.

Appendix

1. Acuña, *Anything but Mexican*, 35; also cited in Pardo, *Mexican American Women Activists*, 40.
2. A pseudonym.
3. A pseudonym.
4. A pseudonym.
5. A pseudonym.

Bibliography

Acuña, Rodolfo F. *Anything but Mexican: Chicanos in Contemporary Los Angeles*. London: Verso, 1996.

African American Registry. "The Black Boy Scout: A History." http://www.aa registry.com/african_american_history/2781/The_Black_Boy_Scout_a_history.

Allen, Theodore W. *The Invention of the White Race*. London: Verso, 1994.

Almaguer, Tomás. *Racial Fault Lines: The Historical Origins of White Supremacy in California*. Berkeley: University of California Press, 1994.

Althusser, Louis. "Ideology and Ideological State Apparatuses (Notes toward an Investigation)." In *Lenin and Philosophy, and Other Essays*, 85–126. New York: Monthly Review Press, 2001.

Anderson, Kay J. "The Idea of Chinatown: The Power of Place and Institutional Practice in the Making of a Racial Category." *Annals of the Association of American Geographers* 77, no. 4 (1987): 580–98.

———. *Vancouver's Chinatown. Racial Discourse in Canada, 1875–1980*. Montreal, Canada: McGill-Queens University Press, 1995.

Arnold, Matthew. *Culture and Anarchy*. New Haven, Conn.: Yale University Press, 1994.

Baldwin, James. *The Fire Next Time*. New York: Vintage, 1963.

Basler, Carleen. "White Dreams and Red Votes: Mexican Americans and the Lure of Inclusion in the Republican Party." *Ethnic and Racial Studies* 31, no. 1 (2007): 123–66.

Becerra, Hector. "East L.A. Speaks from Its Heart." *Los Angeles Times*, October 25, 2011. http://articles.latimes.com/2011/oct/24/local/la-me-eastla-accent-20111025.

———. "Trying to Bridge the Grade Divide in L.A. Schools." *Los Angeles Times*, July 16, 2008. http://www.latimes.com/news/education/la-me-lincoln16-2008 jul16,0,3130880.story.

Benjamin, Walter. "Theses on the Philosophy of History." In *Illuminations*, edited by Hannah Arendt, 253–64. New York: Schocken Books, 1968.

Bhabha, Homi. *The Location of Culture*. New York: Routledge, 1994.

Blanco, Michael A. "Reject Racist Campaigns (Letter to the Editor)." *San Gabriel Valley Tribune*, October 28, 2004. LexisNexis Academic. Web.

Blauner, Robert. *Racial Oppression in America*. New York: Harper and Row, 1972.

Blaut, James. *The Colonizer's Model of the World: Geographical Diffusionism and Eurocentric History*. New York: Guilford Press, 1993.

Bonilla-Silva, Eduardo. *Racism without Racists: Color-Blind Racism and Racial Inequality in the United States*. 3rd ed. Lanham, Md.: Rowman & Littlefield Publishers, 2010.

———. "We Are All Americans!: The Latin Americanization of Racial Stratification in the USA." *Race & Society* 5 (2002): 3–17.

Bonilla-Silva, Eduardo, and David G. Embrick. "Black, Honorary White, White: The Future of Race in the United States?" In *Mixed Messages: Multiracial Identities in the "Color-Blind" Era*, edited by David L. Brunsma, 33–48. Boulder, Colo.: Lynne Rienner, 2006.

Bourdieu, Pierre. "Forms of Capital." In *The Sociology of Economic Life*, edited by Mark Granovetter and Richard Swedberg, 96–111. Boulder, Colo.: Westview Press, 2001.

Boy Scouts of America. "2006–2010 National Strategic Plan Boy Scouts of America." http://www.scouting.org/Media/AnnualReports/2006/05nsp.aspx.

Brenner, Neil. "The Limits to Scale? Methodological Reflections on Scalar Structuration." *Progress in Human Geography* 25, no. 4 (2001): 591–614.

———. "The Urban Question as a Scale Question: Reflections on Henri Lefebvre, Urban Theory and the Politics of Scale." *International Journal of Urban and Regional Research* 24, no. 2 (2000): 361–78.

Brenner, Neil, and Nik Theodore. "Cities and the Geographies of 'Actually Existing Neoliberalism.'" *Antipode* 34, no. 3 (2002): 349–79.

Brooks, Charlotte. *Alien Neighbors, Foreign Friends: Asian Americans, Housing, and the Transformation of Urban California*. Chicago: University of Chicago Press, 2009.

Bunting, Eve. *So Far from the Sea*. New York: Clarion Books, 1998.

Calderón, José Zapata. "'Hispanic' and 'Latino': The Viability of Categories for Panethnic Unity." *Latin American Perspectives* 19, no. 4 (1992): 37–44.

———. "Mexican American Politics in a Multi-Ethnic Community: The Case of Monterey Park: 1985–1990." PhD diss., University of California, Los Angeles, 1991.

Camarillo, Albert. *Chicanos in a Changing Society: From Mexican Pueblos to American Barrios in Santa Barbara and Southern California, 1848–1930*. Cambridge, Mass.: Harvard University Press, 1979.

Campo-Flores, Adrian, and Sarah Kliff. "Campfire Questions." *Newsweek*, January 26, 2009, 66–67.

Carby, Hazel V. "Schooling in Babylon." In *The Empire Strikes Back: Race and Racism in 70s Britain*, edited by the Center for Contemporary Cultural Studies, 183–211. London: Hutchinson, 1982.

Carpenter, Susan. "From Healing Hands to Haute Handbags; Yes, Valley Boulevard in San Gabriel Is a Great Place for Dim Sum, but That's Only the Beginning." *Los Angeles Times*, March 31, 2005, E.30. http://articles.latimes.com/2005/mar/31/news/wk-cover31.

Chakrabarty, Dipesh. *Provincializing Europe: Postcolonial Thought and Historical Difference*. Princeton, N.J.: Princeton University Press, 2000.

Chang, Cindy. "Alhambra Council a House Divided; Tensions Running High in Alhambra." *Pasadena Star-News*, September 28, 2003. LexisNexis Academic. Web.

———. "Alhambra Election Season to Be 'Bloodbath.'" *Pasadena Star-News*, June 23, 2004. LexisNexis Academic. Web.

———. "Alhambra Mayor at Center of Storm." *Pasadena Star-News*, February 20, 2005. LexisNexis Academic. Web.

———. "Alhambra Race Has Been Ugly." *Pasadena Star-News*, October 31, 2004. LexisNexis Academic. Web.

———. "Bribery Scandal Deepens Council Split." *Pasadena Star-News*, September 15, 2004. LexisNexis Academic. Web.

———. "Cities Develop Marketing Plans to Lure Patrons." *Pasadena Star-News*, August 23, 2003.

———. "Column Creates Uproar." *Pasadena Star-News*, March 30, 2005.

———. "Population Gains Slowly Taking Hold." *San Gabriel Valley Tribune*, May 14, 2005.

———. "Talbot Faction Gains Majority on Council." *Pasadena Star-News*, November 4, 2004. LexisNexis Academic. Web.

———. "Turning out the Asian Vote." *Pasadena Star-News*, October 3, 2004. Lexis Nexis Academic. Web.

Charles, Camille Zubrinksy. "The Dynamics of Racial Residential Segregation." *Annual Review of Sociology* 29 (2003): 167–207.

Chavez, Stephanie. "Alhambra Banks on Charming Them." *Los Angeles Times*, August 12, 2002, B1. http://articles.latimes.com/2002/aug/12/local/me -alhambra12.

———. "New Look Reflects an Old Pattern." *Los Angeles Times*, July 25, 2004. http://articles.latimes.com/2004/jul/25/local/me-gabriel25.

Chen, Hsiang-shui. *Chinatown No More: Taiwan Immigrants in Contemporary New York*. Ithaca, N.Y.: Cornell University Press, 1992.

Cheng, Cindy I-Fen. "Out of Chinatown and into the Suburbs: Chinese Americans and the Politics of Cultural Citizenship in Early Cold War America." *American Quarterly* 58, no. 4 (2006): 1067–90.

Cheng, Wendy. "The Model Minority in the Model Home: Geographies of Race in the New Pan-Asian Suburbs." Master's thesis, University of California, Berkeley, 2003.

Chong, Jia-Rui. "Morphing Outrage into Ideas." *Los Angeles Times*, October 12, 2005. http://articles.latimes.com/2005/oct/12/local/me-alhambra12.

Chow, Rey. *The Protestant Ethnic and the Spirit of Capitalism*. New York: Columbia University Press, 2002.

———. *Writing Diaspora: Tactics of Intervention in Contemporary Cultural Studies.* Bloomington and Indianapolis: Indiana University Press, 1993.

Chuh, Kandice. *Imagine Otherwise: On Asian Americanist Critique.* Durham and London: Duke University Press, 2003.

Clark, William A. V. *The California Cauldron: Immigration and the Fortunes of Local Communities.* New York: Guilford Press, 1998.

Cocks, Catherine. *Doing the Town: The Rise of Urban Tourism in the United States, 1850–1915.* Berkeley: University of California Press, 2001.

Cooper, Michael, and Michael Powell. "McCain Camp Says Obama Is Playing 'Race Card.'" *New York Times,* August 1, 2008. http://www.nytimes.com/2008/08/01/us/politics/01campaign.html.

Costello, Daniel. "Some Backers Pull Boy Scouts' Funding after High Court's Ruling on Gay Scouts." *Wall Street Journal,* August 24, 2000, sec. Law.

Crenshaw, Kimberlé W. "Framing Affirmative Action." *Michigan Law Review* (2007). http://michiganlawreview.org/firstimpressions/vol105/crenshaw.pdf.

Dávila, Arlene M. *Barrio Dreams: Puerto Ricans, Latinos, and the Neoliberal City.* Berkeley: University of California Press, 2004.

De Certeau, Michel. *The Practice of Everyday Life.* Translated by Steven Rendall. Berkeley: University of California Press, 1984.

De Genova, Nicholas, ed. *Racial Transformations: Latinos and Asians Remaking the United States.* Durham, N.C.: Duke University Press, 2006.

De Genova, Nicholas, and Ana Y. Ramos-Zayas. *Latino Crossings: Mexicans, Puerto Ricans, and the Politics of Race and Citizenship.* New York: Routledge, 2003.

Deloria, Philip J. *Playing Indian.* New Haven, Conn.: Yale University Press, 1998.

Deverell, William. *Whitewashed Adobe: The Rise of Los Angeles and the Remaking of Its Mexican Past.* Berkeley: University of California Press, 2004.

Di, Minoshi. "San Gabriel Golden Mile Development Project Will Continue." *Alhambra Source,* October 28, 2010. http://www.alhambrasource.org/inthenews/san-gabriel-golden-mile-development-project-will-continue.

Du Bois, W. E. B. *Black Reconstruction in America.* New York: The Free Press, [1935] 1998.

Duncan, James S., and Nancy Duncan. "Aesthetics, Abjection, and White Privilege in Suburban New York." In *Landscape and Race in the United States,* edited by Richard H. Schein. New York: Routledge, 2006.

———. *Landscapes of Privilege: Aesthetics and Affluence in an American Suburb.* New York: Routledge, 2004.

Eng, David. *Racial Castration: Managing Masculinity in Asian America.* Durham, N.C.: Duke University Press, 2001.

Espiritu, Yen Le. *Asian American Panethnicity: Bridging Institutions and Identities.* Philadelphia: Temple University Press, 1992.

Faderman, Lillian. *Surpassing the Love of Men: Romantic Friendship and Love between Women, from the Renaissance to the Present*. New York: Morrow, 1981.

Fanon, Frantz. *The Wretched of the Earth*. New York: Grove Press, 2004.

Fields, Barbara J. "Slavery, Race and Ideology in the United States of America." *New Left Review* 181 (1990): 95–118.

Flores, Adolfo. "Council Keeps 'City with a Mission' as San Gabriel's Official Motto." *Pasadena Star-News*, September 27, 2010. LexisNexis Academic. Web.

———. "Emotional San Gabriel Mayor Announces Resignation after Arrest in Domestic Violence Case." *Whittier Daily News*, October 19, 2010. LexisNexis Academic. Web.

———. "Gabrielinos Balk at San Gabriel's Plan to Change City's Motto." *Pasadena Star-News*, September 8, 2010. LexisNexis Academic. Web.

Foley, Neil. *The White Scourge: Mexicans, Blacks, and Poor Whites in Texas Cotton Culture*. Berkeley: University of California Press, 1997.

Fong, Joe C. *Complementary Education and Culture in the Global/Local Chinese Community*. San Francisco: China Books and Periodicals, 2003.

Fong, Timothy. *The First Suburban Chinatown: The Remaking of Monterey Park, California*. Philadelphia: Temple University Press, 1994.

Foucault, Michel. *The Archaeology of Knowledge and the Discourse on Language*. New York: Pantheon, 1982.

———. *Discipline and Punish: The Birth of the Prison*. Translated by Alan Sheridan. New York: Vintage Books, 1995.

———. *Power/Knowledge: Selected Interviews and Writings, 1972–1977*. New York: Pantheon, 1980.

———. *"Society Must Be Defended": Lectures at the College De France, 1975–1976*. New York: Picador, 2003.

Fredrickson, George M. *White Supremacy: A Comparative Study of American and South African History*. Oxford, U.K.: Oxford University Press, 1981.

Freund, David M. P. *Colored Property: State Policy and White Racial Politics in Suburban America*. Chicago: University of Chicago Press, 2007.

Friends of La Laguna Website. http://www.friendsoflalaguna.org.

Gallay, Alan. *The Indian Slave Trade: The Rise of the English Empire in the American South, 1670–1717*. New Haven: Yale University Press, 2002.

Garcia, Matt. *A World of Its Own: Race, Labor, and Citrus in the Making of Greater Los Angeles, 1900–1970*. Chapel Hill: University of North Carolina Press, 2001.

Gilmore, Ruth Wilson. "Fatal Couplings of Power and Difference: Notes on Racism and Geography." *The Professional Geographer* 54, no. 1 (2002): 15–24.

———. "Forgotten Places and the Seeds of Grassroots Planning." In *Engaging Contradictions: Theory, Politics, and Methods of Activist Scholarship*, edited by Charles Hale, 31–61. Berkeley: University of California Press, 2008.

———. *Golden Gulag: Prisons, Surplus, Crisis, and Opposition in Globalizing California*. Berkeley: University of California Press, 2006.

———. "Profiling Alienated Labor: Scale, Racialization, and Re-Partitioned Geographies." Paper presented at Con/Vergences: Critical Interventions in the Politics of Race and Gender, Center for Race and Gender Inaugural Conference, University of California, Berkeley, February 2004.

———. "Race and Globalization." In *Geographies of Global Change*, edited by Johnson et al., 261–74. Oxford: Blackwell, 2002.

Gilroy, Paul. *Postcolonial Melancholia (The Wellek Lectures)*. New York: Columbia University Press, 2005.

Glenn, Evelyn Nakano. *Unequal Freedom: How Race and Gender Shaped American Citizenship and Labor*. Cambridge, Mass.: Harvard University Press, 2002.

Gold, Lauren. "San Gabriel Makes Deal in Labor Negotiations." *Pasadena Star-News*, May 17, 2012.

Gómez, Laura. *Manifest Destinies: The Making of the Mexican American Race*. New York: New York University Press, 2007.

Gonzalez, Jerry. "'A Place in the Sun': Mexican Americans, Race, and the Suburbanization of Los Angeles, 1940–1980." PhD diss., University of Southern California, 2009.

Gotanda, Neil. "A Critique of 'Our Constitution Is Color-Blind.'" *Stanford Law Review* 44, no. 1 (1991): 1–68.

Gould, Stephen Jay. *The Mismeasure of Man*. Rev. ed. New York: W. W. Norton and Company, 1996.

Gramsci, Antonio. *Selections from the Prison Notebooks*. Translated by Quintin Hoare and Geoffrey Nowell Smith. New York: International Publishers, [1971] 2005.

Greenberg, Miriam. *Branding New York: How a City in Crisis Was Sold to the World*. New York: Routledge, 2008.

Gregory, Steven. *Black Corona*. Princeton, N.J.: Princeton University Press, 1999.

Guevarra, Rudy P., Jr. *Becoming Mexipino: Multiethnic Identities and Communities in San Diego*. New Brunswick: Rutgers University Press, 2012.

Gutiérrez, David. *Walls and Mirrors: Mexican Americans, Mexican Immigrants, and the Politics of Ethnicity*. Berkeley: University of California Press, 1995.

Hackel, Steve W. "Indian Testimony and the Mission San Gabriel Uprising of 1785." *Ethnohistory* 50, no. 4 (2003): 643–69. doi:10.1215/00141801-50-4-643.

Hall, Stuart. "Cultural Identity and Diaspora." In *Identity: Community, Culture, Difference*, edited by Jonathan Rutherford. London: Lawrence & Wishart, 1990.

———. "Gramsci's Relevance for the Study of Race and Ethnicity." In *Stuart Hall: Critical Dialogues in Cultural Studies*, edited by David Morley and Kuan-Hsing Chen, 411–40. London and New York: Routledge, 1996.

————. "Race, Articulation and Societies Structured in Dominance." In *Sociological Theories: Race and Colonialism*, 305–41. Paris: UNESCO, 1980.

————. "Re-Thinking the 'Base-and-Superstructure Metaphor.'" In *Class, Hegemony and Party*, edited by Jon Bloomfield, 43–72. London: Lawrence and Wishart, 1971.

Haney López, Ian F. "Post-Racial Racism: Racial Stratification and Mass Incarceration in the Age of Obama." *California Law Review* 98, no. 3 (2010): 1023.

————. *White by Law: The Legal Construction of Race*. New York: New York University Press, 2006.

Harris, Cheryl. "Whiteness as Property." *Harvard Law Review* 106, no. 8 (1993): 1707–91.

Harvey, David. *The Urban Experience*. Baltimore, Md.: Johns Hopkins University Press, 1989.

Hayden, Dolores. *The Power of Place: Urban Landscapes as Public History*. Cambridge, Mass.: MIT Press, 1995.

Hicks, Joe R. "Drop the Race Card." *Washington Post*, April 15, 2007, B01. http://www.washingtonpost.com/wp-dyn/content/article/2007/04/13/AR2007041302089.html.

Ho, Patricia Jiayi. "Arguello's Road to Re-Election Rocky." *Pasadena Star-News*, September 30, 2006. LexisNexis Academic. Web.

————. "City Wants to Travel Golden Mile." *San Gabriel Valley Tribune*, March 25, 2007. LexisNexis Academic. Web.

————. "Group Rallies to Keep Playground Structures at Park." *San Gabriel Valley Tribune*, December 21, 2006. LexisNexis Academic. Web.

————. "Huang Named to San Gabriel City Council." *Pasadena Star-News*, May 23, 2006. LexisNexis Academic. Web.

————. "Lugo Park Playground Sculptures in Jeopardy." *Pasadena Star-News*, December 2, 2006. LexisNexis Academic. Web.

————. "Revealing Pieces of San Gabriel's Past." *Pasadena Star-News*, March 22, 2007. LexisNexis Academic. Web.

————. "San Gabriel Has Plans for Valley Boulevard Development." *Pasadena Star-News*, September 24, 2006. LexisNexis Academic. Web.

————. "Termed-Out Councilmen Loom Large." *Pasadena Star-News*, December 25, 2006. LexisNexis Academic. Web.

Ho, Pensri. "(E)Racing the Model Minority: Racial Ideology among Young Urbanized Asian American Professionals." PhD diss., University of Southern California, 2000.

Hong, Grace Kyungwon. "'Something Forgotten Which Should Have Been Remembered': Private Property and Cross-Racial Solidarity in the Work of Hisaye Yamamoto." *American Literature* 71, no. 2 (1999): 291–311.

Horsman, Reginald. *Race and Manifest Destiny: The Origins of American Racial Anglo-Saxonism.* Cambridge, Mass.: Harvard University Press, 1981.

Horton, John. *The Politics of Diversity: Immigration, Resistance, and Change in Monterey Park, California.* Philadelphia: Temple University Press, 1995.

HoSang, Daniel Martinez. *Racial Propositions: Ballot Initiatives and the Making of Postwar California.* Berkeley: University of California Press, 2010.

———. "The Rise of Racial Liberalism, the Decline of Racial Justice: Lessons from California." In *Race and American Political Development,* edited by Julie Novkov, Joe Lowndes, and Dorian Warren. New York: Routledge, 2008.

Huang, Albert Y. M. "The Golden Mile of San Gabriel (Proposed)." Personal copy, courtesy of Albert Huang, 2009.

Huhndorf, Shari M. *Going Native: Indians in the American Cultural Imagination.* Ithaca: Cornell University Press, 2001.

Inouye, Kazuo. "Interview with Kazuo K. Inouye Conducted by Leslie Ito." *REgenerations Oral History Project: Rebuilding Japanese American Families, Communities, and Civil Rights in the Resettlement Era, Los Angeles Region: Volume II,* Japanese American National Museum, December 13, 1997. http://content.cdlib.org/xtf/view?docId=ft3580032z1&doc.view=frames&chunk.id=doe8239&toc.depth=1&toc.id=doe8239&brand=calisphere.

Jackson, Kenneth T. *Crabgrass Frontier: The Suburbanization of the United States.* New York: Oxford University Press, 1985.

Jackson, Robert H. and Edward D. Castillo. *Indians, Franciscans, and Spanish Colonization: The Impact of the Mission System on California Indians.* Albuquerque: University of New Mexico Press, 1995.

Jacobson, Matthew Frye. *Whiteness of a Different Color: European Immigrants and the Alchemy of Race.* Cambridge, Mass.: Harvard University Press, 1998.

Jung, Moon-Kie. *Reworking Race: The Making of Hawaii's Interracial Labor Movement.* New York: Columbia University Press, 2006.

KCET. "Life and Times," January 9, 2007. http://kcet.org/lifeandtimes/archives/200701/20070109.php.

———. "Monster Park Headed for Extinction?" January 9, 2007. http://www.kcet.org/lifeandtimes/blog/index.php?p=144&kcet_speed=hi&kcet_play=1.

Kelley, Robin D. G. "Polycultural Me." *ColorLines* (Winter 1999). http://www.utne.com/1999-09-01/the-people-in-me.aspx.

Kibria, Nazli. *Becoming Asian American: Second-Generation Chinese and Korean American Identities.* Baltimore, Md.: Johns Hopkins University Press, 2002.

Kim, Claire Jean. *Bitter Fruit: The Politics of Black-Korean Conflict in New York City.* New Haven: Yale University Press, 2000.

———. "The Racial Triangulation of Asian Americans." *Politics & Society* 27, no. 1 (1999): 105–38.

King, Danny. "Projects Move Forward on Westwood's Golden Mile." *Los Angeles Business Journal*, September 1, 2003, 3.

Koshy, Susan. "Morphing Race into Ethnicity: Asian Americans and Critical Transformations of Whiteness." *boundary 2* 28, no. 1 (2001): 153–94.

Kropp, Phoebe S. *California Vieja: Culture and Memory in a Modern American Place.* Berkeley: University of California Press, 2006.

Kurashige, Scott. "The Many Facets of Brown: Integration in a Multiracial Society." *Journal of American History* 91 (2004): 56–68.

———. *The Shifting Grounds of Race: Black and Japanese Americans in the Making of Multiethnic Los Angeles.* Princeton: Princeton University Press, 2008.

Ladson-Billings, Gloria. "From the Achievement Gap to the Education Debt: Understanding Achievement in U.S. Schools." *Educational Researcher* 35, no. 7 (2006): 3–12.

Lai, Clement. "The Racial Triangulation of Space: The Case of Urban Renewal in San Francisco's Fillmore District." *Annals of the Association of American Geographers* 102, no. 1 (2012): 151–170.

Lee, Stacey. *Unraveling the "Model Minority" Stereotype: Listening to Asian American Youth.* New York: Teachers College Press, 1996.

Lefebvre, Henri. *The Production of Space.* Translated by Donald Nicholson-Smith. Oxford, U.K.: Blackwell, [1974] 1991.

Leonard, Karen. *Making Ethnic Choices: California's Punjabi Mexican Americans.* Philadelphia: Temple University Press, 1992.

Li, Peter S. "Unneighbourly Houses or Unwelcome Chinese: The Social Construction of Race in the Battle over 'Monster Homes' in Vancouver." *International Journal of Comparative Race and Ethnic Studies* 1, no. 1 (1994): 14–33.

Li, Wei. "Beyond Chinatown, Beyond Enclave: Reconceptualizing Contemporary Chinese Settlements in the United States." *GeoJournal* 64 (2005): 31–40.

———. "Building Ethnoburbia: The Emergence and Manifestation of the Chinese Ethnoburb in Los Angeles' San Gabriel Valley." *Journal of Asian American Studies* 2, no. 1 (1999): 1–28.

———. *Ethnoburb: The New Ethnic Community in Urban America.* Honolulu: University of Hawai'i Press, 2009.

———. "Spatial Transformation of an Urban Ethnic Community: From Chinatown to Ethnoburb in Los Angeles." In *From Urban Enclave to Ethnic Suburb: New Asian Communities in Pacific Rim Communities,* edited by Wei Li, 74–94. Honolulu: University of Hawai'i Press, 2006.

Li, Wei, Gary Dymski, Yu Zhou, Maria Chee, and Carolyn Aldana. "Chinese-American Banking and Community Development in Los Angeles County." *Annals of the Association of American Geographers* 92, no. 4 (2002): 777–96.

Li, Wei, and Edward J. W. Park. "Asian Americans in Silicon Valley: High-Technology Industry Development and Community Transformation." In

From Urban Enclave to Ethnic Suburb, edited by Wei Li, 119–33. Honolulu: University of Hawai'i Press, 2006.

Limerick, Patricia Nelson. *The Legacy of Conquest: The Unbroken Past of the American West*. New York: Norton, 1987.

Lin, Jan. *Reconstructing Chinatown: Ethnic Enclave, Global Change*. Minneapolis: University of Minnesota Press, 1998.

Ling, Susie. "The Early History of Chinese Americans in the San Gabriel Valley." *Gum Saan Journal* 29, no. 1 (2005): 25–52.

———. "Pre-War Japanese Americans in the San Gabriel Valley." Unpublished manuscript, 2003.

Lipsitz, George. *How Racism Takes Place*. Philadelphia: Temple University Press, 2011.

———. "Noises in the Blood: Culture, Conflict, and Mixed Race Identities." In *Crossing Lines: Race and Mixed Race across Geohistorical Divide*, edited by Marc Coronado, Rudy P. Guevarra Jr., Jeffrey Moniz, and Laura Furlan Szanto, 19–44. Lanham, Md.: Rowman Altamira, 2003.

———. *The Possessive Investment in Whiteness: How White People Profit from Identity Politics*. Philadelphia: Temple University Press, 1998.

———. "The Racialization of Space and the Spatialization of Race: Theorizing the Hidden Architecture of Landscape." *Landscape Journal* 26, no. 1 (2007): 10–23.

———. "'To Tell the Truth and Not Get Trapped': Why Interethnic Activism Matters Now." In *Orientations: Mapping Studies in the Asian Diaspora*, edited by Kandice Chuh and Karen Shimakawa, 296–309. Durham, N.C.: Duke University Press, 2001.

Little Tokyo Historical Society. "Koyasan Betsuin Temple." http://www.discover nikkei.org/dj/nikkeialbum/files/filemanager/public/active/5/Koyasan%20 Summary.doc.

Liu, Caitlin. "Downtown Alhambra Revival Stirs up Business and Controversy." *Los Angeles Times*, November 9, 1998.

Loewen, James W. *The Mississippi Chinese: Between Black and White*. Long Grove, Ill.: Waveland Press, 1971.

López-Garza, Marta C., and David R. Diaz, eds. *Asian and Latino Immigrants in a Restructuring Economy: The Metamorphosis of Southern California*. Stanford: Stanford University Press, 2001.

Louie, Vivian S. *Compelled to Excel: Immigration, Education, and Opportunity among Chinese Americans*. Stanford: Stanford University Press, 2004.

Lowe, Lisa. *Immigrant Acts: On Asian American Cultural Politics*. Durham and London: Duke University Press, 1996.

———. "The International within the National: American Studies and Asian American Critique." *Cultural Critique* 40 (1998): 29–47.

Lubisich, Senya. "Save 'Monster Park' (Letter to the Editor)." *San Gabriel Valley Tribune*, November 15, 2006.

Lung Amam, Willow S. "Cosmopolitan Suburbs: Race, Immigration, and the Politics of Development in the Silicon Valley." PhD diss., University of California, Berkeley, 2012.

Lynch, Kevin. *The Image of the City*. Cambridge, Mass.: Technology Press, 1960.

MacDonald, Robert H. *Sons of the Empire: The Frontier and the Boy Scout Movement, 1890–1918*. Toronto: University of Toronto Press, 1993.

Macleod, David I. *Building Character in the American Boy: The Boy Scouts, YMCA, and Their Forerunners, 1870–1920*. Madison: University of Wisconsin Press, 1983.

Marcus, Sharon. *Between Women: Friendship, Desire, and Marriage in Victorian England*. Princeton: Princeton University Press, 2007.

Marston, Sallie A. "The Social Construction of Scale." *Progress in Human Geography* 24, no. 2 (2000): 219–42.

Marston, Sallie A., John Paul Jones III, and Keith Woodward. "Human Geography without Scale." *Transactions of the Institute of British Geographers* 30, no. 4 (2005): 416–32.

Marston, Sallie A., and Neil Smith. "States, Scales and Households: Limits to Scale Thinking? A Response to Brenner." *Progress in Human Geography* 25, no. 4 (2001): 615–19.

Massey, Doreen B. *Space, Place, and Gender*. Minneapolis: University of Minnesota Press, 1994.

———. *Spatial Divisions of Labor: Social Structures and the Geography of Production*. 2nd ed. New York: Routledge, 1995.

———. "Travelling Thoughts." In *Without Guarantees: In Honor of Stuart Hall*, edited by Lawrence Grossberg, Paul Gilroy, and Angela McRobbie, 225–32. London: Verso, 2000.

Massey, Douglas S., and Nancy A. Denton. *American Apartheid: Segregation and the Making of the Underclass*. Cambridge, Mass.: Harvard University Press, 1993.

McKittrick, Katherine, and Clyde Woods, eds. *Black Geographies and the Politics of Place*. Cambridge, Mass.: South End Press, 2007.

McWilliams, Carey. *Southern California: An Island on the Land*. Salt Lake City, Utah: Gibbs Smith, [1946] 1973.

Mechling, Jay. *On My Honor: Boy Scouts and the Making of American Youth*. Chicago: University of Chicago Press, 2001.

Mills, Charles W. *The Racial Contract*. Ithaca, N.Y.: Cornell University Press, 1997.

Mitchell, Katharyne. *Crossing the Neoliberal Line: Pacific Rim Migration and the Metropolis*. Philadelphia: Temple University Press, 2004.

Moctezuma, Alessandra, and Mike Davis. "Policing the Third Border." *Colorlines*,

Fall 1999. http://colorlines.com/archives/1999/11/policing_the_third_border .html.

Molina, Natalia. *Fit to Be Citizens? Public Health and Race in Los Angeles, 1879–1939.* Berkeley: University of California Press, 2006.

Muñoz, Jose Esteban. *Disidentifications: Queers of Color and the Performance of Politics.* Minneapolis: University of Minnesota Press, 1999.

Muskal, Michael. "Census Bureau: Minority Births Outnumbered Whites for First Time." *Los Angeles Times,* May 17, 2012. http://www.latimes.com/news/ nation/nationnow/la-na-nn-census-data-20120517,0,7475788.story.

National Public Radio. "Residents Unite to Save Concrete Animal Park." *Day to Day,* December 28, 2006.

Ngai, Mae. *Impossible Subjects: Illegal Aliens and the Making of Modern America.* Princeton and Oxford: Princeton University Press, 2004.

Nguyen, Viet Thanh. *Race and Resistance: Literature and Politics in Asian America.* New York: Oxford University Press, 2002.

Nicolaides, Becky M. *My Blue Heaven: Life and Politics in the Working-Class Suburbs of Los Angeles, 1920–1965.* Chicago: University of Chicago Press, 2002.

O'Brien, Eileen. *The Racial Middle: Latinos and Asian Americans Living beyond the Racial Divide.* New York: New York University Press, 2008.

Ochoa, Gilda L. *Becoming Neighbors in a Mexican American Community: Power, Conflict, and Solidarity.* Austin: University of Texas Press, 2004.

Oliver, J. Eric, and Janelle Wong. "Intergroup Prejudice in Multiethnic Settings." *American Journal of Political Science* 47, no. 4 (2003): 567–82.

Oliver, Melvin L., and Thomas M. Shapiro. *Black Wealth/White Wealth: A New Perspective on Racial Inequality.* New York: Routledge, 1995.

Omi, Michael, and Howard Winant. *Racial Formation in the United States.* New York: Routledge, 1994.

Ong, Aihwa. *Flexible Citizenship: The Cultural Logics of Transnationality.* Durham, N.C.: Duke University Press, 1999.

———, and Donald M. Nonini, ed. *Ungrounded Empires: The Cultural Politics of Modern Chinese Transnationalism.* New York: Routledge, 1997.

Ong, Paul, Edna Bonacich, and Lucie Cheng, eds. *The New Asian Immigration in Los Angeles and Global Restructuring.* Philadelphia: Temple University Press, 1994.

Orenstein, Dara. "Void for Vagueness." *Pacific Historical Review* 74, no. 3 (2005): 367–408.

Osborne, Jason W. "Academics, Self-Esteem, and Race: A Look at the Underlying Assumptions of the Disidentification Hypothesis." *PSPB* 21, no. 5 (1995): 449–55.

Paasi, Anssi. "Place and Region: Looking through the Prism of Scale." *Progress in Human Geography* 28, no. 4 (2004): 536–46.

Paik, Susan J., and Herbert J. Wahlberg, eds. *Narrowing the Achievement Gap: Strategies for Educating Latino, Black, and Asian Students*. New York: Springer, 2007.

Painter, Gary, Stuart Gabriel, and Dowell Myers. "Race, Immigrant Status, and Housing Tenure Choice." *Journal of Urban Economics* 49 (2001): 150–67.

Palumbo-Liu, David. *Asian/American: Historical Crossings of a Racial Frontier*. Stanford: Stanford University Press, 1999.

Pardo, Mary S. *Mexican American Women Activists: Identity and Resistance in Two Los Angeles Communities*. Philadelphia: Temple University Press, 1998.

Pasadena Star-News. "Around Pasadena," September 6, 2007.

Pascoe, Peggy. *What Comes Naturally: Miscegenation Law and the Making of Race in America*. Oxford, U.K.: Oxford University Press, 2009.

Pattillo-McCoy, Mary. *Black Picket Fences: Privilege and Peril among the Black Middle Class*. Chicago: University of Chicago Press, 1999.

Peschiutta, Claudia. "City Playing Active Role in Revitalization of Main Street (Spotlight on Alhambra)." *Los Angeles Business Journal*, January 21, 2002.

Peterson, Robert W. *The Boy Scouts: An American Adventure*. New York: American Heritage, 1984.

———. "Scouting in World War II Detention Camps." *Scouting Magazine*, November–December 1999. http://scoutingmagazine.org/issues/9911/d-wwas.html.

Pierson, David. "Dragon Roars in San Gabriel." *Los Angeles Times*, March 31, 2006. http://articles.latimes.com/2006/mar/31/local/me-sangabriel31.

———. "Chi Mui, 53; Was the First Mayor of Asian Descent in San Gabriel's History." *Los Angeles Times*, April 28, 2006, B-11. http://articles.latimes.com/2006/apr/28/local/me-mui28.

Pitt, Leonard. *The Decline of the Californios: A Social History of the Spanish-Speaking Californians, 1846–1890*. Berkeley: University of California Press, 1998.

Portes, Alejandro, and Ruben G. Rumbaut. *Legacies: The Story of the Immigrant Second Generation*. Berkeley: University of California Press, 2001.

Powers, Jeanne. "Mendez V. Westminster (1946) as a Window into Mid-Century Racial Ideologies." Paper presented at Annual Meeting of the American Sociological Association, New York, N.Y., August 11, 2007. http://www.allacademic.com/meta/p110773_index.html.

Prado, Jose Miranda. "A Critical Social Capital Analysis of Educational Tracking in the West San Gabriel Valley." PhD diss., University of Southern California, 2006.

Pulido, Laura. *Black, Brown, Yellow, and Left: Radical Activism in Los Angeles*. Berkeley: University of California Press, 2006.

———. "Development of the 'People of Color' Identity in the Environmental Justice Movement of the Southwestern U.S." *Socialist Review* 96, no. 4 (1996): 145–80.

———. "Rethinking Environmental Racism: White Privilege and Urban Development in Southern California." *Annals of the Association of American Geographers* 90, no. 1 (2000): 12–20.

Pulido, Laura, Laura Barraclough, and Wendy Cheng. *A People's Guide to Los Angeles*. Berkeley: University of California Press, 2012.

Quintana, Isabella Seong-Leong. "National Borders, Neighborhood Boundaries: Gender, Space and Border Formation in Chinese and Mexican Los Angeles, 1871–1938." PhD diss., University of Michigan, 2010.

Rees, Brenda. "Fairy-Tale Ending: A California Playground Gets a Second Chance." In *Preservation Magazine*, March 30, 2007. http://www.preservation nation.org/magazine/story-of-the-week/2007/fairy-tale-ending.html.

Ringle, Ken. "The Patriot; Norman Mineta Was Interned by His Country, but Still He Loved It. Then He Changed It." *Washington Post*, August 21, 2000.

Robinson, Cedric J. *Black Marxism: The Making of the Black Radical Tradition*. Chapel Hill: University of North Carolina Press, [1983] 2000.

Robinson, Toni, and Greg Robinson. "The Limits of Interracial Coalitions: Mendez V. Westminster Reexamined." In *Racial Transformations: Latinos and Asians Remaking the United States*, edited by Nicholas De Genova, 93–119. Durham, N.C.: Duke University Press, 2006.

Robles, Rowena A. *Asian Americans and the Shifting Politics of Race: The Dismantling of Affirmative Action at an Elite Public High School*. New York: Routledge, 2006.

Rodriguez, Clara E. *Changing Race: Latinos, the Census, and the History of Ethnicity in the United States*. New York: New York University Press, 2000.

Roediger, David R. *The Wages of Whiteness: Race and the Making of the American Working Class*. London and New York: Verso, 1991.

———. *Working toward Whiteness: How America's Immigrants Became White: The Strange Journey from Ellis Island to the Suburbs*. New York: Basic Books, 2005.

Rojas, James. "The Cultural Landscape of a Latino Community." In *Landscape and Race in the United States*, edited by Richard H Schein, 177–85. New York: Routledge, 2006.

Root, Maria P. P. *Love's Revolution: Interracial Marriage*. Philadelphia: Temple University Press, 2001.

Rosenthal, Elisabeth. "American Dream, Chinese Style; California Mansions Sprout up on the Outskirts of Beijing." *New York Times*, February 5, 2003.

Said, Edward. *Orientalism*. New York: Vintage Books, 1978.

Saito, Leland T. "The Political Significance of Race: Asian American and Latino Redistricting Debates in California and New York City." In *Racial Transformations: Latinos and Asians Remaking the United States*, edited by Nicholas De Genova. Durham, N.C.: Duke University Press, 2006.

———. "The Politics of Adaptation and the 'Good Immigrant': Japanese Americans and the New Chinese Immigrants." In *Asian and Latino Immigrants in a Restructuring Economy: The Metamorphosis of Southern California*, edited by Marta C. López-Garza and David R. Diaz, 332–50. Stanford: Stanford University Press, 2001.

———. *Race and Politics: Asian Americans, Latinos, and Whites in a Los Angeles Suburb*. Urbana: University of Illinois Press, 1998.

Sánchez, George J. *Becoming Mexican American: Ethnicity, Culture and Identity in Chicano Los Angeles, 1900–1945*. Oxford and New York: Oxford University Press, 1993.

———. "'What's Good for Boyle Heights Is Good for the Jews': Creating Multiracialism on the Eastside during the 1950s." *American Quarterly* 56, no. 3 (2004): 633–62.

San Gabriel Mission District Partnership. "Business Plan, 2005." http://www.san gabrielcity.com/pointsofinterest/documents/Missiondistrictbusinessplan.pdf.

San Gabriel Valley Tribune. "Alhambra Factionalism (Editorial)," November 5, 2004. LexisNexis Academic. Web. August 4, 2009.

———. "Harrington, Costanzo Win Bids in San Gabriel," March 9, 2011. LexisNexis Academic. Web. August 4, 2009.

———. "San Gabriel Council Race Too Close to Call Early," March 8, 2011. LexisNexis Academic. Web. August 4, 2009.

Saxton, Alexander. *The Indispensable Enemy: Labor and the Anti-Chinese Movement in California*. Berkeley: University of California Press, [1971] 1995.

Schein, Richard, ed. *Landscape and Race in the United States*. New York: Routledge, 2006.

———. "Normative Dimensions of Landscape." In *Everyday America: Cultural Landscape Studies after J. B. Jackson*, edited by Chris Wilson and Paul Groth, 199–218. Berkeley: University of California Press, 2003.

SGV Website. http://www.sgvforlife.com.

Shah, Nayan. *Contagious Divides: Epidemics and Race in San Francisco's Chinatown*. Berkeley: University of California Press, 2001.

———. *Stranger Intimacy: Contesting Race, Sexuality, and the Law in the North American West*. Berkeley: University of California Press, 2011.

Shapiro, Thomas M. *The Hidden Cost of Being African American: How Wealth Perpetuates Inequality*. New York: Oxford University Press, 2004.

Sheppard, Eric, and Robert McMaster, eds. *Scale and Geographic Inquiry: Nature, Society, and Method*. Oxford, U.K.: Blackwell, 2004.

Shirey, John F. "Show Me the Money: The Economic Impact of Redevelopment." *Western City Magazine*, May 2005.

Sides, Josh. *L.A. City Limits: African American Los Angeles from the Great Depression to the Present*. Berkeley: University of California Press, 2003.

Slotkin, Richard. *The Fatal Environment: The Myth of the Frontier in the Age of Industrialization, 1800–1890.* New York: Atheneum Press, 1985.

———. *Gunfighter Nation: The Myth of the Frontier in Twentieth-Century America.* New York: Atheneum Press, 1992.

———. *Regeneration through Violence: The Mythology of the American Frontier, 1600–1860.* Middletown, Conn.: Wesleyan University Press, 1973.

Smith, Neil. "Contours of a Spatialized Politics: Homeless Vehicles and the Production of Geographical Scale." *Social Text* 33 (1992): 55–81.

Smith, Stacey L. *Freedom's Frontier: California and the Struggle over Unfree Labor, Emancipation, and Reconstruction.* Chapel Hill: University of North Carolina Press, 2013.

Spickard, Paul R. *Mixed Blood: Intermarriage and Ethnic Identity in Twentieth-Century America.* Madison: University of Wisconsin Press, 1989.

Spivak, Gayatri Chakravorty. "Subaltern Studies: Deconstructing Historiography." In *Selected Subaltern Studies,* edited by Ranajit Guha and Gayatri Spivak, 3–32. Oxford, U.K.: Oxford University Press, 1988.

Stanton-Salazar, Richard D. *Manufacturing Hope and Despair: The School and Kin Support Networks of U.S.-Mexican Youth.* New York: Teachers College Press, 2001.

Steele, Claude M. "Race and the Schooling of Black Americans." *The Atlantic Monthly,* April 1992, 68–78.

Sugrue, Thomas. *The Origins of the Urban Crisis: Race and Inequality in Postwar Detroit.* Princeton: Princeton University Press, 1996.

Swyngedouw, Erik. "6 Scaled Geographies: Nature, Place, and the Politics of Scale." In *Scale and Geographic Inquiry: Nature, Society, and Method,* edited by Eric Sheppard and Robert B. McMaster, 129–53. Oxford, U.K.: Blackwell, 2004.

Takagi, Dana Y. *The Retreat from Race: Asian-American Admissions and Racial Politics.* New Brunwsick, N.J.: Rutgers University Press, 1992.

Takaki, Ronald, ed. *Debating Diversity: Clashing Perspectives on Race and Ethnicity in America.* 3rd ed. New York: Oxford University Press, 2002.

Tongson, Karen. *Relocations: Queer Suburban Imaginaries.* New York: New York University Press, 2011.

Townley, Alvin. *Legacy of Honor: The Values and Influence of America's Eagle Scouts.* New York: Thomas Dunne Books, 2007.

Toyota, Tritia. *Envisioning America: New Chinese Americans and the Politics of Belonging.* Stanford: Stanford University Press, 2010.

Tseng, Yen-Fen. "Suburban Ethnic Economy: Chinese Business Communities in Los Angeles." PhD diss., UCLA, 1994.

Tuan, Mia. *Forever Foreigners or Honorary Whites? The Asian Ethnic Experience Today.* New Brunswick, N.J.: Rutgers University Press, 1998.

Valenzuela, Angela. *Subtractive Schooling: U.S.-Mexican Youth and the Politics of Caring*. Albany, N.Y.: State University of New York Press, 1999.

Valle, Victor M., and Rodolfo D. Torres. *Latino Metropolis*. Minneapolis: University of Minnesota Press, 2000.

Varzally, Allison. *Making a Non-White America: Californians Coloring outside Ethnic Lines, 1925–1955*. Berkeley: University of California Press, 2008.

Villa, Raul Homero. *Barrio-Logos: Space and Place in Urban Chicano Literature and Culture*. Austin: University of Texas Press, 2000.

Vincent, Roger. "Big Condo Complex Planned for Alhambra." *Los Angeles Times*, October 10, 2006. http://articles.latimes.com/2006/oct/10/business/fi -alhambra10.

Warren, Jonathan W., and France Winddance Twine. "White Americans, the New Minority? Non-Blacks and the Ever-Expanding Boundaries of Whiteness." *Journal of Black Studies* 28, no. 2 (1997): 200–218.

Waters, Mary C. *Ethnic Options: Choosing Identities in America*. Berkeley: University of California Press, 1990.

Weber, Rachel. "Extracting Value from the City: Neoliberalism and Urban Redevelopment." *Antipode* 34, no. 3 (2002): 519–40.

Weglyn, Michi. *Years of Infamy: The Untold Story of America's Concentration Camps*. Seattle: University of Washington Press, 1976.

Weiss, Richard. *The American Myth of Success: From Horatio Alger to Norman Vincent Peale*. Urbana: University of Illinois Press, 1988.

Widener, Daniel. "'Perhaps the Japanese Are to Be Thanked?' Asia, Asian America, and the Construction of Black California." *positions: east asia cultures critique* 11, no. 1 (2003): 135–81.

Wiese, Andrew. *Places of Their Own: African American Suburbanization in the Twentieth Century*. Chicago: University of Chicago Press, 2004.

Wild, Mark. *Street Meeting: Multiethnic Neighborhoods in Early Twentieth-Century Los Angeles*. Berkeley: University of California Press, 2008.

Williams, Eric. *Capitalism and Slavery*. Chapel Hill: University of North Carolina Press, 1994.

Williams, Linda. *Playing the Race Card: Melodramas of Black and White from Uncle Tom to O. J. Simpson*. Princeton: Princeton University Press, 2001.

Williams, Raymond. *Marxism and Literature*. Oxford: Oxford University Press, 1977.

Williams-León, Teresa, and Cynthia L. Nakashima. *The Sum of Our Parts: Mixed-Heritage Asian Americans*. Philadelphia: Temple University Press, 2001.

Willis, Paul. *Learning to Labour: How Working Class Kids Get Working Class Jobs*. Westmead, Farnborough, Hants, England: Saxon House, 1977.

Wise, Tim. *Colorblind: The Rise of Post-Racial Politics and the Retreat from Racial Equity*. San Francisco: City Lights Books, 2010.

Wong, Janelle. *Democracy's Promise: Immigrants and American Civic Institutions.* Ann Arbor: University of Michigan Press, 2006.

Woods, Clyde. *Development Arrested: Race, Power, and the Blues in the Mississippi Delta.* London: Verso, 1998.

Yamamoto, Hisaye. *Seventeen Syllables and Other Stories.* New Brunswick, N.J.: Rutgers University Press, 1998.

Yancey, George A. "Racial Justice in a Black/Nonblack Society." In *Mixed Messages: Multiracial Identities in the "Color-Blind" Era,* edited by David L. Brunsma, 49–62. Boulder, Colo.: Lynne Rienner, 2006.

———. *Who Is White?: Latinos, Asians, and the New Black/Nonblack Divide.* Boulder, Colo.: L. Rienner, 2003.

Zhao, Xiaojian. *The New Chinese America: Class, Economy, and Social Hierarchy.* New Brunswick, N.J.: Rutgers University Press, 2010.

Zhou, Min. *Contemporary Chinese America: Immigration, Ethnicity, and Community Transformation.* Philadelphia: Temple University Press, 2009.

Zhou, Min, Yen-Fen Tseng, and Rebecca Kim. "Rethinking Residential Assimilation: The Case of a Chinese Ethnoburb in the San Gabriel Valley, California." *Amerasia Journal* 34, no. 3 (2008): 53–83.

Zhou, Yu. "How Do Places Matter? A Comparative Study of Chinese Ethnic Economies in Los Angeles and New York City." *Urban Geography* 19, no. 6 (1998): 531–53.

Zhou, Yu, and Yen-Fen Tseng. "Regrounding the 'Ungrounded Empires': Localization as the Geographical Catalyst for Transnationalism." *Global Networks: A Journal of Transnational Affairs* 1, no. 2 (2001): 131–54.

Index

achievement gap, 63, 68, 70; at
Alhambra High School, 63, 79, 113;
common sense explanations of, 64,
72, 73, 74; naturalization of, 73–74;
racialized discourse of, 84, 89
affiliation: multiracial/ethnic, 174
affirmative action: and Asian
Americans, 237–38n58; and "Black
entitlement," 120; and Latina/o
stereotypes, 79–80; *Regents of the
University of California v. Bakke*,
237–38n58; as reverse racism, 237–
38n58; and white women, 243n81
African Americans: in BSA, 91–94,
112–27; and color-blind discourse,
243n69; property rights of, 230n42;
Woods on, 12. *See also* Blackness
Aguilar, Laura, 1
Ahn, Grace, 55–56, 58, 203, 204, 217;
cognitive map by, 218 fig. 26
Alhambra (CA), 8 fig. 4, 9 fig. 5, 144
fig. 15, 221–22n16, 254n33; chamber
of commerce, 148; as core West
SGV city, 3; demographics of,
233n2; diversity campaign, 129–30,
131 fig. 11, 137–41, 139–41 fig. 13a–e,
170; eminent domain, use of,
147; Main Street, redevelopment
of, 137–38, 141, 143, 144, 146–47;
map of, 137 fig. 12; "Mosaic on
Main" banners in, 148, 169; racial

composition of, 43 fig. 9; and racial
exclusion, 37; Spanish past, myth
of, 148–49; white political power
in, 136. *See also* Alhambra High
School
Alhambra High School, 2;
achievement, racialized character
of, 76, 79; achievement gap at,
63, 79, 113; AP courses at, 63–64,
68; demographics, racial, 64,
66–67; Latina/o performance at,
69; mascot of, 248–49n65; open
enrollment at, 88–89, 239n79;
tracking at, 68; Zhou column
controversy, 63–64, 69–70, 81–
86, 88, 89–90, 239n79. *See also*
Alhambra; education; schools
Althusser, Louis, 18, 63, 88; "ideology
cop fable," 87
Alvarez, Gina, 57, 59–60, 210–11
Alvarez, Milo, 23–24, 39–41, 40–41, 57,
175, 181, 211
Amam, Willow Lung, 232n91
American Dream: and assimilation,
94, 103; and color-blind
discourse, 94, 95, 127; and
Golden Mile campaign, 151–52;
and homeownership, 40, 61;
and individualism, 94; and
multiculturalism, 138; as myth of
success, 95; and white privilege, 110

sedimentation, 60; social relations, metaphor for, 10–11

segregation: of Black people, 33; resegregation, 24; residential, 229n31. *See also* segregation, school

segregation, school: *Brown v. Board of Education*, 70, 230–31n45; desegregation, 68; *Mendez v. Westminster*, 230–31n45

SGV (clothing brand), 1, 2, 189; "SGV dreamgirl" shirt, 171, 172 fig. 19

Shah, Nayan, 252n4

Sham, Stephen, 136, 214 fig. 22, 216

Shapiro, Thomas, 33

Smith, Neil, 199

Solis, Hilda, 121

Song, Alfred, 32, 246n29

South El Monte, 3

South Pasadena, 3, 185–86, 254n33; school district, 185, 254n34

South San Gabriel, 1–2, 3, 49, 221n8; and homeownership, 30, 48

space: differentiated, moral geography of, 25, 26, 60, 197; and history, 170; and neoliberalism, 131, 248n61; and race, 19, 21, 22, 171, 223–24n34; and race consciousness, 173, 207; and racial formation, regional, 21–22; social production of, 223n33; as white, 45; and whiteness, 25, 39, 60; and white privilege, 230n38. *See also* space, Chinese

space, Chinese, 132; Chinatowns, 133, 134, 209; Eurocentric conceptions of, 133. *See also* space

Spanish fantasy past, 130, 167; in Alhambra, 148–49; Indians, erasure of, 134; and manifest destiny, 134; and Mexican

Americans, 16, 18, 132; Mexicans, erasure of, 134; and white power, 134; and whites, 132

Spickard, Paul, 173

Steele, Claude, 79, 86, 237n51

suburbanization, 24, 27

Sugrue, Thomas, 227n82

Taiwanese Americans, vii–viii, 152–53, 159; immigration to United States, 6; politicians, 130, 135, 157, 169; in West SGV, 4, 6, 10, 41, 57, 181, 183, 203, 221n10, 254–55n51. *See also* Asian Americans; Chinese, ethnic; Chinese Americans

Takagi, Dana Y., 237–38n58, 238–39n63

Talbot, Paul, 245–46n26, 246n27

Thomas, Gregory, 138

Toguchi, Ed, 2, 29, 30–31

Toguchi, Karen, 2, 29, 30–31, 46, 216; cognitive map by, 214 fig. 21

Tong, David, 30–32, 36, 37–38, 40, 221–22n16

Tong, Soume, 36, 37–38, 40

Toyota, Tritia, 10

Tran, John, 245n20

Treaty of Guadalupe Hidalgo, 35

Tuan, Mia, 74, 75, 236n39, 253n23; racial privilege, theorization of, 236n39

UCLA, 203

United States: demographics, racial, 13

University of California (UC): admission policies, 69, 235n22

urban renewal, 24

Uyehara, Romy, 46, 216; cognitive map by, 217 fig. 25

Valenzuela, Angela, 80, 237n50

Varzally, Allison, 253n16

WENDY CHENG is assistant professor of Asian Pacific American studies and justice and social inquiry in the School of Social Transformation at Arizona State University. She is coauthor, with Laura Pulido and Laura Barraclough, of *A People's Guide to Los Angeles*.